THESAURUS

of the

SENSES

THESAURUS

of the

SENSES

_____

LINDA HART

The universe is full of magical things
patiently waiting for our wits to grow sharper.

—*Eden Phillpotts, A Shadow Passes*

See
Well   Hear
Well   Touch
Well   Taste
Well   Smell
Well

How to Use This Thesaurus

Thesaurus of the Senses is an instrument for your writing success. Whether you are seeking just the right word or need a bit of inspiration, this reference tool can guide your literary travels.

Connect with the Senses. Use the words and exercises in this book to connect with one of your most valuable assets as a writer: your ability to engage physically and emotionally with the world through your senses. Grounding yourself in the senses and seeking out new ways to become aware of sensory experiences can help you connect with readers and find your writing voice.

Expand your perspective. Broaden your viewpoint by using all of your senses to build vibrant descriptions. Browse the different facets of each sense in the book to find rich complexities that will engage readers. Consider shapes, textures, aromas, colors, facial expressions, flavors, and sounds in your word choices. Add spark and zing to your work during the editing process.

Get inspired. Rummage through the word list for inspiration and encouragement. Delight in the *fiery, frothy, furrowed,* and *fluttering* words—all collected in one place. Use your favorite words as writing prompts to launch your next story or poem.

Find the apt word. Explore the word and subject indexes in the back to locate more relevant and impactful words for your writing tasks. Discover new associations and connections.

Contents

Introduction

Certain words rattle the ground beneath you. They startle, intoxicate, beckon, electrify. They reverberate with excitement and shimmer with emotion. They poke you in the rib cage and entice your tongue. They arouse the senses. These special words, collected like jewels by wordsmiths and poets, in journals and notebooks or on scraps of paper for later use, enliven writing with their astonishing beauty and power. They instill in readers a sense of place rooted in the physical world, and they command attention and respect.

Thesaurus of the Senses is a collection of some of the best English sensory words, curated for their whimsy, grandeur, and resonance. Unlike ordinary thesauri that contain all manner of words—the mesmerizing as well as the mundane—this thesaurus contains the gems of the literary world. Here writers will find excellent company among the *careening, clanging, unflinching, splendorous,* and *velvety* words that add depth, inspiration, and spice to their work.

This collection is intended as a resource for writers, poets, teachers, students, storytellers, and word lovers alike who want to bring sparkle to their writing or who simply want to delight in the rich kinship of language. The words in this thesaurus are often simple and unpretentious. They are not esoteric oddities or corporate "power words," even though they are powerful. Their use is not meant to help win TV game shows or stump dinner companions. Yet, these words can stop readers in their tracks with their passion and panache.

Organized loosely by each of the five senses—see, hear, touch, taste, smell—as well as subcategories of the main qualities and dimensions of those senses, this book offers tools to build vivid descriptions and bring rhythm and crackle to writing. These words can also serve as writing prompts to discover hidden connections and unleash creativity.

Rather than an exhaustive collection of words, shades of meaning, and precise definitions, it is a collection of loosely related words intended to spark imagination, serendipity, and association by highlighting the breadth and interconnections of sensory experiences.

Not surprisingly, the largest collection of words is the seeing words—*glisten, bedraggled, willowy*. Visual words have special impact because they can provide the first, and sometimes the fullest, impression to a reader. They are especially useful for sketching the physical outlines and unspoken emotional texture of a scene quickly through which readers can envision the rest of the story.

Acoustic words add to the music, pace, and rhythm of a work, particularly when combined with crisp dialogue and action. When used sparingly and to great effect, hearing words provide force, surprise, tone, lilt, melody—and a bit of drama.

Tactile words bring immediacy and presence to writing because, like something *prickly, frothy*, or *clammy* touching your skin, they cannot be ignored. Like a marinade, they also combine well with other sensory words such as those describing taste and smell.

Taste words, though sometimes overlooked as descriptors unless actual food is involved, can be very tempting, even tantalizing, in writing. Some readers will find it impossible to read through the list of taste words without salivating.

And, smells. Ah, smells! Smells offer a primal and direct connection to memory, pleasure, and revulsion. Along with tastes, scents can captivate our senses, turning a simple walk in a forest or bakery into an emotional and sensual extravagance. From floral to peppery words, the smell list is not exhaustive, but readers can get a whiff of some of its more pungent odors.

Finally, each of our senses is not experienced in isolation. The miracle of our combined senses is how they blend and trigger thoughts and emotions to create meaningful impressions of the world—sometimes a profound kinesthetic and even synesthetic experience.

And on the edge of our five senses is an inexplicable, unnamed sixth sense: our deep insight into and connection with the unknown. Many words in this thesaurus cannot be pinned down to one particular sense or quality. They glimmer in that unfathomable space between the sensory and mystical worlds—a poetic and spiritual wonder.

From the weighty to the wispy, senses are how we perceive and understand the world and how readers come to know an imagined world. When we are acutely attuned, our senses catapult us directly into creative realms. They intermingle to add color, shape, sound, depth, texture, taste, and aroma to our experiences. I invite you to explore the exquisite and intricate world of sensory words and let them infuse your writing with their magic.

Connecting *with the* Senses: Exercises

These exercises are meant to ground you in the senses so that you can more easily connect with and describe your experiences. While doing these exercises, it is handy to have a writing journal or recorder nearby so you can capture your thoughts and feelings more easily.

1. Has something you've seen or heard brought you to tears? How about something you've smelled? Or tasted? Describe your experiences.

2. Of the five senses, what is your strongest sense? What is your weakest or most underdeveloped sense? To pique your weakest sense, write down five intense sensations or experiences that would enliven that sense. What words or descriptions come to mind to describe those heightened experiences?

3. Words carry emotion, melody, and rhythm—sometimes contrary to their actual meaning. Listen to the following words and write about the types of music, sensations, and feelings they convey or evoke: *cataclysmic, resplendent, muddled, precipitous, swirling, cacophony, succulent.*

4. Sensory experiences are both qualitative and quantitative. Quantitatively, they can range from barely perceptible to overwhelmingly intense. Qualitatively, they can range from rich and riveting to dull and bland. In addition, sometimes sensory experiences are a curious mixture of opposites— discordant and harmonious, enticing and repulsive, sweet and sour, etc. Pick a few sensory words and for each word explore its similar and opposite states and the layers of complexity within it.

5. Wherever you are right now, stop to listen. See if you can isolate each separate sound in your space. Write down all sounds that you can identify.

6. Write a five-sentence poem using each of the five senses in a separate line. In the next line, write about a sixth sense you've experienced. In the following lines of the poem, write how the senses you wrote about are connected.

7. Pick a large object in your environment and picture it very small; pick a small object and see it suddenly gigantic.

8. Look at various things and people through different objects such as a vase, colored glass, mirror, magnifying glass, long tube, etc. What do you notice about your perception and reaction to these transformations?

9. Find an exotic fruit or vegetable that you have never tasted before. Write about your first experience of seeing, touching, smelling, and tasting it. What places, emotions, and memories does eating it invoke?

10. Describe how you feel when you unexpectedly get caught in a rainstorm, windstorm, or snowstorm.

11. Describe what you are feeling right now using only a whisper.

12. Take a walk outside at your normal pace. Now decrease your pace by half. Now by half again. Continue decreasing your pace by half until you are no longer moving. Describe your sensations and observations at each stage of the process. Now try this exercise (with care) walking backwards.

13. Politely eavesdrop on a conversation and listen to the kinds of words and expressions of the people talking. What tone and volume do they use? Is one person dominating the conversation? How do the others respond? What words describe their interaction? See if you can imagine and describe their facial expressions and gestures without looking at them.

14. The five basic elements of water, earth, fire, air, and space drive our senses. Pick one of these elements and describe your physical and emotional connections to it. Then explore different combinations of these elements, such as water/fire, fire/air, earth/water, etc., and their dynamic effect on you.

15. Describe an outdoor scene using only your sense of smell or taste. What emotions and memories do these smells and tastes trigger?

16. Stimulate your senses by visiting a coffee shop that sells whole beans that you can smell. Or sniff different kinds of spices in a spice store or soaps in a bath store. What are your favorite and least favorite smells? Are you surprised by how complex the smells are?

17. Build a poem or some prose using the following instructions:
- Begin with a physical object and describe in separate lines what the object looks, sounds, feels, tastes, and smells like.
- What are the object's strengths and weaknesses?
- Describe what is true about the object.
- What is unknowable, indescribable, or hidden about the object?
- Have a character interact with the object and tell you what it means to him/her.
- What would happen if the object became lost or destroyed?
- How can the object be transformed into something else?

18. Make sounds vocally or using your body or an object that express your mood. What words come to mind as you make these sounds?

19. In synesthesia, one sense can trigger another. For example, a sound can trigger certain colors, or certain words can trigger specific tastes or smells. Have you ever had experiences like these? During your day, observe how your senses overlap, bend, and expand. See if you can extend your awareness of your sensory experiences beyond your normal perception. Can you hear grass, smell sunlight, taste wind, etc.?

20. Sometimes one sense magnifies our other senses and emotions, for example, sounds that help us see better or smells that expand our taste. Find other examples. Can smell help us hear something better? Can taste enliven how we see or hear something?

21. When we are intensely using one of our senses, we sometimes block out the other senses, for example, closing our eyes when we experience an intense sound, taste, smell, or touch. What are examples you have experienced?

22. Write about a character and describe how he or she fully senses the world and how others sense him or her.

23. Smells are sometimes difficult to describe and are often based on what something smells like (flowers, gasoline, skunk, etc.) instead of their actual essence. English words for describing smells are surprisingly limited. However, some languages have richer vocabularies for describing smells. For example, the Jahai language of the inhabitants of the Malay Peninsula has a smell word that translates into "to have a bloody smell which attracts tigers." What new, richer ways can you describe smells that you encounter or imagine?

24. Have a companion pick a half dozen foods or condiments and offer them to you to taste one at a time while you keep your eyes closed. How accurately can you describe these tastes?

25. Describe these sensory experiences: riding with a caravan of mules down a Grand Canyon trail, playing in a bell choir in an echo chamber, licking a lizard's skin, driving a spacecraft near Saturn's rings, singing with a pack of coyotes, lighting the torch at the Olympics ceremony, using only your sense of smell to imagine where an old book has been, becoming a river.

SEE

We eat light, drink it in through our skins... Seeing is a very sensuous act—there's a sweet deliciousness to feeling yourself see something.
—James Turrell, American artist

LIGHT *and* DARK - COLORS *and* HUES - SIZES *and* AMOUNTS -
SPACE, LOCATION, *or* POSITION - SHAPES *and* STRUCTURES -
TEXTURES, DESIGNS, *and* PATTERNS - FACIAL EXPRESSIONS -
MOTION - DISTINCTIVE QUALITY *or* IMPRESSION -
GENERAL APPEARANCE - VISION *and* SIGHT

Seeing is a faulty sense. Anyone who has ever fallen victim to a magic trick knows that vision is not always trustworthy. It can be a slight of hand. We can haplessly plunge through optical trapdoors or fail to recognize blind spots. Our expectations and beliefs can lead us down blind alleys or into hallucinatory flights of fancy. We see only what we want to see. Or turn a blind eye. Our sight can deceive us, mesmerize us, haunt us.

On the other hand, we can perceive and interpret a phenomenal amount of information in just one glance—patterns, shapes, colors, movements, impressions—and from there accurately assess our surroundings. We can also have exceptional vision beyond sight—a beholder of beauty and possessor of insight, of the unseen and the invisible. We can read between the lines, visualize the impossible, and imagine in our mind's eye elaborate worlds of our own making. We can also display visual virtuosity in the form of extraordinary foresight or hindsight. Or vividly recall an event using photographic memory.

Our world relies heavily on visual impressions, in mass media, advertising, film, art, sports, fashion, music, etc. Some images leave an indelible mark upon us, providing lifelong inspiration or conversely leaving us scarred. As our dominate sense, sight allows us continually record rich visual tapestries and unspoken messages around us. We can visually play back pleasant memories and envision our future from many vantage points. In addition, our eyes can perceive intangible, elusive qualities in people and situations such as allure, charisma, and *je ne sais quoi*, a certain indescribable something.

We constantly project an image of ourselves onto the world. We see and are seen. Yet, the mystery of sight is that we never truly get an accurate glimpse of ourselves as others see us. Though we carry a mental picture of ourselves, and an idealized vision, we remain always behind the mirror, looking out.

In this section, set your sights on words showcasing the many dimensions of visual perception—size, shape, color, design, etc.—that combine into the marvel of seeing. This section also includes words that describe facial expressions—human visuals to which we are acutely attuned—and multifaceted words that reflect a distinctive visual quality or impression.

LIGHT *and* DARK

ablaze
> burning, fiery, flaming, glowing, aglow, shimmering, bright, shining

aglow
> glowing, shimmering, radiant, ablaze, luminous, luminescent, flaming, bright, shining, fiery

angelic
> celestial, ethereal, shining, heavenly, radiant, glorious, luminous, divine

aura
> brightness, glow, halo, ambiance, mood, atmosphere

beam, beaming
> luster, rocket, spark, gleaming, flaring, glaring, blazing, scorching, flaming, lucid, luminous, brilliant, radiant

blackened
dark, heavy, shadowy, inky, darkened, dimmed, shaded

blaze, blazing
rocket, luster, wildfire, flaring, glaring, beaming, flaming, gleaming, scorching, spark, burst

bright
illuminated, ablaze, burning, aura, shining, glowing, aglow, flashy, shimmering, scintillating, dazzling

brilliant
lucid, bright, illustrious, radiant, vivid, dazzling, golden, luminous, sparkling, lustrous, bold

burning
fiery, smoking, blackened, flaming, ablaze, glowing, aglow, bright, shining

candescent
bright, illuminated, shining, glowing, dazzling, luminescent

celestial
angelic, ethereal, shining, divine, glowing, astral, starlike, luminous, stellar

clarify, clarified
sheer, crystalline, refined, purified, illuminate, elucidate

crystalline
clarified, clear, translucent, glassy, sparkling, lucid, pure

crystallize
clarify, refine, purify, materialize, coalesce

dappled
speckled, spotted, filtered, stippled, blotchy, mottled, flecked

dark, darkly
heavy, shadowy, black, inky, glowering, scowling, sullen, dense, murky, brooding, shady, clouded, curtained, sulky, gloomy, morose, moody

dazzle, dazzling
shining, brilliant, spellbinding, hypnotic, radiant, sparkling, flickering, glittering, glimmering, glinting, glistening, shimmering, twinkling, lively

enlighten, enlightening
illuminate, brighten, shining, glowing, clarify, elucidate

ethereal
angelic, celestial, shining, unearthly, volatile, changeable, heavenly, divine, airy, ephemeral

fiery
flaming, glowing, aglow, ablaze, burning, bright, shining, inflamed, impassioned, passionate

flame
> spark, flare, blaze, scorch, gleam, luster, rocket

flaming
> burning, bright, shining, fiery, glowing, aglow, ablaze, shimmering

flare, flaring
> glare, blaze, flame, gleam, luster, scorch, rocket, spark, flicker, sparkle, beam

flash, flashy, flashing
> flamboyant, bright, colorful, elaborate, eye-catching, splashy, shimmering, vivid, dashing, showy

flick, flicker
> flare, spark, glare, glint, shimmer, twinkle, sparkle, blink, dazzle, glimmer, glisten, glitter, flitter, pulse

glassy
> glazed, filmy, glossy, luster, mirrored, gleaming, sleek

gleam, gleaming
> flare, glare, beam, blaze, flame, luster, sparkle, glimmer, glint, glow

glimmer, glimmering
> glint, gleam, glisten, sparkle, twinkle, inkling, flicker, shimmer

glint, glinting
> sparkle, flash, flicker, flare, shine, glare, shimmer, glimmer

glisten, glistening
> glimmer, glint, gleam, sparkle, twinkle, shimmer, glitter

glitter, glittering
> showy, flashy, frilly, glimmer, shimmer, glisten, sparkle

glossy
> shiny, sheen, sleek, glassy, iridescent, opalescent, pearly, gleaming, glaze, slick

glow, glowing
> illuminated, ablaze, shimmering, burning, bright, shining, fiery, flaming, aglow, glimmering

heavy
> shadowy, dense, murky, shady, clouded, curtained, gloomy, moody, brooding

illuminate, illuminated
> bright, shining, glowing, clarify, enlighten, spotlight

illumine
> illuminate, brighten, flash, light, irradiate, clarify, gleam

illustrious
> dazzling, shining, lively, brilliant, spellbinding, hypnotic, radiant, esteemed, eminent, preeminent, renowned, magical, splendorous, wondrous, resplendent

inky
heavy, shadowy, black, dark, pitch-black, dense, murky, shady

lackluster
dull, dim, vapid, drab, colorless, bland, flat, dreary

lightning
spark, flash, charge, bolt, thunderbolt

lucid
beaming, bright, brilliant, crystal-clear, incandescent, luminous, gleaming

luminous
lucid, beaming, bright, brilliant, shining, radiant, glowing, incandescent

luster
gleam, spark, radiance, flare, glare, blaze, flame, sheen, sparkle, beam, gloss

lustrous
glamorous, alluring, beaming, dazzling, enchanting, shining, radiant, luminous, magnetic, stunning, gleaming, polished

mirrored
reflecting, shiny, shimmering, glassy, glossy, shining

murky
shadowy, black, inky, dense, shady, clouded, brooding, moody

nebulous
shadowy, foggy, hazy, obscure, dim, fuzzy, faint

opaque
cloudy, shaded, murky, hazy, muddied, foggy, blurry

radiant, radiance
stunning, shining, sparkling, splendorous, brilliant, luminous

ray
beam, spark, glimmer, flicker

reflecting
mirrored, shiny, shimmering, glassy, flashing

resplendent
splendorous, dazzling, shining, brilliant, sublime, glimmering, spellbinding, radiant

searchlight
beacon, torch, lamplight, moonlight, firelight, lantern, flame, flash

shadowy
heavy, black, brooding, murky, shady, clouded, curtained, gloomy, moody, dense, inky

shady
> heavy, shadowy, black, sullen, murky, clouded, curtained, gloomy, moody, inky, brooding, dense

sheen
> glossy, shiny, slick, sleek, glassy, polish, gloss, shine, gleam, glint

shimmer, shimmering
> glowing, aglow, shining, flaming, shiny, ablaze, bright, glimmering, flickering

shine, shiny
> bright, illuminated, glowing, polished, refined, mirrored, reflecting, glaze, sheen

spark
> flame, gleam, scorch, rocket, flare, glare, beam, blaze, torch

sparkle, sparkling
> dazzling, flickering, glimmering, glinting, glistening, glittering, shimmering, twinkling, effervescent, vivacious

torch
> beacon, searchlight, lamplight, moonlight, firelight, lantern

twinkle, twinkling
> shimmering, glistening, glittering, flickering, sparkling, blinking, dazzling, glimmering, glinting

COLORS *and* HUES

abloom
> bright, flowery, showy, blossomy, blooming

alabaster
> ivory, pale, fair, translucent, creamy

amber
> honey-yellow, yellow-orange, golden

apricot
> peach, light-orange, orange-yellow

aquamarine
> blue-green, sea-green

ashen
> pale, sickly, dreary, ghostly, pallid, sallow, anemic, bland, gray, faded, colorless, peaked, ghastly, pasty, gaunt

auburn
> light-brown, coppery, reddish-brown, tawny

azure
    sky-blue, cyan, cerulean, aquamarine, turquoise

beige
    tawny, hazel, nut-brown, walnut

black, blackened
    dark, heavy, raven, jet-black, sable, ebony, pitch-black, shadowy, inky

blanched
    pale, white, faded, washed out, clammy, ashen, pallid, pasty

bland
    colorless, ashen, anemic, pale, dreary, faded, lifeless, pallid, sallow

blood-red
    crimson, ruddy, flame-red, fiery, cherry-red, port-wine, scarlet, maroon, ruby

bloom, blooming
    abloom, bright, flowery, showy, blossomy, rosy, blush

blossomy, blossoming
    flowery, showy, abloom, blooming, radiant

blush, blushing
    rosy, blooming, radiant, reddened, vibrant

brindle
    beige, hazel, nut-brown, walnut, russet, coppery, tawny, flecked, multicolored, rusty

bronze
    yellowish-brown, metallic, copper, brass, rust, chestnut, tanned

carmine
    ruby, cherry, cherry-red, ruddy, scarlet, crimson, flame-red

cerulean
    sky-blue, azure, cyan, deep-blue, aquamarine

chalky
    dusty, pale, ashen, snowy, silvery, frosty, milky, powdery

charcoal
    dark gray, gray, gray-black

chartreuse
    pale green, green-yellow, lemon-lime

cherry, cherry-red
    scarlet, ruby, crimson, ruddy, inflamed, flame-red, fiery, port-wine, maroon

colorless
    ashen, anemic, bland, insipid, dreary, faded, lifeless, pallid, sallow, pale

copper, coppery
    rusty, tawny, russet, bronze, metallic, chestnut, auburn

coral
    pinkish-red, pinkish orange, salmon

crimson
    ruby, ruddy, flame-red, fiery, cherry-red, port-wine, scarlet, blood-red, maroon

dingy
    drab, grungy, shabby, discolored, faded, dreary, muddy, colorless, dull

discolored
    stained, tarnished, faded, yellowed, blemished, dingy

drab
    dingy, dull, grungy, shabby, faded, lackluster, gray

drained
    colorless, faded, bleary, empty, void, pale, dim, faint

dreary
    bleak, grim, colorless, ashen, bland, pale, faded, drab, pallid, sallow, dull

dull
    bland, faded, colorless, drab, bleached, faint, washed-out, pale, ashen, blanched, pallid, sallow, gray

ebony
    dark, heavy, shadowy, raven, jet-black, sable, pitch-black, charcoal, onyx, inky

emerald
    green, verdant, foliaged, grassy, leafy, mossy, forest, jade

faded
    drab, gray, faint, washed-out, yellowed, blanched, withered, bleached, colorless, ashen, bland, dreary, pallid, sallow, pale

flamboyant
    bright, flowery, bold, elaborate, showy, flashy, garish, splashy, ornate, dashing

flame-red
    crimson, ruddy, fiery, cherry-red, scarlet, maroon

flashy
    flamboyant, bright, colorful, bold, elaborate, eye-catching, splashy, garish, showy, dashing, brazen

floral
    flowery, abloom, showy, blossomy, blooming, verdant

florid
    adorned, flowery, fanciful, frilly, blooming, lush, rosy, ornate

flowery
>floral, florid, adorned, fanciful, frilly, lush, rosy, ornate, abloom, resplendent, showy, blossomy, blooming

foliaged
>grassy, leafy, verdant, vernal, lush, green, emerald

frosty
>snowy, silvery, chalky, fleecy, milky, icy

ghostly
>ashen, pale, pallid, sallow, shadowy

ginger, gingered
>reddish-yellow, saffron, golden

gold, golden
>brilliant, dazzling, flaxen, glorious, saffron, shining, shimmering, glistening

grassy
>vernal, lush, mossy, verdant, green, emerald, foliaged, leafy

gray
>pallid, faded, silvery, ashen, pale, steel-gray, charcoal

hazel
>tawny, beige, drab, nut-brown, walnut, chestnut

heavy
>dark, dense, murky, blackened, gray

hoary
>snowy, silvery, frosty, gray, graying, gray-haired

hue
>shade, tint, wash, stain, blush, varnish, tinge, tone

hued
>imbued, colored, stained, tinted, dyed, tinged, shaded

imbued
>dyed, tinted, hued, colored, stained, saturated, tinged

indigo
>purplish-blue, dark-blue, violet, violet-blue, aquamarine, azure, purplish

infused, infusion
>tincture, dye, tint, immersion

inky
>dark, heavy, shadowy, raven, jet-black, sable, ebony, pitch-black, onyx, murky

insipid
>monochrome, lifeless, unimaginative, dull, banal, colorless, dreary, spiritless, vapid

iridescent
opalescent, pearly, soft-hued, moire, glossy, opaline

ivory
cream, creamy-white, off-white, alabaster, fair, pale

jade
blue-green, light-green, emerald, forest, moss

jet-black
dark, heavy, shadowy, inky, raven, sable, ebony, pitch-black, black

kaleidoscope, kaleidoscopic
multicolored, psychedelic, vivid, chromatic, colorful

khaki
brownish-yellow, sandy, camel, biscuit, tan, taupe

lavender
purple-blue, mauve, lilac, violet

leafy
emerald, green, verdant, grassy, lush, foliaged, meadowy, mossy

lilac
light-purple, pale purple, violet, pink, mauve

lurid
gaudy, bright, blinding, intense, vivid, glaring, shocking, flaming, loud, garish

lush
green, verdant, florid, flowery, blooming, rosy, emerald, foliaged, grassy, leafy, botanical

magenta
purplish-red, rose, fuchsia, purple, plum, mulberry

mahogany
reddish-brown, maroon, cherry, brick, bronze, russet, amber, auburn

maroon
brownish-red, mahogany, cherry, ruby, scarlet

milky
turbid, cloudy, thick, opaque, murky, muddy

mousy
brown, grayish-brown, dull, lackluster, drab, plain, colorless

navy
dark-blue, blue-black

ochre
golden-yellow, gold, yellow-brown, golden

olive
green, grayish-green, muddy green, sage

opalescent
iridescent, pearly, subtle, soft-hued, moire, glossy, opaline

pale
ashen, gray, ghostly, pallid, sallow, blanched, faded, faint, dim

pallid, pallor
pale, bland, dreary, faded, lifeless, ashen, ghostly, sallow, colorless, anemic, pasty, gray, gaunt

pastel
pale, light, soft, muted, soft-hued

pasty
ashen, pale, ghostly, bland, dreary, faded, wan, sallow, colorless, anemic, gray

peaked
ashen, sickly, gray, pale, ghostly, pallid, sallow, colorless, anemic, dreary, faded

pearly
opalescent, iridescent, lustrous, frosted, milky, ivory

periwinkle
mauve, lavender, lilac, purple, violet

pewter
gray, tin, gun-metal, silver

pitch-black
dark, heavy, shadowy, inky, raven, jet-black, sable, ebony, black

plum
deep purple, reddish-purple, magenta

raven
dark, heavy, shadowy, inky, jet-black, sable, ebony, pitch-black, onyx

rose
deep-red, pinkish red, blush, maroon, red-violet, magenta

rosy
florid, flowery, blooming, blushing, coral, peach, pinkish

ruby
carmine, cherry, cherry-red, fiery, ruddy, scarlet, crimson, flame-red, blood-red

ruddy
scarlet, crimson, flaming, maroon, flame-red, fiery, cherry-red, port-wine, ruby

russet
tawny, coppery, bronze, chestnut, auburn

rust, rusty
   tawny, russet, coppery, bronze

sable
   dark, heavy, shadowy, inky, raven, jet-black, ebony, pitch-black

saffron
   golden, orange-yellow, bright, creamy, gold

sallow
   ashen, pale, gray, ghostly, pallid, colorless, bland, dreary, faded

salmon
   pinkish-orange, pale pink, coral, terra cotta, apricot

sandy
   light-brown, walnut, yellowish-brown, khaki

scarlet
   ruby, carmine, crimson, flame-red, cherry, ruddy, cherry-red, maroon, blood-red, fiery

sepia
   reddish-brown, amber, drab, coffee, monochrome, tawny, chestnut

shade
   cast, hint, shadow, streak, tinge, stain, hue

sienna
   reddish-brown, yellow-brown, rust

silver, silvered, silvery
   hoary, snowy, frosty, gray, frosted, metallic, grayish-white, shiny, mirrored

sky-blue
   cyan, azure, cerulean, bright blue

slate
   blue-gray, azure, purple-gray, purple-blue, pewter, charcoal

snowy
   silvery, frosty, fleecy, milky, icy

stained
   hued, tinted, dyed, imbued, discolored, splattered

steel-blue
   bluish gray, metallic, pewter

taupe
   grayish-brown, gray-brown, khaki, camel, cream

tawny
   beige, hazel, nut-brown, walnut, rusty, russet, coppery, brindle, drab

teal
blue-green, cyan, turquoise

terra cotta
brownish-red, brownish-orange, salmon

tincture
dye, tint, infusion, extract, pigment, stain

tinted
stained, dyed, imbued, colored, hued

translucent
clear, crystalline, luminous, transparent, sheer

transparent
translucent, clear, luminous, glassy, sheer

turbid
cloudy, thick, milky, opaque, murky, muddy, obscure, sludgy

turquoise
blue-green, sky-blue, cyan, teal

vapid
dull, colorless, lifeless, bland, insipid

verdant
grassy, leafy, green, emerald, foliaged, meadow, lush, mossy

violet
indigo, purple-blue, lilac, lavender

vivid
vibrant, rich, striking, dazzling, glaring, deep, intense, bold, bright, colorful

walnut
tawny, beige, drab, hazel, nut-brown, khaki, camel

SIZES *and* AMOUNTS

abound, abounding
plentiful, abundant, bountiful, copious, flourishing, swarming, profuse, teeming, thriving, bristling, bursting, ample, overflowing

abundant
rich, profuse, fruitful, copious, bountiful, teeming, lavish, plentiful, abounding, ample, flourishing, thriving, generous

aerial
elevated, atmospheric, majestic, visionary, panoramic, lofty, flying

Thesaurus of the Senses

ample
plentiful, abounding, abundant, bountiful, copious, teeming

ascendant
rising, preeminent, momentous, stellar, towering, transcendent, grand

balloon, ballooning
inflated, overblown, swollen, swelling, bulging, skyrocketing, mounting, soaring

bare
meager, gaunt, scant, skimpy, spare, vacant, barren, empty, void, blank

behemoth
monstrosity, enormous, colossal, gargantuan, gigantic, mammoth, giant

booming
flourishing, bounding, teeming, thriving, swarming, bristling, mushrooming, bursting, overflowing, burgeoning, vigorous

bottomless
yawning, gaping, cavernous, immense, plunging, vast, endless, unfathomable

boundless
limitless, infinite, innumerable, measureless, unbridled, eternal, unbounded, vast, unrestrained, immeasurable

bountiful
abundant, fruitful, copious, teeming, lavish, plentiful, abounding, ample, prolific, flourishing, profuse, thriving

brimming
overflowing, abundant, teeming, copious, bristling, gushing, awash, swarming

burgeoning
flourishing, booming, abounding, teeming, thriving, swarming, bristling, bursting, overflowing, vigorous

cavernous
gaping, yawning, immense, spacious, mammoth, echoing, hollow

colossal
gigantic, massive, enormous, immense, gargantuan, mammoth, grandiose, vast, majestic, titanic, monumental, towering, behemoth

commanding
sweeping, powerful, expansive, decisive, imposing, lofty, superior, impressive, soaring

compact
concise, condensed, crammed, tight, dense, compressed, succinct

compressed
compact, condensed, crammed, dense, squeezed, constricted, abbreviated, dense

SEE: SIZES *and* AMOUNTS

condensed
concise, truncated, compact, concentrated, succinct

copious
abundant, profuse, fruitful, bountiful, plentiful, abounding, rampant, teeming, swarming, bristling, bursting, ample, exuberant, flourishing, overflowing

deepening
expanding, intensifying, heightening, magnifying, mounting

diffuse
sparse, scanty, scarce, spotty, sporadic, thin, scattered, strewn

diminutive
tiny, miniscule, minute, microscopic, teeny, petite, miniature

dinky
meager, paltry, piffling, puny, dainty, petit, miniature, trifling, trivial

elephantine
colossal, gigantic, immense, mammoth, monstrous, humongous, towering, massive

elevated
highfalutin, majestic, lofty, visionary, superlative, colossal, grandiose, noble, aerial

enormous
colossal, gigantic, massive, immense, vast, towering, gargantuan, mammoth, behemoth

exhaustive
sweeping, far-reaching, expansive, intensive, full-blown, extensive, wide-ranging

exorbitant
extravagant, enormous, inflated, inordinate, outrageous, excessive, preposterous, steep

expansive, expanding
sweeping, extensive, roomy, voluminous, spacious, panoramic, vast, far-reaching, gathering

gaping
yawning, cavernous, immense, enormous, vast, gigantic, colossal, wide

gargantuan
massive, towering, mammoth, colossal, enormous, behemoth, immense, prodigious, staggering, astounding

gigantic
behemoth, titanic, colossal, massive, enormous, immense, vast, towering, monumental, whopping

hair's breadth
> tiny, narrow, by a whisker, miniscule, slight

immense
> enormous, towering, colossal, gigantic, massive, gaping, yawning, cavernous, vast

infinite
> boundless, innumerable, unending, measureless, limitless, eternal, everlasting, perpetual, untold, incalculable, inexhaustible

infinitesimal
> minute, miniscule, meager, negligible, imperceptible, insignificant, tiny

inflated
> extravagant, enormous, exorbitant, overblown, ballooning, excessive, bloated, exaggerated

innumerable
> limitless, boundless, infinite, measureless, countless, incalculable, untold

insurmountable
> impossible, overwhelming, overpowering, hopeless, unassailable, devastating

limitless
> inexhaustible, boundless, incalculable, infinite, innumerable, unending, ceaseless, measureless, perpetual

mammoth
> gargantuan, colossal, enormous, massive, towering, staggering, prodigious, immense

massive
> colossal, enormous, immense, towering, gargantuan, mammoth, vast

meager
> scant, skimpy, spare, trifling, infinitesimal, sparse, paltry, measly

measly
> paltry, piffling, puny, quibbling, superficial, stingy, trivial

miniscule
> tiny, minute, microscopic, insignificant, slight, hair's breadth

momentous
> crucial, pivotal, earth-shattering, eventful, preeminent, ascendant, stellar, grand, towering, transcendent, seminal

monumental
> titanic, colossal, gigantic, immense, massive, towering, vast

overflowing
> cascading, torrential, rushing, swarming, abounding, bristling, bursting, abundant

SEE: SIZES *and* AMOUNTS

oversized
cumbersome, unwieldy, ungainly, expanding, eclipsing, ballooning, protruding, bulky

paltry
miserly, piffling, puny, quibbling, superficial, stingy, trivial, measly

panoramic
sweeping, commanding, expansive, aerial, vast, comprehensive, far-reaching

petty
trivial, dinky, paltry, piffling, superficial, measly, trifling

piffling
quibbling, superficial, petty, dinky, paltry, puny, measly, trivial, trifling

plunging
plummeting, nose-diving, yawning, sinking, tumbling, descending, dipping

precipitous
steep, abrupt, headlong, dizzying, sharp, sheer, swift

prodigious
gargantuan, mammoth, colossal, massive, towering, immense, staggering, astounding, enormous, behemoth

profuse
bountiful, teeming, abundant, copious, lavish

puny
trivial, measly, petty, dinky, paltry, trifling, quibbling, superficial

roomy
voluminous, spacious, expansive, vast, extensive, generous, sizable, ample

scant, scanty
meager, skimpy, spare, spindly, paltry, sparse, insufficient, stingy, bare

seismic
huge, earth-scattering, enormous, colossal, massive, mammoth, tectonic, weighty, tumultuous, profound

spacious
roomy, voluminous, expansive, vast, sweeping, ample, sizable, extensive

spare
scant, unadorned, stark, fine, thin, confined, meager, bare, slight

sprawling
spreading, stretched, extended, scattered, rambling, draping

steep
precipitous, abrupt, headlong, sheer, sharp, elevated, extreme

swarming
  abounding, bristling, bursting, copious, flourishing, overflowing, brimming, thriving, booming, prospering, teeming, vigorous

sweeping
  far-reaching, expansive, commanding, vast, spacious, panoramic, exhaustive

tectonic
  earth-scattering, enormous, massive, seismic, momentous, weighty

teeming
  plentiful, thriving, prospering, swarming, vigorous, abundant, profuse, fruitful, copious, bountiful, lavish, roaring

titanic
  colossal, gigantic, immense, massive, monumental, towering, vast, herculean, elephantine

towering
  enormous, immense, vast, colossal, gigantic, massive, gargantuan, mammoth, preeminent, momentous, grand, ascendant, stellar, transcendent, titanic, behemoth

unfathomable
  immeasurable, inscrutable, incomprehensible, mystifying, deep, unplumbed, boundless

ungainly
  cumbersome, oversized, bulky, clumsy, unwieldy, awkward

vast
  massive, enormous, voluminous, spacious, expansive, colossal, gigantic, immense, towering

vanishing
  evanescent, ephemeral, melting, fleeting, ethereal, transient, fading

voluminous
  roomy, spacious, expansive, billowing, vast, copious, swelling, massive, ample

yawning
  gaping, cavernous, immense, bottomless, plunging, echoing

SPACE, LOCATION, *or* POSITION

abandoned
  isolated, disjointed, detached, estranged, alienated, godforsaken, remote, empty, stranded, sealed off, separated, rootless, secluded, vacant, barren

abyss
  gulf, cavern, chasm, pit, gorge, schism, fissure, crevasse, void

aligned
symmetrical, proportional, even, uniform, balanced, centered, geometrical

askance
skewed, unbalanced, crooked, lopsided, uneven, misaligned, awry, askew, slanted, oblique, sidelong, twisted

askew
crooked, unbalanced, skewed, lopsided, uneven, awry, cockeyed, askance, tilted, oblique, sidelong

barren
desolate, empty, dreary, forlorn, godforsaken, void, abandoned, deserted, bare, remote, gaunt, stark, vacant

blockaded
confined, constricted, enclosed, trapped, barricaded, caged

caged
enclosed, trapped, cramped, blockaded, confined, constricted

canyon
gulch, gulf, chasm, gorge, ravine, gully, valley

cavern
gulf, chasm, abyss, gorge, ravine, gully, cave

chasm
gulf, cavern, abyss, gorge, rift, schism, void

cloistered
sheltered, confined, enclosed, curtained

confined
caged, enclosed, cramped, blockaded, constricted

constricted
caged, confined, enclosed, tightened, hampered

crammed
cramped, wedged, compact, tight, squeezed

cramped
blockaded, caged, confined, constricted, enclosed, crammed

crevasse
abyss, gorge, fissure, void, gulf, cavern, chasm, cleft

disconnected
isolated, stranded, secluded, detached, separated, alienated

discrete
distinct, separate, disconnected, detached

distant
forbidding, guarded, impassive, remote, stern, unapproachable, uninviting

distinct
discrete, pronounced, clear, refined, separate, precise

encased
confined, constricted, caged, enclosed, wrapped, sheathed, covered

enclosed
cramped, blockaded, caged, confined, constricted, encased, embedded

estranged
disjointed, detached, alienated, abandoned, isolated, remote, stranded, sealed off, separated

faraway
far-flung, remote, outlying, far-off, afar, yonder, obscure, distant

far-flung
exotic, remote, distant, outlandish, far-reaching, widespread

gorge
gulf, cavern, chasm, rupture, abyss, schism

gulf
cavern, chasm, rupture, abyss, gorge, schism

isolated
remote, stranded, sealed off, secluded, abandoned, disjointed, detached, estranged, alienated

jammed
obstructed, cemented, compressed, seized, immobilized, blocked

oblique, obliquely
tangential, sidelong, askew, pitching, crooked, leaning, slanting, sloped, awry

peripheral
sideways, tangential, outlying, incidental, remote, oblique, sidelong

precipice
cliff, brink, bluff, crag, steep, drop, steer

remote
abandoned, isolated, exotic, far-flung, distant, secluded, detached, stranded, separated

schism
gulf, cavern, chasm, rupture, abyss, gorge, rift

secluded
remote, stranded, separated, abandoned, isolated, disjointed, detached

sheltered
> cloistered, enclosed, curtained, protected, insulated, sequestered

sidelong
> oblique, askance, indirect, backhanded

skewed
> unbalanced, crooked, lopsided, uneven, misaligned, askew, askance, sidelong, oblique, twisted, slanted, awry

stranded
> estranged, secluded, isolated, alienated, disjointed, detached, remote, sealed off

tangential
> peripheral, sideways, outlying, incidental, remote, oblique, sidelong

vacant
> abandoned, bare, barren, empty, deserted, void

void
> vacuum, abyss, gulf, cavern, nothingness

SHAPES *and* STRUCTURES

aerodynamic
> sleek, elegant, smooth, fluid, streamlined

airy
> gauzy, delicate, fine-spun, gossamer, lacy, dainty, willowy, wispy, fragile

amalgamation
> blend, mixture, fusion, combination, synthesis

amorphous
> nebulous, blurry, formless, fuzzy, shapeless, murky, vague

angular
> forked, bent, bony, rawboned, jagged, pointed

anomalous
> irregular, twisted, peculiar, deviating, incongruous, divergent

asymmetrical
> unbalanced, crooked, lopsided, misaligned, skewed, askance, uneven

atrophied
> wasting, emaciated, shrinking, withering, disintegrating

ballooning
> swelling, swollen, inflated, bursting, bloated, enlarged, expanding, distended

barbed
> spiny, prickly, thorny, spiky, spiked, sharp

battered
  crumbling, ravaged, dilapidated, beat-up, rickety, deteriorated, aged, ramshackle

bifurcated
  forked, divided, branched, divergent, split

billow, billowy
  fluffy, puffy, rippling, swirling, streaming, ballooning, spewing, rolling, wavy, undulating

bloated
  swollen, bulging, distended, turgid, inflated, puffy, engorged

bony
  gangly, lanky, spindly, gawky, scrawny, angular, rawboned, skinny, lean

branched, branching
  twiggy, gawky, reedy, spidery, twisting, snaking, bifurcated, forked, split

brawny
  burly, hefty, stocky, robust, hearty, muscular, sinewy, steely, rugged, sturdy

breakable
  flimsy, brittle, fragile, rickety, shaky, willowy, frail, wobbly, delicate, weak

brittle
  rickety, splintering, shaky, flimsy, fragile, breakable

bulbous
  bulging, swollen, distended, rotund, round, globular, orbed, curved

bulging
  puffy, distended, swollen, turgid, inflated, bloated, protruding

bulky
  clunky, heavy, hefty, unwieldy, awkward, cumbersome, ungainly, oversized

burly
  hefty, stocky, brawny, fleshy, beefy, weighty, meaty, portly

byzantine
  intricate, complex, convoluted, serpentine, tangled, knotty, elaborate

chunky
  paunchy, rotund, plump, bulbous, round, pudgy, stout, stocky, portly

clunky
  bulky, awkward, heavy, hefty, unwieldy, leaden

coiled
  twisted, bent, looped, curled, spiraled, corkscrew, helical

concave
  curved, recessed, hollow, sunken, indented

contorted
twisted, disfigured, distorted, deformed, gnarled, misshapen, crooked, warped

contoured
curved, shaped, smoothed, outlined, formed, molded

convoluted
tangled, complicated, elaborate, snaking, intricate, serpentine

corrugated
grooved, ridged, fluted, creased, puckered

cracked
crumble, fractured, chipped, fissured, ruptured, gaping, cratered, dented, pitted, splintered, shattered

craggy
steep, rough, rugged, weathered, ragged

crater
hollow, gaping, crack, abyss, cavern, pit

creased
grooved, ridged, fluted, puckered, corrugated, pleated, rumbled, folded, wrinkled

crooked
contorted, warped, lopsided, uneven, misaligned, skewed, twisted, misshapen, tortuous, winding, meandering, slanted, distorted, gnarled

crumbling
battered, dilapidated, decaying, deteriorated, eroded, collapsing, disintegrating

cumbersome
unwieldy, awkward, blundering, lumbering, ungainly, oversized, bulky

curly
wavy, rippled, kinked, swirled, spiralled, looped

curved, curvaceous
winding, wavy, circuitous, meandering, twisting

curvy
shapely, curvaceous, curving, voluptuous, bending, twisting, corkscrew, wavy

dangling
slack, baggy, drooping, floppy, limp, hanging

deformed
contorted, twisted, disfigured, distorted, grotesque, misshapen, gnarled, marred, warped

delicate
intricate, fine, exquisite, dainty, gauzy, willowy, fine-spun, gossamer, lacy, sheer, wispy, threadlike, airy

dense
heavy, dark, weighty, ponderous, opaque, packed, impenetrable

dented
hollow, cracked, sunken, marred, concave, gouged, indented

deviating
twisted, anomalous, divergent, circuitous, tortuous, meandering, winding

dilapidated
decrepit, shabby, disheveled, battered, decaying, aged, deteriorated, ruined, rickety

disfigured
misshapen, crooked, contorted, twisted, distorted, deformed, gnarled, warped, marred

disjointed
disconnected, alienated, isolated, detached, separated, fragmented, jumbled

dislocated
disordered, distorted, disarray, displaced, jumbled

distended
bloated, inflated, engorged, swollen, bulging, puffy

distorted
contorted, twisted, disfigured, deformed, crooked, awry, warped, misshapen, marred

doughy
flabby, fleshy, mushy, pasty, thick, chunky, paunchy

drooping, droopy
dangling, slack, baggy, floppy, limp, wilted

elliptical, ellipsoidal
oblong, oval, elongated, ellipse

faceted
multi-sided, complex, multi-stranded, multi-dimensional

feeble
flaccid, limp, weak, frail, flimsy, failing, decrepit

fine
narrow, precise, thin, slender, slight, spare, tenuous, fragile, flimsy, exquisite, fine-spun

flabby
flaccid, floppy, slack, sagging, doughy, fleshy, mushy, paunchy

flaccid
feeble, limp, droopy, weak, flabby, floppy, flimsy

flattened
compressed, crushed, compact, squashed, pressed

fleshy
heavy, weighty, brawny, meaty, paunchy, plump, jowly, doughy, flabby, mushy, pasty, thick, burly

flexible
fluid, flowing, resilient, stretchy, adaptable, pliable, supple, elastic, bendable

flimsy
brittle, fragile, breakable, rickety, shaky, willowy, frail, wobbly, wispy, floppy

floppy
flabby, flaccid, flimsy, malleable, slack, baggy, dangling, drooping, limp

fluid
flexible, flowing, liquid, watery, shifting, molten, runny, changeable

fluted
grooved, creased, corrugated, wrinkled, furrowed, puckered, ridged

forked
bifurcated, branching, pronged, split, divided

formless
amorphous, nascent, unformed, nebulous, chaotic, shapeless

fragile
flimsy, brittle, shaky, willowy, frail, breakable, rickety, wobbly, wispy

fragmented
uneven, choppy, frayed, spotty, erratic, haphazard, splintered, broken

frail
shaky, willowy, wobbly, fragile, flimsy, brittle, breakable, rickety, wispy

full-bodied
robust, dynamic, hearty, sturdy, vibrant, vigorous, zestful

fused, fusion
mixture, synthesis, amalgamation, melding, mingling, integration, blended

gangly
bony, lanky, spindly, gawky, scrawny, long-legged, leggy, skinny

gashed
jagged, spiky, serrated, rough, ragged, gouged, lacerated, split, ripped

gawky
gangly, bony, lanky, spindly, scrawny, twiggy, reedy, scraggly

geometrical
symmetrical, proportional, aligned, balanced

globular
　spherical, rounded, bulbous, orb, circular

gnarled
　disfigured, contorted, distorted, knotty, twisted, knobby, crooked, misshapen, deformed, marred, warped

grooved
　corrugated, ridged, fluted, creased, puckered, crimped, sculpted, carved

gutted
　destroyed, demolished, wrecked, ransacked, ravaged, decimated, looted, ruined, stripped

heavy, heavy-set
　fleshy, weighty, brawny, meaty, paunchy, plump, dense, stocky, stout, portly, burly

hefty
　bulky, clunky, heavy, portly, chunky, massive, weighty

hollow
　sunken, concave, deep-set, recessed, vacant, empty

impenetrable
　impervious, indestructible, persistent, resistant, dense, bulletproof, unyielding

impervious
　indestructible, impenetrable, persistent, resistant, unyielding, inflexible, immune, refractory, watertight

inflexible
　taut, intractable, stiff, unbending, unyielding, hardened, tough, rigid

intractable
　unbending, unmanageable, inflexible, obstructive, stiff, unyielding

jagged
　spiky, serrated, rough, angular, broken, forked, gashed, ragged, saw-toothed

knobby
　bumpy, gnarled, rough, lumpy

knotty
　elaborate, twisted, gnarled, thorny, tangled, convoluted

lanky
　gawky, scrawny, gangly, bony, spindly, twiggy, reedy

lean
　angular, slender, lanky, wiry, sinewy, brawny, ropy

leggy
　shapely, overgrown, stringy, bony, spindly

See: Shapes *and* Structures

limp
> drooping, floppy, flaccid, slack, baggy, dangling

lithe
> sinuous, flexible, supple, willowy, graceful, pliable

lopsided
> unbalanced, crooked, uneven, misaligned, skewed, asymmetrical, askew, tilted

malleable
> pliable, flexible, supple, moldable, yielding, elastic, workable, springy, bendable

marred
> gnarled, warped, misshapen, disfigured, contorted, deformed

matted
> rumpled, crinkled, tousled, knotted, tangled, flattened

misaligned
> unbalanced, crooked, lopsided, uneven, skewed, askew, irregular, awry

misshapen
> contorted, warped, twisted, buckled, skewed, crooked, disfigured, deformed, distorted, gnarled, marred

muscular
> robust, brawny, full-bodied, hearty, sinewy, rugged, strapping

mushy
> doughy, squishy, flabby, fleshy, pasty, thick, spongy

narrow
> fine, precise, thin, slender, slight, spare, slim, tight, hair's breadth

nebulous
> formless, amorphous, fuzzy, chaotic, shapeless, hazy, ambiguous, shadowy

papery
> lacy, slinky, wispy, airy, delicate, dainty, gauzy, willowy

paunchy
> rotund, plump, bulbous, round, chunky, stout, stocky, portly, meaty, doughy, fleshy, heavy, burly

perforated
> riddled, punctured, pitted, punched, pierced

pliable
> flexible, supple, malleable, elastic, limber, lithe, willowy

plump
> paunchy, fleshy, heavy, weighty, burly, brawny, meaty, chunky, beefy

pointed, pointy
> jagged, spiny, thorny, barbed, spiked, edged

puffy

inflated, swollen, bulging, bloated, distended, enlarged

punctured

riddled, perforated, torn, ripped, pierced, ruptured

ragged

jagged, spiky, serrated, rough, angular, forked, gashed, slipshod, tattered, scruffy, shredded, scraggly, ratty, torn

rambling

twisting, winding, meandering, tortuous, sprawling, disconnected, circuitous, serpentine, roundabout

ramshackle

tottering, rickety, shifting, wobbly, crumbling, shabby, tumbledown, dilapidated, shaky, flimsy

ravaged

blighted, corrosive, devastated, disintegrating, haggard, plagued, ruinous, wasted, wrecked

rawboned

angular, bony, gaunt, scrawny, gawky, skinny, lanky

reedy

twiggy, branching, gawky, lanky, gangly, leggy

resilient

adaptable, flexible, mobile, changeable, responsive, pliable, supple, durable, sturdy

rickety

dilapidated, decrepit, shabby, flimsy, brittle, fragile, breakable, battered, decaying, deteriorated, shaky, wobbly, tottering, aged, ramshackle, tumbledown

riddled

perforated, punctured, saturated, pierced, peppered, pelted, marred

ridged

grooved, fluted, creased, puckered, corrugated, ribbed, toothed, jagged

rigid

immobile, immovable, stagnant, unmoving, changeless, stiff, unyielding

robust

brawny, dynamic, full-bodied, hearty, muscular, sinewy, staunch, rugged, sturdy, vibrant, vigorous

ropy

wiry, lean, sinewy, stringy, thready, fibrous

rotund

plump, bulbous, round, chunky, paunchy, stout, portly

rough-hewn
chiseled, angular, rawboned, sharp, coarse, unrefined, unfinished, unpolished

rounded
spherical, globular, bulbous, orb, circular

rubbery
malleable, elastic, pliable, spongy, springy, stretchy

rugged
rough, resistant, robust, durable, sturdy, enduring, craggy, steep, hearty, muscular

rutted
rough, craggy, rugged, irregular, grooved, knobby, bumpy, uneven, choppy

scraggly
scrawny, gawky, bedraggled, ragged, threadbare, unkempt, disheveled, frayed, frazzled, shoddy

scrawny
spindly, gangly, bony, lanky, gawky, scraggly, rawboned, ragged, meager, stunted

sculpted
chiseled, shaped, carved, molded

serpentine
snaking, meandering, convoluted, circuitous, twisted, winding, wavy, curvaceous

serrated
jagged, spiky, ragged, toothed, notched, saw-toothed

shaky
flimsy, wobbly, fragile, breakable, rickety, ramshackle, tottering, unsteady

shallow
empty, flimsy, superficial, flat, hollow

shapely
leggy, curvy, curvaceous, buxom, graceful, balanced, elegant

silhouette
contour, outline, shadow, etching, profile

sinewy
muscular, burly, robust, brawny, full-bodied, hearty, sturdy

sinuous
billowy, flexible, supple, lithe, curving, coiling, twisting

skew, skewed
unbalanced, crooked, lopsided, uneven, misaligned, slanted, distorted, askew, awry

skimpy
scant, spare, spindly, meager, thin, paltry, skinny

skinny
wiry, lean, sinewy, ropy, thread, gawky, bony

slack
baggy, dangling, drooping, floppy, limp, lax

sleek
elegant, smooth, fluid, streamlined, aerodynamic

slender
thin, slight, spare, narrow, fine, precise, lean, slim

slight
narrow, fine, precise, thin, slender, spare

slinky
supple, willowy, sinuous, smooth, sleek

snaking
serpentine, circuitous, curvaceous, meandering, twisted, twisting, winding, wavy, convoluted

spidery
webby, twiggy, branching, angular

spiked, spiky
jagged, serrated, angular, forked, gashed, ragged, spiny, prickly, thorny, barbed, pointy

spindly
gangly, bony, lanky, gawky, scrawny, leggy, bare, gaunt

spiny
prickly, thorny, barbed, spiky, pointed, sharp

spiral, spiralled
coiled, twisted, bent, looped, curled, rolled, curved, arched, furled, corkscrew

splintering, splintered
fragmented, fractured, disintegrating, frayed, crumbling, shattered, disconnected, broken

springy
fluid, stretchy, elastic, supple, flexible, rubbery

statuesque
majestic, shapely, stately, elegant, towering

stiff
inflexible, unbending, recalcitrant, rigid, wooden

stocky
brawny, burly, hefty, sturdy, chunky, stubby, squat

stout
rotund, plump, burly, round, chunky, paunchy, portly

streamlined
sleek, elegant, smooth, fluid, aerodynamic, refined

stretchy
elastic, springy, supple, bouncy, pliable, malleable

strewn
dispersed, scattered, unleashed, flung, tossed, littered

stringy
fibrous, flossy, wiry, sinewy, ropy, thread, gangly, leggy

sturdy
robust, hearty, muscular, rugged, vibrant, unyielding, durable

sunken
hollow, gaping, cracked, dented, submerged, indented, recessed, concave

supple
sinuous, muscular, flexible, lithe, pliable, resilient, bendable, elastic, stretchy

swollen
bulging, bursting, distended, bloated, inflated, puffy, engorged, turgid

symmetrical
proportional, even, aligned, uniform, balanced

tattered
ripped, torn, shredded, shabby, ragged, ratty, holey, threadbare

tenuous
fragile, slender, fine, delicate, thin, shaky, airy, flimsy

thicket
grove, clump, underbrush, shrub, tangle

thorny
spiny, prickly, barbed, spiky, pointy

thready
wiry, lean, sinewy, coarse, brawny, ropy, stringy

toothed
serrated, notched, ragged, ridged, saw-toothed

tortuous
crooked, twisting, winding, meandering, convoluted, curving, serpentine, snaking

turgid
distended, bulged, inflated, puffy, swollen, engorged, bloated

twiggy
branching, lean, gawky, lanky, leggy, reedy, spidery, tenuous

twisted, twisting
coiled, bent, looped, curled, spiraled, crooked, tortuous, winding, entangled, intertwined, contorted, deformed, distorted, gnarled, convoluted, meandering, rambling

unbroken
continuous, constant, unified, sound, solid, whole

uneven
asymmetrical, disproportional, misaligned, lopsided, irregular, crooked, askew

ungainly
cumbersome, oversized, bulky, clumsy, unwieldy, awkward

uniform
even, constant, steady, unbroken, consistent, smooth, symmetrical

unwieldy
awkward, ungainly, cumbersome, oversized, massive, burdensome, bulky

voluptuous
curvaceous, shapely, curvy, buxom

warped
deformed, distorted, gnarled, misshapen, disfigured, contorted, crooked, marred, twisted

wavy
meandering, serpentine, snaking, winding, circuitous, curvaceous, curvy, curved, undulating, rippled

webbed
interwoven, intertwined, entangled, twisted, braided, enlaced, fretted, interlaced, woven

whorl, whorled
spiraled, curled, looped, ringed, twisted, helical, eddy, whirlpool, corkscrew, coiled

willowy
delicate, dainty, wispy, airy, graceful, lithe, lacy, papery, slinky

winding
curvaceous, meandering, serpentine, snaky, twisted, circuitous, wavy, convoluted

wiry
lean, sinewy, coarse, brawny, ropy, stringy, thready, wavy

wispy
airy, brittle, delicate, dainty, gauzy, lacy, papery, slinky, willowy

withered
decaying, gaunt, haggard, emaciated, shriveled, wrinkled, wizened

wizened
shriveled, creased, withered, shrunken, gnarled, wrinkled

wobbly
ambling, doddering, faltering, tottering, oscillating, toppling, rickety, bobbling, capsizing, tumbling, careening

Textures, Designs, *and* Patterns

adorn, adorned
decorate, embellish, festoon, garnish, wreathe, bejeweled, flowery, fanciful, frilly, lush, ornate, luxuriant, lavish, resplendent, beaded, fancy, ornamented, trimmed

beaded
jeweled, adorned, bejeweled, embellished, festooned, ornamented

bejeweled
jeweled, embellished, festooned, adorned, beaded, ornamented, trimmed, bespangled, studded, spangled

bespangled
spangled, embellished, studded, bejeweled, glittering, adorned, glimmering, sprinkled, trimmed, sequinned

blotched, blotchy
marked, patchy, uneven, tarnished, besmirched, blemished, spotty, smudged, tainted, fragmented

burnish, burnished
buff, finish, glaze, gloss, luster, polish, shine, varnish, wax, patina

bushy
woolly, hairy, unruly, thick, shaggy, disheveled, scruffy, scrubby

checkered
patterned, multicolored, decorative, motley, quilted, patchwork

coating, coated
patina, burnish, wear, finish, glaze, veneer, polish, shine, gloss

corroded
tarnished, damaged, rusted, eroded, deteriorated, rotted, worn

cottony
silky, fine-spun, satiny, sleek, velvety, plush, delicate, fluffy

craggy
weathered, weather-beaten, rugged, rough, stony, rocky

creased
> crinkled, weathered, wrinkled, craggy, rumpled, shriveled, pleated

crinkled
> wrinkled, scrunched, creased, shriveled, rumpled, ruffled

dainty
> delicate, intricate, fine, exquisite, wispy, airy, gauzy, lacy, papery, slinky, willowy

decorated, decorative
> adorned, embellished, festooned, garnished, wreathe, gilded, ornamental

delicate
> intricate, willowy, exquisite, dainty, gauzy, airy, fine-spun, gossamer, lacy, sheer, wispy, threadlike, fine

dense
> heavy, dark, weighty, thick, opaque, compressed, solid

dog-eared
> threadbare, worn, rickety, battered, run-down, ragged, ramshackle, scruffy, ratty

durable
> sturdy, enduring, indestructible, impervious, persistent, resistant, rugged, vital, unchanging

earthen, earthy
> hearty, clay, muddy, natural, rocky, stony

elaborate
> extravagant, showy, intricate, ornate, embellished, adorned, flowery, grandiose, fanciful, resplendent, frilly

embellished
> adorned, decorated, festooned, garnished, wreathed, luxuriant, lavish, elaborate, resplendent, ornate, adorned, flowery, fanciful, fancy, frilly

enlaced
> intertwined, entangled, twisted, braided, fretted, interlaced, woven, interwoven, webbed

eroded
> rusted, corroded, tarnished, oxidized, ravaged, degraded

extravagant
> showy, ornate, flamboyant, flashy, adorned, elaborate, lavish

fanciful
> elaborate, whimsical, extravagant, imaginative, dreamy, adorned, flowery, frilly, lush, ornate, romantic, resplendent, embellished

festoon, festooned
> garnish, wreathe, trim, adorn, decorate, embellish, jewel, ornament

filigree, filigreed
lace, ornamented, lattice, interlaced, lacy

filmy
translucent, fine-spun, fragile, chiffon, gossamer, sheer, dainty, wispy, transparent

fine
narrow, precise, thin, slender, slight, spare, tenuous, fragile

fine-spun
gauzy, airy, delicate, gossamer, lacy, fragile, wispy, filmy

finish
patina, coating, gloss, burnish, glaze, veneer, polish, shine

flecked
freckled, marbled, blotchy, spotted, streaked, checkered

freckled
flecked, spotted, blotchy, checkered, speckled

fretted
enlaced, interlaced, webbed, interwoven, braided, woven, twisted, intertwined, entangled

frilly
fanciful, embellished, fancy, lacy, gossamer, delicate, fine-spun, threadlike, fine, ornate, adorned, flowery, resplendent, elaborate

frothy
effervescent, airy, breezy, bubbling, fizzy, sparkling, sudsy, foamy

furry
hairy, fuzzy, bearded, shaggy, fleecy, downy, woolly

fuzzy
foggy, cloudy, murky, blurry, opaque, muddy, obscured, nebulous, amorphous, shadowy, furry, hairy, bearded, shaggy, hazy

garland
wreathe, twine, lace, ribbon, festoon, laurel, crown

garnish
festoon, wreathe, adorn, decorate, embellish, trim

gauzy
airy, delicate, gossamer, lacy, sheer, filmy, translucent, wispy, dainty, papery

gilded
golden, embellished, decorative, embroidered, festooned, luxurious, adorned, ornate

glaze
glassy, tint, varnish, film, gloss, luster, shine, finish, veneer, polish

gossamer
delicate, fine-spun, lacy, threadlike, sheer, airy, fine, filmy, silky

hairy
fuzzy, bearded, furry, shaggy, woolly, whiskered

insignia
emblem, regalia, badge, symbol, seal, crest

interlaced
entangled, twisted, intertwined, interwoven, woven, braided

intertwined
braided, enlaced, interlaced, interwoven, entangled, woven, twisted, webbed

interwoven
intertwined, entangled, twisted, braided, enlaced, fretted, woven, interlaced, webbed

intricate
ornate, exquisite, dainty, elaborate, complex, entangled

jagged
rugged, craggy, weathered, weather-beaten, pitted, irregular, uneven, ridged, spiked, rough

jeweled
adorned, beaded, bejeweled, embellished, festooned, ornamented, trimmed

lace
wreathe, garland, twine, ribbon, thread, filigree, mesh, trim, mesh, tie, border

lacy
dainty, gauzy, papery, slinky, threadlike, frilly, gossamer, fine, delicate, fine-spun

luxuriant, luxurious
rich, thick, adorned, embellished, festooned, lavish, sumptuous, stately, glorious, majestic

mosaic
patchwork, collage, pattern, montage, melange, pastiche, medley

mottled
dappled, spotted, blotchy, speckled, stippled, streaked, checkered, freckled

ornamented
bejeweled, embellished, jeweled, adorned, beaded, festooned, trimmed, gilded, ornate

ornate
adorned, flowery, fanciful, elaborate, embellished, fancy, frilly, resplendent

patchy
uneven, fragmented, choppy, frayed, spotty, haphazard, blotchy, irregular

pastiche
mosaic, motif, patchwork, collage, synthesis, montage, melange, medley, blend

patina
coating, wear, finish, burnish, glaze, veneer, polish, shine, gloss

peppered
riddled, pelted, stippled, perforated, punctured, saturated

pitted
rugged, pockmarked, pocked, craggy, weathered, weather-beaten, rough, jagged, uneven

plumage
feathers, cluster, clump, shock, tuft, strand

plush
opulent, rich, lavish, luscious, luxuriant, sumptuous, showy, posh, elegant, fancy

pocked, pockmarked
rugged, pitted, craggy, weathered, weather-beaten, rough, jagged

polish
patina, glaze, shine, finish, sheen, gloss

polished
refined, glossy, impeccable, smooth, buffed, burnished, tasteful, shiny

prickly
spiny, thorny, barbed, spiky, pointy, bristly, knotty

regalia
insignia, finery, emblem, crown, badge, crest

ribbon
twine, lace, thread, wreathe, garland

rough
craggy, steep, rugged, irregular, stony, rutted, uneven

rugged
craggy, weathered, weather-beaten, rough, pitted, jagged, bumpy, coarse, worn

rumpled
creased, crinkled, matted, tousled, wrinkled, trampled, flattened

rusted
corroded, tarnished, oxidized, eroded, pitted, decaying

satin, satiny
silky, fine-spun, sleek, velvety, shiny, silken, smooth, glossy

scrawl, scrawled
scribble, hieroglyphics, symbol, stylized, illegible

scribble
scrawl, hieroglyphics, illegible, graffiti

sheer
airy, gossamer, clarified, translucent, gauzy, chiffon, thin, flimsy, see-through, crystalline

showy
flashy, frilly, glittering, ornate, garish, luxurious, plush, opulent, rich, lavish

shredded
torn, tattered, ragged, chopped, frayed, ripped

shriveled
crinkled, wrinkled, creased, weathered, withered, shrunken

silky
cottony, fine-spun, satin, sleek, velvety, fleecy, silken

sleek
silky, fine-spun, satin, velvety, glossy, shiny, sheen, slick, glassy

slick, slickness
glossy, shiny, sheen, sleek, glassy, slippery

slippery
slick, shiny, glassy, lubricated, slimy, oily, greasy, smooth

spangled
studded, bejeweled, glittering, adorned, glimmering

spare
scant, unadorned, stark, fine, precise, thin, bare, gaunt

sparse
diffuse, scanty, scarce, spotty, sporadic, stark, thin

speckled
dappled, spotted, blotchy, mottled, stippled, freckled, checkered, flecked, studded

spotted
flecked, dotted, dappled, speckled, splotchy, freckled, sprinkled, blotchy, patchy

sprinkled
spotted, sprayed, peppered, dappled, speckled, splotchy, freckled, flecked, studded, dotted

stippled
speckled, dappled, spotted, blotchy, mottled, dotted, blotted

studded
flecked, mottled, spotted, variegated, bespangled, bejeweled, spangled

tableau
scene, spectacle, view, montage, melange

tapestry
fabric, design, regalia, finery, screen, pattern, valance, textile

tarnished
besmirched, blemished, blotchy, debased, scorched, smudged, tainted, eroded, corroded, rusty

threadbare
shopworn, tattered, torn, worn, dull, scruffy, dog-eared, ragged

torn
shredded, holey, tattered, patchy, ragged, threadbare, frayed, ripped

trimmed
festooned, ornamented, jeweled, adorned, beaded, bejeweled, embellished

unadorned
natural, stark, spare, unvarnished, stripped, austere, unembellished, pure, plain

variegated
mottled, checkered, speckled, striped, patchy, flecked, dappled, hued

varnish
glaze, glassy, tint, film, finish, coat, luster, polish, gloss

velvety
silky, cottony, fine-spun, satin, sleek, silken

veneer
finish, glaze, polish, patina, burnish, coating, wear, shine

weathered
wrinkled, craggy, creased, crinkled, shriveled, scraggy, withered, weather-beaten, worn

withered
decaying, gaunt, haggard, barren, stark, desolate, emaciated

wizened
shriveled, creased, withered, shrunken, wilted, gnarled, winkled

worn
threadbare, shopworn, tattered, torn, dog-eared, frayed, ragged

woven
interwoven, intertwined, entangled, twisted, braided, enlaced, fretted, interlaced

wreathe
garland, twine, lace, ribbon, crown, festoon

wrinkled
rumpled, creased, crinkled, tousled, craggy, shriveled, scraggy, aged, weathered

FACIAL EXPRESSIONS

abashed
> shamefaced, regretful, pitiable, sorrowful, sheepish, mortified, remorseful

affable
> jovial, gleeful, joyous, hearty, light-hearted, congenial, pleasant, good-humored, amiable

agape
> appalled, dismayed, astonished, aghast, open-mouthed, wide-eyed, incredulous, awed

agitated
> disturbed, tumultuous, frenzied, hysterical, flustered, tempestuous, stormy, frantic, turbulent, distracted, disquieted, rattled

alert
> perceptive, sharp, discerning, vigilant, cogent, penetrating, piercing, watchful, guarded, mindful, observant

amazed
> wide-eyed, astonished, dumbstruck, flabbergasted, astounded, bedazzled, awed, surprised, startled, stupefied

anguished
> distressed, devastated, inconsolable, grief-stricken, heart-broken, woeful, bleak, dismal, mournful, sorrowful, morose

animated
> expressive, vibrant, lively, exuberant, vivacious, passionate, spirited

assured
> self-possessed, composed, balanced, equanimous, unflappable, unruffled, calm, poised

astonished
> flabbergasted, amazed, astounded, awed, bedazzled, wide-eyed, dumbstruck, surprised, startled, stupefied

astounded
> bedazzled, perplexed, wide-eyed, dumbstruck, surprised, startled, stupefied, flabbergasted, amazed, astonished, awed

austere
> stern, unapproachable, uninviting, grave, resolute, strict, taciturn, unbending, staid, cold

awed
> surprised, startled, wide-eyed, bedazzled, astonished, amazed, dumbstruck, astounded, flabbergasted, stupefied

See: Facial Expressions

baffled

puzzled, perplexed, bewildered, confounded, confused, stumped, befuddled, dazed

bedazzled

wide-eyed, astonished, dumbstruck, dazzled, amazed, astounded, stupefied, stunned, mesmerized, captivated, awed, enchanted

befuddled

bewildered, flustered, confounded, dazed, agitated, baffled

belligerent

hostile, menacing, forbidding, unfriendly, threatening, pugnacious

bewildered

confounded, stunned, baffled, puzzled, perplexed, dazed, rattled, befuddled

bitter

icy, cold, cutting, dispassionate, distant, impassive, numb, reticent, sharp, stony, detached

blank

empty, glazed, void, bare, stony, impassive, deadpan

breathless

headlong, panting, breakneck, dashing, gasping, wheezing

brooding

sulky, morose, sullen, moody, despondent, languishing, gloomy, dark

cagey

guarded, cunning, crafty, wary, sneaky, evasive, secretive, cautious, wily

composed

poised, refined, unruffled, unflappable, self-possessed, assured, balanced, calm, equanimous, placid

contemplative

wistful, longing, yearning, wishful, thoughtful, pining, musing, nostalgic, ruminating

contemptuous

disdainful, scoffing, scornful, sneering, mocking, derisive, insulting

contorted

twisted, disfigured, distorted, deformed, convulsed, writhing, tortured, wrenched

convulsed, convulsing

twisted, shuddering, contorted, shuddering, writhing, tormented, agitated, unsettled, disturbed, pained

crafty

cagey, cunning, sneaky, evasive, secretive, sly, calculating, devious, scheming

cunning
crafty, cagey, sneaky, guarded, evasive, secretive, canny

deadpan
blank, empty, glazed, void, stony, glassy, vacuous, emotionless

defiant
resistant, stubborn, obstinate, bull-headed, willful, headstrong, rigid

delirious
deranged, frantic, raving, crazed, manic, unhinged, wild, howling, demented

deranged
raving, savage, wild, fierce, delirious, frantic, howling, demented

despairing
despondent, mournful, melancholy, dispirited, brooding, forlorn, inconsolable

despondent
mournful, inconsolable, despairing, melancholy, forlorn, dispirited, morose,
doleful, dejected, disheartened

detached
stoic, impassive, lethargic, withdrawn, stony, callous, dry

dim-witted
foolish, absurd, vacuous, inane, fatuous, empty, vapid

disdainful
contemptuous, haughty, arrogant, pompous, scornful, derisive, indifferent,
sneering

dispirited
despondent, inconsolable, despairing, melancholy, forlorn, mournful, teary-eyed

dizzy
woozy, befuddled, unsteady, witless, whirling, confused, dazed, giddy, groggy

dramatic
stagy, cinematic, histrionic, melodramatic, theatrical, overblown

dreamy
contemplative, languid, meditative, wide-eyed, peaceful, romantic, placid,
tranquil, whimsical

droll
quirky, wry, comical, dry, witty, amusing, eccentric

drunken
boozy, carousing, inebriated, sloshed, bumbling

dumbstruck
surprised, startled, amazed, stupefied, wide-eyed, astonished, flabbergasted,
bedazzled, perplexed, awed

ecstatic
blissful, exultant, jubilant, rejoicing, euphoric, joyous, triumphant, rapturous, beaming, dreamy, elated, enraptured

elated
triumphant, exultant, jubilant, rejoicing, ecstatic, joyous, delirious, delighted, enraptured

emotional
dramatic, hysterical, histrionic, melodramatic, cinematic, moving, sentimental, impassioned, tender, poignant, tearful, weepy, stagy, teary-eyed

empty
blank, void, vacant, glassy, glazed, deadpan, vacuous, hollow

enigmatic
mysterious, secretive, perplexing, puzzling, obscure, mystifying, cryptic

equanimous
poised, composed, assured, balanced, unruffled, unflappable, self-possessed, calm, placid

euphoric
ecstatic, blissful, exultant, jubilant, rejoicing, elated, enraptured, joyous

evasive
sneaky, secretive, cagey, guarded, cunning, crafty, deceptive, elusive

exasperated
aggravated, disturbed, galled, irked, provoked, weary, troubled, vexed, incensed

exhilarated
vivacious, intoxicated, elated, delighted, invigorated, animated, euphoric

expressive
animated, vibrant, exuberant, vivacious, spirited, lively, colorful, striking, energetic

expressionless
blank, emotionless, deadpan, inscrutable, vacant, impassive, stony, wooden

exuberant
jaunty, cheerful, buoyant, ebullient, exhilarated, elated, animated, lively

ferocious
barbaric, beastly, belligerent, fierce, monstrous, raging, terrifying

fidgety
jittery, flustered, quivering, restless, trembling, twitchy, jumpy, uneasy, shaky

fierce
raging, forceful, wild, howling, savage, ferocious, barbaric, beastly, belligerent, intense

flabbergasted
> astonished, dumbstruck, amazed, wide-eyed, bedazzled, perplexed, surprised, startled, awed, stupefied, astounded, gobsmacked

flinty
> unyielding, hardened, immovable, steely, unflappable, unbending, stern, stony, rigid

flustered
> uneasy, jittery, fidgety, quivering, restless, nervous, shaky, jumpy, trembling, twitchy, turbulent

forlorn
> despondent, inconsolable, despairing, melancholy, mournful, dispirited, dejected, hopeless

frantic
> agitated, distracted, feverish, tumultuous, turbulent, frenzied, distressed, frenetic, hysterical, panic-stricken, panicky, distraught, wild

fraught
> distraught, frantic, panicky, overwrought, panic-stricken, agitated, overwrought, distressed

frightened
> spooked, disturbed, alarmed, appalled, startled, fearful, terrorized, frozen

frightening
> creepy, spooky, disturbing, chilling, alarming, hideous, terrifying, eerie, freaky

gaunt
> haggard, withered, somber, hollow, scrawny, emaciated, angular, bony, stark

ghostly
> ashen, pale, spooky, pallid, sallow, eerie, murky

glassy
> vacant, blank, empty, glazed, expressionless, dazed

glazed
> empty, glassy, vacant, blank, vacuous, dazed, dumbfounded

gleeful
> jovial, joyous, blissful, elated, delighted, jubilant, exuberant

gloomy
> dismal, somber, forlorn, sulky, morose, dark, sullen, moody, dour, brooding

glowering
> dark, scowling, sullen, glaring, brooding, gloomy, skulking, angry, frowning

grim
> dreary, forlorn, bleak, forbidding, stony, stern, cold

groggy
    dizzy, woozy, befuddled, unsteady, witless, confused, dazed, giddy, disoriented

guarded
    distant, remote, unapproachable, cautious, leery, uninviting, defensive, watchful, alert, vigilant, cagey, evasive, stern, wary

haggard
    gaunt, withered, stark, exhausted, emaciated, hollow, pale

hardened
    flinty, unyielding, immovable, steely, unflappable, unbending, stern

haughty
    pompous, arrogant, disdainful, contemptuous, scornful

histrionic
    hysterical, cinematic, showy, melodramatic, operatic, dramatic, stagy, theatrical

hostile
    malicious, menacing, belligerent, forbidding, unfriendly, vicious, threatening, pugnacious, cold

hysterical
    frantic, frenetic, frazzled, wild, histrionic, dramatic, melodramatic, inconsolable, tumultuous, frenzied, raging

icy
    frozen, biting, bitter, detached, cold, cutting, dispassionate, distant, frosty, stony, impassive, numb, reticent, sharp, shivery

immovable
    unyielding, hardened, steely, unflappable, unbending, motionless

impassive
    distant, expressionless, remote, stony, icy, frozen, detached, reticent, stoic, stern, dispassionate, numb, cold

inconsolable
    hysterical, frantic, despondent, despairing, melancholy, dispirited, wild, mournful

indecipherable
    puzzling, enigmatic, inscrutable, cryptic, mystifying, perplexing

inflamed
    prickly, festering, crimson, smoldering, feverish, fiery, flushed, heated, ignited, livid, raw

inscrutable
    enigmatic, indecipherable, mystifying, incomprehensible, cryptic, puzzling, perplexing

jovial
    festive, gleeful, joyous, affable, hearty, light-hearted, delighted

joyous
> hearty, light-hearted, jovial, gleeful, affable, elated, ecstatic

jubilant
> elated, triumphant, exultant, joyous, gleeful, rapturous, delighted

leery
> guarded, wary, apprehensive, cautious, uncertain, suspicious

listless
> languid, dull, lumbering, sleepy, poky, lethargic, shuffling, spiritless, slumberous, fatigued

longing
> wistful, yearning, wishful, thoughtful, mournful, contemplative, pining, pensive, regretful, musing, nostalgic, ruminating

melancholy
> despondent, inconsolable, despairing, mournful, forlorn, gloomy, dispirited, woeful

menacing
> intimidating, threatening, hostile, glowering, frightening, ominous, vicious, scowling

moody
> sulky, gloomy, morose, dark, sullen, brooding, glowering, dour, melancholy

morose
> brooding, moody, sulky, gloomy, dark, melancholy, sullen, mournful, dour

mortified
> shamefaced, regretful, pitiable, sorrowful, sheepish, remorseful, abashed, rueful

mournful
> forlorn, rueful, musing, nostalgic, gloomy, ruminating, melancholy, regretful, despondent, teary-eyed, pensive

musing
> contemplative, pining, nostalgic, wishful, thoughtful, pensive, wistful, longing, yearning, meditative, ruminating

nostalgic
> musing, ruminating, wistful, contemplative, longing, yearning, wishful, pensive, thoughtful, pining, regretful

open-mouthed
> flabbergasted, astonished, dumbstruck, amazed, wide-eyed, awed, bedazzled, surprised, startled, stupefied, astounded

overwrought
> fraught, distraught, frantic, panicky, distressed, uneasy, exhausted

panicky, panicked
> frenzied, fraught, distraught, frantic, distressed, overwrought, desperate, panic-stricken

peevish
> sullen, petulant, cantankerous, testy, prickly, acrimonious, irritable

penetrating
> sharp, discerning, keen, piercing, biting, fierce, intense

pensive
> longing, yearning, wishful, thoughtful, mournful, contemplative, wistful, pining, regretful, musing, nostalgic, ruminating

perplexed
> baffled, bewildered, confounded, cryptic, enigmatic, puzzled

piercing
> penetrating, perceptive, keen, shrewd, sharp, fierce, intense

pining
> longing, yearning, wistful, wishful, thoughtful, musing, pensive, contemplative, nostalgic, ruminating

placid
> poised, self-possessed, composed, assured, balanced, equanimous, unruffled, unflappable, tranquil, calm

poised
> elegant, graceful, stylish, tasteful, self-possessed, composed, assured, unruffled, balanced, equanimous, refined, unflappable, placid, calm

pugnacious
> hostile, aggressive, bullying, menacing, combative, bellicose

puzzled
> baffled, perplexed, bewildered, confounded, rattled, confused

puzzling
> baffling, cryptic, mysterious, quizzical, enigmatic, perplexing, bewildering, inexplicable, confounding, mystifying

quizzical
> puzzling, enigmatic, bizarre, curious, eccentric, odd, sardonic

raging
> ranting, raucous, raving, ferocious, barbaric, beastly, belligerent, fierce, monstrous

rapturous
> ecstatic, euphoric, blissful, jubilant, elated, triumphant, exultant, joyous, gleeful, rhapsodic

regretful
yearning, wishful, wistful, longing, thoughtful, pensive, pining, musing, rueful, mournful, contemplative, nostalgic, ruminating, remorseful, sorrowful

rueful
shamefaced, regretful, pitiable, sorrowful, sheepish, mortified, abashed, remorseful

ruminating
contemplative, pining, wistful, longing, yearning, wishful, musing, mournful, thoughtful, pensive, nostalgic

sardonic
scornful, disdainful, mocking, bitter, caustic, sneering, cynical

savage
howling, raving, wild, fierce, delirious, deranged, frantic, ferocious, vicious

scornful
disdainful, contemptuous, scoffing, sneering, scowling, withering, rude, haughty

scowling
glowering, sneering, glaring, moody, surly, gloomy, frowning, sullen

secretive
cagey, guarded, sneaky, evasive, cunning, crafty, wary, enigmatic, furtive

self-possessed
composed, assured, balanced, poised, unruffled, unflappable, equanimous, calm, placid

shamefaced
rueful, regretful, pitiable, sorrowful, sheepish, mortified, abashed, remorseful

sheepish
shamefaced, regretful, pitiable, sorrowful, mortified, abashed, remorseful, rueful

sickly
emaciated, feeble, ashen, pallid, sallow, peaked, languid, peaked, pale, gaunt

sorrowful
shamefaced, regretful, sheepish, mortified, abashed, remorseful, rueful

spiritless
languid, lumbering, sapless, shuffling, slumberous, apathetic, listless

spiteful
edgy, huffy, snappish, cantankerous, feisty, fractious, testy, ill-tempered

startled
wide-eyed, astonished, dumbstruck, flabbergasted, astounded, bedazzled, perplexed, surprised, stupefied, awed

SEE: FACIAL EXPRESSIONS

steadfast
unyielding, adamant, headstrong, inflexible, ironfisted, resolute, unflappable, unflinching, rapid

steely
cold, flinty, unyielding, hardened, immovable, unflappable, stony, unbending, icy, callous, stern

stern
unapproachable, uninviting, staid, austere, grave, unbending, taciturn, stern, stony

stoic
detached, impassive, lethargic, withdrawn, unexpressive, resigned, unemotional, indifferent

stony
steely, frozen, biting, callous, detached, dispassionate, distant, frosty, impassive, numb, reticent, icy, cold

stunned
bewildered, stupefied, confused, dumbfounded, astonished, numb, astounded, dismayed, startled, dazed

sulky
sullen, moody, gloomy, morose, dark, brooding, dour, morose, frowning, sour

sullen
moody, glowering, brooding, scowling, morose, sulky, gloomy, dark

surly
sulky, sullen, sour, scowling, testy, morose, rude, gruff, dour, irritable

teary, teary-eyed
despondent, inconsolable, despairing, melancholy, mournful, tearful, forlorn

tempestuous
tumultuous, agitated, frazzled, frenzied, hysterical, passionate, stormy, turbulent, volatile, fiery, raving

testy
bad-tempered, cantankerous, cranky, crotchety, crusty, feisty, spiteful, fractious, ill-tempered, edgy, huffy, irritable, snappish

thoughtful
wistful, longing, yearning, wishful, pensive, contemplative, pining, musing, nostalgic, ruminating

tormented
agonized, haunted, pained, tortured, twisted, anguished, vexed, distressed

tortured
tormented, convulsed, haunted, twisted, contorted, disturbed, distressed, pained

tranquil
languid, meditative, dreamy, contemplative, peaceful, soothing, placid, calm

transfixed
mesmerized, hypnotized, enchanted, captivated, engrossed, fascinated, riveted

trembling
twitchy, turbulent, quivering, jittery, flustered, fluttery, fidgety, restless, shaky, uneasy, nervous, jumpy

unbending
recalcitrant, inflexible, hostile, willful, flinty, hardened, immovable, steely, stiff, unflappable

uncertain
ambiguous, dubious, hesitant, doubtful, reluctant, tentative, faltering, vacillating, skeptical

undaunted
brazen, unblinking, unabashed, bold, fearless, intrepid, unflinching

uneasy
fidgety, restless, quivering, jittery, flustered, shaky, jumpy, twitchy, turbulent, trembling

unflappable
immovable, steely, flinty, unyielding, hardened, unbending, cool, unruffled, unflinching, cool-headed

unflinching
unyielding, adamant, headstrong, fearless, impervious, stern, resolute

unglued
crazed, unmoored, unhinged, unsteady, unstable, unraveled

unhinged
unmoored, unglued, deranged, unstable, demented, unraveled, crazed

unruffled
unflappable, composed, balanced, equanimous, placid, poised, cool-headed, collected, calm

unsteady
dazed, woozy, dizzy, befuddled, giddy, erratic, wobbly, shaky

unyielding
adamant, headstrong, inflexible, steadfast, unflinching, flinty, hardened, steely, immovable, unflappable, unbending

vacuous
inane, fatuous, empty, vapid, foolish, dim-witted, absurd

vapid
lifeless, empty, absurd, vacuous, fatuous, foolish, dim-witted, colorless, inane

vengeful
vindictive, unforgiving, spiteful, hostile, avenging

vindictive
vengeful, unforgiving, spiteful, hateful, malicious, ruthless

wary
guarded, leery, apprehensive, cautious, distrustful, suspicious

weary
exhausted, drained, frazzled, bewildered, fatigued, worn

wide-eyed
perplexed, surprised, startled, stupefied, astonished, dumbstruck, astounded, flabbergasted, amazed, awed, bedazzled

willful
defiant, inflexible, hostile, stiff, unbending, stubborn

wistful
longing, yearning, wishful, thoughtful, pensive, contemplative, pining, regretful, musing, nostalgic, ruminating

withdrawn
stoic, detached, impassive, taciturn, aloof, restrained, distant

woeful
anguished, dismal, sorrowful, heart-broken, miserable, pitiful, morose, bleak

wolfish
feral, barbaric, predatory, greedy, vicious, ferocious

wooden
stilted, awkward, glazed, empty, glassy, vacant, blank, vacuous

woozy
dizzy, befuddled, unsteady, dazed, unstable, tipsy, groggy, confused

wry
mocking, displeased, disgusted, vexed, unimpressed, annoyed

yearning
musing, nostalgic, wistful, longing, wishful, thoughtful, pensive, mournful, contemplative, pining, regretful, ruminating

MOTION

abound, abounding
plentiful, abundant, bountiful, flourishing, profuse, overflowing, swarming, teeming, thriving, bristling, bursting, copious

amble, ambling
rambling, dawdling, sauntering, drifting, meandering, strolling

balloon, ballooning
soar, rocket, distend, surge, swell, billow, spiral, bloat

blunder, blundering
lurching, lumbering, bungling, bumbling, floundering

bobble, bobbling
careening, staggering, tottering, toppling, capsizing, plunging, tumbling, wobbling, bungling, floundering

breakneck
headlong, breathless, dashing, impulsive, plunging, precipitous, rash, reckless, heedless

brim, brimming
overflowing, abundant, teeming, copious, bristling, gushing

bristle, bristling
overflowing, boiling, seething, fuming, ruffled, flaring, infuriated, raging

bubble, bubbling
churning, burbling, boiling, seeping, trickling, fizzing, percolating, foaming, frothing

bungle, bungling
botched, blundering, fumbling, bumbling

burst, bursting
cascade, flow, overflow, pour, spout, slosh, spew, spill, waterfall, torrent, rush, plummet, explosive, volcanic, swarming, copious, overflowing, gushing

capsize, capsized
toppling, bobbling, careening, tottering, plunging, tumbling, wobbling, upended

careen, careening
swaying, tilting, pitching, tottering, toppling, bobbling, plunging, tumbling, wobbling, lurching

cascade, cascading
flow, burst, overflow, pour, spout, slosh, spew, spill, waterfall, rush, torrent, plummet

cataclysm, cataclysmic
upheaval, catastrophe, apocalyptic, disastrous, calamitous, ruinous

chaotic, chaos
random, erratic, disarray, pandemonium, confused, disordered, frantic, frenetic, tumultuous, haphazard, clamorous, frenzied, hysterical, stormy, tempestuous, turbulent, raucous

choppy
patchy, uneven, fragmented, frayed, wobbly, erratic, haphazard, hitching, jolting, halting, jarring

circuitous
serpentine, twisted, winding, convoluted, meandering, snaking, rambling, wavy, circular

clumsy
bungling, bumbling, blundering, gawkish, ungainly, awkward

convulse, convulsing
jerking, thrashing, twisting, shuddering, writhing, agitated

disarray
chaos, pandemonium, confusion, turmoil, disorder

dodder, doddering
ambling, faltering, oscillating, tottering, shaking, quivering, shifting, shuffling, swaying, staggering

ebb, ebbing
dwindling, receding, waning, subsiding, diminishing, shrinking, slackening, fading

explosive
bursting, edgy, passionate, volcanic, volatile, changeable, impulsive, mercurial

falter, faltering
floundering, wobbling, tottering, ambling, doddering, oscillating, stumbling, shifting, lurching

fidget, fidgety
quivering, restless, jittery, flustered, fluttery, trembling, twitchy, jumpy, turbulent, uneasy, shaky

fleeting
vanishing, evanescent, ephemeral, melting, ethereal, transient, fading, short-lived

flitter, flittering
flit, fling, quiver, pulse, flicker, dart, swoop, ripple

float, floating
buoyant, fluid, effervescent, bouncy, ebullient, springy, breezy, drifting, hovering, airy

flourish, flourishing
thriving, swarming, bristling, bursting, overflowing, teeming

flow, flowing
cascade, burst, overflow, pour, spout, slosh, spew, spill, waterfall, torrent, rush, plummet

Thesaurus of the Senses

fluttery, fluttering
flustered, fidgety, quivering, jumpy, turbulent, restless, trembling, jittery, twitchy, shaky

frenetic
frenzied, chaotic, frantic, hysterical, manic, uproarious, furious, wild, obsessive

frenzy, frenzied
chaotic, frantic, frenetic, hysterical, manic, crazed, tumultuous, agitated, wild, turbulent

fumble, fumbling
awkward, blundering, bungling, stumbling, grappling, groping, floundering, bumbling, clumsy

gyrate, gyrating
lurching, pitching, reeling, swirling, throbbing, twirling, whirling, undulating

halting
choppy, hitching, jolting, jarring, stumbling, faltering, bumbling, vacillating

haphazard
chaotic, aimless, careless, irregular, random, erratic, reckless, disordered

headlong
breathless, breakneck, dashing, impulsive, plunging, precipitous, rash, reckless, heedless

heedless
rash, reckless, careless, headlong, impulsive, aimless

hitching
choppy, jolting, halting, jarring, stumbling, glitchy, sputtering

immobile
crippled, incapacitated, paralyzed, rigid, stagnant, unmoving

incapacitated
crippled, immobile, paralyzed, debilitated, impaired

jammed
blocked, cemented, compressed, seized up, immobilized, frozen, obstructed, clogged

jarring
jolting, choppy, hitching, grating, halting, disturbing, clashing, grinding

jittery
shaky, trembling, twitchy, jumpy, flustered, fluttery, fidgety, restless, quivering, turbulent, uneasy

jolting
jarring, alarming, choppy, hitching, halting, knocking, shaking, jostling

jumpy
twitchy, turbulent, uneasy, flustered, fluttery, fidgety, quivering, restless, shaky, trembling, jittery

lapping
splashing, swishing, sloshing, licking, swallowing, rolling

lumber, lumbering
plodding, slogging, shuffling, trudging, lurching

lurch, lurching
rolling, careening, gyrating, pitching, undulating, swirling, throbbing, twirling, whirling, reeling

meander, meandering
crooked, twisted, tortuous, winding, snaking, convoluted

oscillate, oscillating
tottering, pitching, vacillating, wobbling, faltering, shifting, seesawing, wavering

overflow, overflowing
cascading, spouting, spewing, spilling, rushing, swarming, abounding, bursting, waterfall, torrent

pandemonium
chaos, disarray, confusion, turmoil, disorder, commotion, bedlam, turbulence

paralyzed
immobilized, stunned, crippled, incapacitated, numb, frozen

plunge, plunging
plummet, hurtle, nosedive, careen, topple, tumble, sink, lunge, pitch

quiver, quivering
flustered, fluttery, jumpy, turbulent, uneasy, jittery, fidgety, restless, shaking, trembling, twitchy

rampant
unrestrained, unbridled, uncontrolled, unrestricted, runaway

restless
uneasy, quivering, jittery, flustered, fluttery, trembling, twitchy, fidgety, jumpy, shaky

rolling
billowy, careening, gyrating, lurching, pitching, reeling, swirling, throbbing, thundering, twirling, undulating, whirling

shuffle, shuffling
dragging, limping, lumbering, stumbling, ambling, scraping

slosh, sloshing
cascading, overflowing, pouring, spouting, spewing, splattering, rushing, spilling

spew, spewing
spout, slosh, spill, burst, overflow, pour, belch, gush, spit, cascade, expel

spill, spilling
overflow, pour, spout, slosh, spew, cascade, burst, torrent, rush, slop, squirt, disgorge

spiral, spiralling
balloon, soar, rocket, surge, swell, billow, roll, curled, corkscrew

splash, splashing
splatter, dapple, shower, speckle, slosh, sprinkle, splurge, burst, dash, slop

splatter, splattering
splash, splotch, swish, slosh, spew, spill, douse, drench, plunge

sporadic
sparse, diffuse, patchy, spotty, haphazard, fitful, irregular, scattered

spout, spouting
burst, overflow, cascade, flow, spew, spill, waterfall, torrent, rush, pour, slosh, gush, emit, spray, squirt

stagnant
immobile, rigid, unmoving, immovable, static, dormant

stagnate, stagnating
deteriorating, declining, languishing, festering, stalling

stymie, stymied
obstructed, hindered, hampered, thwarted, impeded, confounded, crimped, hamstring

swarm, swarming
abounding, bursting, copious, flourishing, overflowing, brimming, thriving, prospering, roaring, teeming

swirl, swirling
billowing, careening, gyrating, twirling, undulating, whirling, rolling

taper, tapering
diminishing, dwindling, narrowing, waning, slackening

teeming
plentiful, thriving, prospering, swarming, vigorous, bountiful, abundant, robust, profuse, fruitful, copious

thwart, thwarted
obstructed, hindered, hampered, stymied, impeded, circumvented, foiled

topple, toppling
plunging, tumbling, wobbling, careening, staggering, tottering, bobbling, capsized

torrent
cascade, burst, overflow, spout, spew, waterfall, rush, downpour, deluge

totter, tottering
wobbling, ambling, doddering, faltering, oscillating, shifting, careening, toppling, bobbling, plunging, tumbling

tumble, tumbling
plunging, wobbling, careening, staggering, tottering, toppling, bobbling, flopping

tumult, tumultuous
turmoil, havoc, upheaval, mayhem, volatile, agitated, frenzied, hysterical, chaotic, explosive, tempestuous, turbulent

turbulent
stormy, trembling, unstable, jumpy, tumultuous, agitated, chaotic, frenzied, tempestuous

twitchy, twitching
trembling, jumpy, quivering, jittery, flustered, fluttery, fidgety, restless, shaky, turbulent, uneasy

unbridled
boundless, irrepressible, unrestrained, unchecked, uncontrolled, riotous, chaotic

undulate, undulating
rolling, billowing, careening, twirling, whirling, gyrating, pitching, swirling

unravel, unraveling
decipher, untangle, unscramble, unwind, disentangle, collapse, decode, untie

unrestrained
unbridled, boundless, excessive, irrepressible, rampant, unchecked

unscramble
decipher, unravel, untangle, decode

unspool
unravel, untangle, unwind, disengage, untwist

untangle
unscramble, unsnarl, decipher, unravel, decode, disentangle

upend, upended
capsized, overturned, inverted, unsettled, pitched, topsy-turvy, cockeyed, jumbled, toppled

volatile
changeable, effervescent, ephemeral, explosive, charged, fluid, mercurial, erratic, wavering, turbulent

volcanic
explosive, bursting, passionate, fiery, violent, excitable, volatile, turbulent

wane
ebb, dwindle, recede, taper, fade, slacken, subside, wither, diminish

whirl, whirling
swirl, twirl, gyrate, flurry, whirlwind, stir, spin, orbit, twist, revolve

DISTINCTIVE QUALITY *or* IMPRESSION

abominable
atrocious, wretched, vile, despicable, detestable, odious, loathsome

absorbing
engrossing, enriching, gripping, inspiring, riveting, captivating, compelling, enthralling

absurd
preposterous, senseless, ridiculous, ludicrous, foolish, outlandish, wacky

abysmal
woeful, abominable, anguished, bleak, dismal, dreadful, deplorable, pitiful, appalling

airy
buoyant, effervescent, breezy, exhilarating, frothy, sparkling, lively, vivacious, floating

alchemy
magic, transformation, sorcery, wizardry

allure, alluring
enticing, captivating, charming, enchanting, fascinating, seductive, hypnotic, beguiling, arresting, bewitching, engrossing, enthralling, gripping, intriguing, magnetic, mesmerizing, disarming

ambiance
aura, mood, atmosphere, tone, impression

anomaly
oddity, aberration, curiosity, peculiarity, deviation, freak

aplomb
poise, composure, equanimity, elegance, grace, serenity, tact

appalling
egregious, frightful, outrageous, atrocious, detestable, wretched, dreadful, hideous, ghastly

appealing
alluring, tempting, arousing, captivating, charming, fascinating, enchanting, seductive, enticing

SEE: DISTINCTIVE QUALITY *or* IMPRESSION

arousing
thrilling, captivating, enchanting, enlivening, gripping, rousing, evocative

arresting
hypnotic, beguiling, alluring, bewitching, captivating, engrossing, enthralling, enchanting, enticing, gripping, intriguing, magnetic, mesmerizing, striking, stunning, impressive

artistry
brilliance, drama, flourish, style, finesse, flair, virtuosity

atmosphere
aura, mood, tone, ambiance, climate, color, scene

atrocious
appalling, egregious, frightful, outrageous, ghastly, detestable, dreadful, hideous, wretched

august
stately, courtly, dignified, gallant, glorious, kingly, lofty, majestic, noble, striking, distinguished

baffling
puzzling, perplexing, bewildering, disconcerting, mystifying, incomprehensible, cryptic, unfathomable

barbaric
ferocious, beastly, belligerent, fierce, monstrous, raging, inhumane, savage, cruel

beastly
belligerent, fierce, ferocious, barbaric, monstrous, raging, savage, abominable

bedraggled
disheveled, unkempt, scruffy, untidy, tousled, mangy, scraggly, shabby, messy, ragged

beguiling
enchanting, charming, alluring, bewitching, arresting, disarming, hypnotic, captivating, engrossing, enticing, gripping, intriguing, magnetic, mesmerizing

bewilder, bewildering
convoluted, confounding, inexplicable, mystifying, perplexing, puzzling, stunning, baffling

bewitch, bewitching
enchanting, beguiling, mysterious, entrancing, captivating, magical, charming, fascinating, hypnotic, alluring, arresting, engrossing, gripping, intriguing, magnetic, mesmerizing, tantalizing, enticing, enrapturing, enthralling

bizarre
unearthly, uncanny, freakish, mysterious, peculiar, outlandish, surreal

bleak
desolate, stark, dreary, gloomy, barren, forlorn, godforsaken, deplorable, woeful, dismal, dreadful, grim, abysmal

blithe
effervescent, breezy, exhilarating, carefree, sparkling, vivacious, joyous, buoyant, exuberant, lively, perky, bouncy, ebullient, airy, jaunty

bodacious
bold, daring, remarkable, audacious, assured, unabashed, intrepid, gutsy

bold
flamboyant, bright, colorful, showy, flashy, splashy, unabashed, brazen

bouncy
ebullient, floating, jaunty, springy, effervescent, breezy, buoyant, exhilarating, sparkling, lively, perky, blithe, vivacious, exuberant, airy, light-hearted

brash
energetic, assertive, bold, brazen, cocky, impulsive, rude, reckless

brassy
saucy, flashy, brazen, brash, cheeky, daring, sassy, gaudy, jarring, cocky, pushy

brazen
bold, unblinking, undaunted, saucy, flashy, brash, unabashed, showy, splashy, audacious

breathtaking
captivating, spectacular, extraordinary, magnificent, stunning, wondrous, astounding

breezy
effervescent, airy, exhilarating, frothy, sparkling, vivacious, lively, blithe, light-hearted

bucolic
rustic, rural, pastoral, woodsy, serene, peaceful, tranquil

bumptious
pompous, overbearing, swaggering, pushy, obnoxious, haughty, cocky

bungling
clumsy, messy, careless, botched, inelegant, awkward, blundering, fumbling, graceless, bumbling, ungainly, sloppy

buoyant
energetic, joyful, lively, jaunty, exuberant, ebullient, effervescent, fluid, bouncy, blithe

canny
skillful, deft, shrewd, astute, crafty, wily

SEE: DISTINCTIVE QUALITY *or* IMPRESSION

cantankerous
> testy, bad-tempered, crotchety, fractious, ill-tempered, irritable, edgy, huffy, surly, snappish, spiteful, feisty, crusty, cranky, grumpy, ornery

captivate, captivating
> charming, enchanting, fascinating, alluring, enticing, appealing, tempting, attractive, seductive, compelling, riveting, enthralling, tantalizing, enrapturing, bewitching, thrilling, arousing, enlivening, gripping, rousing

charismatic
> magical, bewitching, enchanting, seductive, charming, magnetic

charming
> disarming, arresting, delightful, alluring, enticing, appealing, tempting, hypnotic, captivating, enchanting, fascinating

cinematic
> dramatic, theatrical, vivid, stellar, operatic, animated, colorful, picturesque

clumsy
> awkward, bungling, bumbling, blundering, gauche, ham-handed

commanding
> sweeping, powerful, expansive, decisive, superior, compelling, assertive, forceful, imposing, impressive

compelling
> absorbing, engrossing, enriching, captivating, enthralling, gripping, inspiring, riveting, moving, powerful

composed
> poised, refined, unruffled, unflappable, self-possessed, balanced, equanimous, calm, self-assured, placid

confounded
> bewildered, baffled, puzzled, perplexed, befuddled, startled, mystified

contemptible
> obnoxious, abhorrent, repugnant, offensive, deplorable, repellent, vile

courtly
> kingly, lofty, stately, august, dignified, gallant, glorious, majestic, noble, striking

creepy
> spooky, frightening, freaky, disturbing, eerie, ghoulish, hair-raising

crotchety
> cranky, crusty, ill-tempered, feisty, fractious, testy, bad-tempered, cantankerous, edgy, huffy, irritable, snappish, spiteful, grouchy

crusty
> ill-tempered, edgy, huffy, irritable, snappish, spiteful, testy, bad-tempered, feisty, cantankerous, cranky, crotchety, fractious

Thesaurus of the Senses

cultured
> polished, refined, accomplished, graceful, impeccable, tasteful, sophisticated

curious
> aberrant, odd, peculiar, strange, deviating, freakish, puzzling, exotic

dashing
> sporty, dynamic, stylish, elegant, dazzling, flashy, showy, eye-catching, splashy, dapper, flamboyant, lively

daunting
> formidable, intimidating, imposing, dismaying, ominous, forbidding, fearsome

decrepit
> decaying, rickety, battered, ramshackle, crumbling, degraded, tottering, aged, dilapidated, worn

deft
> masterful, accomplished, brilliant, consummate, superlative, skillful, proficient, superb

delirious
> fierce, deranged, frantic, howling, raving, savage, unhinged, ecstatic, blissful, rapturous, blissful, ecstatic, wild

desolate
> forlorn, abandoned, empty, dreary, godforsaken, bleak, deserted, grim, barren, remote, stark

despicable
> abominable, atrocious, contemptible, despairing, dreadful, monstrous, miserable, worthless, repugnant, abhorrent, heinous, vicious, vile

devastated
> ruined, wasted, wrecked, ravaged, blighted, demolished

diabolical
> fiendish, demonic, villainous, devious, dastardly, vile, wicked

dignified
> gallant, glorious, stately, august, courtly, kingly, striking, majestic, noble, lofty

disarming
> beguiling, charming, arresting, stunning, striking, irresistible, bewitching

disheveled
> bedraggled, unkempt, disarrayed, messy, sloppy, untidy, scruffy, wrinkled, rumbled

dismal
> bleak, dreary, miserable, woeful, abominable, anguished, dreadful, sorrowful, tragic, deplorable, abysmal

distasteful

unsavory, obnoxious, offensive, repulsive, repugnant, unpleasant, displeasing

dizzying

woozy, befuddled, unsteady, dazed, witless, whirling, bewildering, giddy

dramatic

climactic, cinematic, thrilling, stirring, stellar, sensational, striking, startling, impressive, vivid

dreadful

atrocious, hideous, grim, ghastly, grisly, grotesque, gruesome, vile, heinous, horrendous, horrifying, loathsome, monstrous, odious

dreary

desolate, forlorn, godforsaken, bleak, grim, colorless, dismal, lifeless, gloomy

droll

quirky, wry, comical, dry, witty, amusing, eccentric, absurd, farcical, whimsical

ebullient

effervescent, lively, buoyant, exuberant, irrepressible, elated

edgy

explosive, bursting, volcanic, testy, feisty, restless, nervous, high-strung, uptight

eerie

mysterious, peculiar, strange, creepy, freakish, spooky, scary, spine-chilling, bone-chilling

effervescent

breezy, exhilarating, frothy, sparkling, vivacious, buoyant, ebullient, exuberant, lively, blithe, jaunty, bubbly

elegant

graceful, tasteful, refined, poised, polished, stylish

elevated

highfalutin, majestic, lofty, superlative, noble, grandiose, exalted, grand, eminent, dignified

eminent

outstanding, preeminent, illustrious, renowned, pre-eminent, distinguished, famed, esteemed

enamored

engrossed, riveted, beguiled, bewitched, enthralled, captivated, smitten, enchanted, charmed

enchanting, enchanted

captivating, bewitching, enlivening, riveting, mesmerizing, magical, beguiling, entrancing, charismatic, enamored

enduring

durable, sturdy, indestructible, impervious, persistent, resistant, unchanging, profound, unforgettable, inextinguishable, unfading, vital, indelible

engrossing, engrossed

enriching, gripping, compelling, enthralling, absorbing, riveting, captivating

enraptured

enthralled, thrilled, enamored, captivated, bewitched, delighted

enriching

engrossing, inspiring, elevating, nourishing, stimulating

entrancing, entranced

bewitching, enchanting, beguiling, mysterious, captivating, mesmerized, hypnotized

evanescent

ephemeral, fading, vanishing, short-lived, fleeting, ethereal, transient, tenuous

evocative

powerful, vivid, stirring, moving, expressive, suggestive, graphic, haunting

exotic

mysterious, mystical, striking, curious, fascinating, alluring

exquisite

delicate, intricate, fine, dainty, elegant, polished, striking, charming, ornate, intense

extravagant

showy, ornate, fanciful, flamboyant, flashy, adorned, elaborate, ostentatious, indulgent

exultant

triumphant, elated, jubilant, euphoric, ecstatic, enraptured, joyous

fanciful

elaborate, whimsical, extravagant, imaginative, adorned, flowery, ornate, resplendent, frilly, embellished

fanfare

celebration, glitz, flourish, pageantry, splendor, spectacle

fastidious

exacting, finicky, meticulous, scrupulous, discriminating

fearsome

frightful, terrifying, imposing, intimidating, formidable, menacing, alarming, shocking

feisty

testy, touchy, edgy, spunky, gritty, gutsy, spirited, scrappy

ferocious
> barbaric, beastly, belligerent, fierce, monstrous, raging, savage

festive
> joyful, light-hearted, lively, gleeful, joyous, blithe, celebratory, jovial, jubilant

fiendish
> diabolical, demonic, villainous, devious, dastardly, nefarious

finesse
> artistry, mastery, flair, panache, craft, elegance, polish, wizardry, excellence, savvy

flair
> artistry, brilliance, daring, drama, flourish, panache, style, savvy, polish, glitz, craft

flamboyant
> bright, colorful, flowery, elaborate, showy, flashy, garish, splashy, glamorous, extravagant, dazzling, theatrical, bold

flashy
> flamboyant, bright, colorful, bold, elaborate, eye-catching, splashy, garish, showy, dashing, brazen

flaunting
> ostentatious, flamboyant, frilly, flashy, blatant, glaring, pretentious

flawless
> impeccable, immaculate, exquisite, meticulous, pristine, spotless, unmarred, unblemished

flourish, flourishing
> flair, brilliance, luxuriant, plentiful, abounding, lavish, teeming, thriving, copious, swarming, bristling, bursting, exuberant, overflowing

forbidding
> gloomy, spooky, distant, menacing, remote, foreboding, unpleasant, uninviting, sinister, ominous, stern

forlorn
> desolate, deserted, remote, dejected, dreary, abandoned, barren, grim, hopeless, despondent, bleak

formidable
> imposing, intimidating, threatening, dismaying, daunting

freakish, freaky
> strange, curious, peculiar, aberrant, creepy, eerie, surreal, uncanny, odd, bizarre

frightful
> hideous, disturbing, appalling, alarming, shocking, calamitous, dreadful, ghastly

frothy
> effervescent, bubbly, breezy, exhilarating, sparkling, vivacious, fizzy, foamy, soapy

gallant
fearless, dauntless, valorous, valiant, courageous, unflinching, bold, undaunted

galling
irksome, provoking, vexing, aggravating, wearisome, troubling, bothersome, disturbing, exasperating, tiresome

garish
gaudy, flashy, tacky, tawdry, lurid, vulgar, glaring, ostentatious, showy

gauche
tasteless, awkward, gawky, inelegant, uncouth, unpolished, tactless, crude, unsophisticated

gaudy
garish, tacky, showy, tawdry, ostentatious, flashy, harsh, tasteless, lurid

gawky
awkward, ungainly, unpolished, uncouth, ungraceful, clumsy

ghastly
appalling, dreadful, frightening, horrendous, hideous, horrifying, ghoulish, gruesome, grisly

glamorous
alluring, beguiling, dazzling, enchanting, lustrous, elegant, stylish, glittering, magnetic, stunning

glorious
luxurious, illustrious, majestic, striking, radiant, gallant, wondrous, noble

goon, goony
nincompoop, ninny, blockhead, imbecile, simpleton, nitwit, sap, dimwit, foolish, buffoon

gorgeous
exquisite, radiant, stunning, sparkling, dazzling, opulent, brilliant, luxurious, splendid, sumptuous

graceful
elegant, stylish, tasteful, refined, poised, polished, cultured, sophisticated

graceless
inelegant, awkward, blundering, bungling, fumbling, indelicate, loutish, ungainly, bumbling, clumsy

grand
momentous, preeminent, ascendant, towering, stately, impressive, stellar, lavish, transcendent, magnificent

grandiose
elaborate, majestic, lofty, ostentatious, colossal, elevated, visionary, highfalutin, noble, grand, superlative

gripping

> hypnotic, arresting, bewitching, engrossing, enthralling, magnetic, mesmerizing, thrilling, arousing, enlivening, rousing

grisly

> ghastly, appalling, horrific, dreadful, frightening, horrendous, gruesome

gritty

> feisty, spunky, gutsy, spirited, scrappy, tenacious, fierce, dogged, determined, plucky

grotesque

> deformed, gruesome, monstrous, twisted, contorted, misshapen, gnarled, mangled, hideous

gruesome

> dreadful, frightening, appalling, horrific, horrendous, hideous, ghastly, grisly

hapless

> forlorn, doomed, hopeless, cursed, wretched, disastrous, woeful

haunted

> tormented, cursed, tortured, possessed, frightful, creepy, obsessed, anguished, troubled

haunting

> eerie, nagging, indelible, frightful, unforgettable, stirring, poignant, moving

hazardous

> perilous, treacherous, uncertain, precarious, risky, unsound

hideous

> heinous, horrendous, horrifying, grim, atrocious, dreadful, ghastly, grisly, vile, grotesque, monstrous, odious, appalling, wretched, gruesome, loathsome

histrionic

> stagy, hysterical, cinematic, melodramatic, emotional, operatic, sensational, dramatic, showy

horrendous

> hideous, grim, atrocious, heinous, horrifying, loathsome, dreadful, ghastly, grisly, grotesque, gruesome, monstrous, odious, vile

horrifying

> gruesome, loathsome, vile, heinous, horrendous, dreadful, ghastly, monstrous, odious, hideous, grim, atrocious, grisly, grotesque

howling

> raving, wild, fierce, delirious, deranged, frantic, savage, wailing, barking

hypnotic

> beguiling, alluring, arresting, bewitching, captivating, engrossing, enthralling, enchanting, intriguing, magnetic, mesmerizing, riveting

idyllic

picturesque, ornate, charming, quaint, scenic, vivid, striking

impassioned

forceful, intense, fiery, passionate, rousing, stirring, fierce, vehement, fervent

impeccable

flawless, exquisite, meticulous, pristine, refined, precise, faultless, unblemished

indelible

enduring, keen, ingrained, poignant, profound, unforgettable, inextinguishable, pervading, piercing, unfading

indelicate

bungling, inelegant, awkward, blundering, fumbling, bumbling, graceless, clumsy, ungainly

inelegant

indelicate, loutish, ungainly, tasteless, awkward, graceless, clumsy, bungling, fumbling, blundering, uncouth

inscrutable

enigmatic, indecipherable, mystifying, puzzling, perplexing, incomprehensible

insolent

saucy, cocky, rude, ill-mannered, insulting, impertinent, brazen, arrogant

intriguing

enticing, magnetic, mesmerizing, hypnotic, beguiling, enthralling, arresting, bewitching, captivating, engrossing, alluring, enchanting

irksome

vexing, aggravating, bothersome, disturbing, exasperating, galling, provoking, tiresome, wearisome, troubling

ironfisted

adamant, unyielding, steadfast, headstrong, impervious, inflexible, unflinching, refractory, resistant

irreparable

irrevocable, ruined, unsalvageable, impossible, hopeless, broken, irretrievable, irreversible, irreplaceable

irrepressible

unrestrained, ebullient, exuberant, unbridled, boundless, buoyant, bubbling, vivacious

jaunty

cheerful, lively, buoyant, ebullient, effervescent, breezy, sparkling, vivacious, exuberant, perky, bouncy, blithe, light-hearted

kingly

stately, august, courtly, dignified, gallant, glorious, lofty, majestic, noble, striking

lackadaisical
indifferent, careless, lazy, dreamy, halfhearted, apathetic, lethargic, idle, listless, spiritless, lax

languid
listless, lumbering, sleepy, shuffling, leisurely, unhurried, poky, lazy, idle

languish, languishing
deteriorating, listless, withering, drooping, wasting, dwindling

lavish
luxuriant, adorned, embellished, extravagant, grand, lush, opulent, sumptuous, plush

lively
buoyant, exuberant, cheerful, ebullient, spirited, sparkling, cheery, uplifting, bustling, animated, vigorous, bubbly

lofty
elevated, grandiose, aerial, colossal, highfalutin, majestic, noble, soaring, stately, superlative, visionary, glorious

loony
kooky, batty, cuckoo, daffy, flaky, crazy, unbalanced, unhinged, nutty

lurid
gaudy, bright, blinding, intense, vivid, glaring, shocking, flaming, dazzling, loud, garish

luscious
opulent, lavish, luxuriant, plush, sumptuous, showy, exquisite

magical
bewitching, charismatic, enchanting, radiant, wondrous, wizardly, splendorous

magnetic
hypnotic, alluring, arresting, engrossing, enthralling, beguiling, bewitching, captivating, enticing, gripping, intriguing, enchanting, mesmerizing

majestic
gallant, glorious, elevated, grandiose, highfalutin, noble, visionary, superlative, stately, august, courtly, dignified, kingly, luxurious, lofty

masterful, masterly
accomplished, brilliant, consummate, deft, superb, superlative

mercurial
volatile, changeable, explosive, impulsive, wavering, erratic, flighty

mesmerize, mesmerizing
enthralling, enchanting, hypnotic, riveting, beguiling, gripping, arresting, bewitching, captivating, engrossing, enticing, alluring, intriguing, magnetic

meticulous

flawless, impeccable, scrupulous, precise, scrutinizing, exacting, conscientious

momentous

crucial, pivotal, earth-shattering, eventful, grand, preeminent, ascendant, stellar, towering, transcendent, seminal

monstrous

ferocious, vile, atrocious, heinous, vicious, barbaric, beastly, fierce, belligerent, raging

mysterious

cryptic, secret, enigmatic, perplexing, puzzling, obscure, baffling, inexplicable, inscrutable

mystifying

puzzling, baffling, cryptic, mysterious, secret, enigmatic, quizzical, perplexing, bewildering, inexplicable, confounding

noble

majestic, superlative, visionary, lofty, elevated, grandiose, kingly, highfalutin, stately, august, courtly, dignified, gallant, glorious

noxious

obnoxious, abhorrent, repugnant, toxic, odious, offensive, vile, repellent

obnoxious

abhorrent, repugnant, contemptible, odious, offensive, noxious, repellent, vile

odd, oddity

aberrant, curious, peculiar, freakish, irregular, bizarre, offbeat

odious

foul, obnoxious, abhorrent, repugnant, contemptible, offensive, noxious, vile, repellent

onerous

grueling, laborious, rigorous, vigorous, exhausting, formidable, arduous

operatic

cinematic, showy, histrionic, melodramatic, emotional, sensational, dramatic, stagy

opulent

rich, affluent, lavish, luscious, luxuriant, plush, sumptuous, showy, grand

ostentatious

flamboyant, frilly, flashy, flaunting, showy, pretentious

other-worldly

mystical, supernatural, unearthly, ethereal, dreamy, mysterious

outlandish

absurd, bizarre, wondrous, weird, preposterous, peculiar, fantastic, outrageous

outrageous

appalling, egregious, frightful, preposterous, exorbitant

passionate

explosive, bursting, volcanic, forceful, impassioned, vehement, fervent, spirited, ardent, intense

pastoral

rustic, bucolic, rural, woodsy, scenic, peaceful

peculiar

odd, aberrant, curious, strange, deviating, freakish, outlandish

perilous

hazardous, treacherous, uncertain, precarious, menacing, unsound, risky

perplexing

baffling, bewildering, confounding, cryptic, mysterious, secret, enigmatic, puzzling, inexplicable

pervading

indelible, enduring, ingrained, piercing, penetrating, permeating, keen, transfused

picturesque

idyllic, luxuriant, ornate, charming, quaint, scenic, pastoral, bucolic, vivid

plagued

disintegrated, ravaged, blighted, corrosive, devastated, ruinous, wasted, wrecked

poignant

moving, touching, indelible, enduring, profound, unforgettable, pervading, unfading

ponderous

heavy, weighty, unwieldy, plodding, dreary, tedious, burdensome

precarious

hazardous, perilous, treacherous, uncertain, delicate, tenuous, unstable, tricky

preeminent

momentous, grand, ascendant, stellar, towering, transcendent, distinguished, illustrious

preposterous

outlandish, absurd, impossible, ludicrous, staggering, unthinkable, outrageous, shocking

provoking

galling, irksome, vexing, aggravating, exasperating, bothersome, disturbing, tiresome, wearisome, troubling

puzzling

baffling, mysterious, enigmatic, perplexing, bewildering, obscure, inexplicable, confounding, cryptic

quaint
picturesque, idyllic, charming, scenic, whimsical, pleasing

racy
bawdy, fiery, lusty, juicy, provocative, risqué, spicy, saucy, vivacious

ravening
raging, ravenous, ferocious, voracious, predatory, greedy, savage

raving
howling, savage, barking, wild, fierce, ranting, delirious, deranged, frantic, unhinged

reckless
impulsive, headlong, dashing, plunging, rash, heedless, careless, thoughtless

refined
poised, elegant, graceful, stylish, tasteful, self-possessed, balanced, composed, assured, calm

repellent
repugnant, contemptible, odious, obnoxious, abhorrent, offensive, noxious, vile

repugnant
offensive, noxious, obnoxious, abhorrent, contemptible, repellent, vile, odious

resplendent
luxuriant, splendorous, radiant, dazzling, shining, spellbinding, brilliant, sublime, lively

rhapsodic
blissful, euphoric, elated, ecstatic, exhilarated, joyous, rapturous

rich
lavish, bountiful, abundant, profuse, opulent, intense, luscious, vibrant, vivid

risqué
racy, bawdy, fiery, lusty, juicy, provocative, salty, spicy, spirited, tart, saucy

riveting, riveted
enthralling, mesmerizing, hypnotic, thrilling, gripping, engrossing, spellbinding, enchanting, captivating, beguiling, magnetic, alluring, arresting, enticing

roaring
thriving, flourishing, uproarious, robust, swarming, teeming, vigorous, rowdy, boisterous

rotten
appalling, atrocious, decayed, detestable, dreadful, putrid, rancid, sordid, spoiled, wretched

rousing
thrilling, arousing, captivating, enchanting, enlivening, gripping, stirring, impassioned, animated

saucy

brash, brazen, cheeky, daring, sassy, rude, flippant

savage

howling, raving, ferocious, fierce, delirious, deranged, frantic, vicious, wild

scintillating

flashy, brilliant, sparkling, gleaming, glistening, effervescent, lively, dazzling, glimmering

scrupulous

impeccable, meticulous, flawless, precise, scrutinizing, unsparing, conscientious

seedy

chintzy, cheap, ragged, ratty, slipshod, squalid, tattered, tawdry, disreputable

shady

unsavory, disreputable, slippery, unscrupulous, shoddy, suspicious, fishy, shifty

showy

flashy, frilly, brash, ornate, garish, luxurious, plush, lavish, opulent, glittering

sophisticated

cultured, graceful, impeccable, polished, refined, accomplished, tasteful

sorcery

wizardry, witchcraft, magic, alchemy, incantation, mystique

sordid

seedy, vile, sleazy, unsavory, squalid, grimy, foul, filthy, wretched

spectacle

array, display, splendor, extravagance, drama, curiosity, parade

spectacular

breathtaking, phenomenal, extraordinary, magnificent, stunning, wondrous, astounding, sublime

spellbinding

absorbing, alluring, beguiling, enchanting, engrossing, gripping, mesmerizing, enthralling

spirited

animated, ebullient, lively, vivacious, passionate, dynamic, vibrant

splashy

flashy, glittering, showy, glitzy, opulent, sensational, eye-catching

splendorous

extravagant, magical, bewitching, charismatic, enchanting, radiant, brilliant, wondrous, glorious

sprightly

lively, spirited, vigorous, animated, ebullient, vivacious

staggering
   astonishing, stunning, aghast, startling, astounding, unthinkable, alarming, shocking

stagy
   cinematic, dramatic, histrionic, melodramatic, showy, operatic

stately
   august, courtly, dignified, glorious, kingly, lofty, impressive, majestic, noble, distinguished, striking

stellar
   preeminent, momentous, grand, ascendant, towering, sterling, transcendent, cinematic, dramatic, superlative

sterling
   pure, refined, absolute, stellar, exceptional, superior, stunning

stormy
   tumultuous, agitated, frenzied, raging, blustery, wild, passionate, turbulent, tempestuous

striking
   disarming, beguiling, charming, arresting, stunning, extraordinary, compelling, dazzling, wondrous, vivid

stunning
   striking, disarming, beguiling, charming, arresting, astonishing, phenomenal, tremendous, vivid

stylish
   elegant, graceful, tasteful, poised, dapper, polished, refined

sublime
   superb, glorious, transcendent, grand, heavenly, majestic, elevated

sumptuous
   luxuriant, lavish, luscious, resplendent, stately, opulent, rich, plush, showy

superficial
   petty, flat, hollow, shallow, tacky, frivolous, trivial

superior, superlative
   majestic, noble, visionary, grandiose, masterful, brilliant, elevated, consummate, deft, superb

surreal
   unearthly, bizarre, uncanny, freakish, dreamlike, odd, fantastic, peculiar

tacky
   garish, gaudy, tawdry, cheap, tasteless, shoddy, sleazy, crude, seedy, run-down, trashy

tantalizing

captivating, enrapturing, bewitching, alluring, enticing, appealing, tempting, fascinating, seductive, compelling, charming, riveting, enchanting, enthralling

tasteful

refined, polished, elegant, graceful, stylish, cultured, sophisticated, poised

tawdry

gaudy, tacky, shoddy, shabby, garish, sleazy, tasteless, cheap, vulgar, crude

thrilling

arousing, captivating, enchanting, enlivening, gripping, rousing, electrifying, riveting

thriving

radiant, flourishing, robust, swarming, teeming, vigorous

transcendent

preeminent, momentous, ascendant, stellar, towering, unparalleled, unmatched, grand, mystical

treacherous

precarious, hazardous, perilous, deceitful, deceptive, menacing, two-faced

treasure

gem, jewel, riches, masterpiece, fortune, prize

triumphant

elated, exultant, euphoric, delighted, jubilant

unabashed

bold, brazen, unblinking, undaunted, shameless, flagrant

uncanny

surreal, unearthly, bizarre, freakish, mysterious, unnatural, ghostly, magical, eerie, unsettling

uncouth

gauche, boorish, crass, crude, tacky, clumsy

unearthly

dreamy, otherworldly, whimsical, mysterious, surreal, ethereal

unflappable

immovable, steely, unyielding, hardened, unbending, unruffled, flinty

unflinching

unyielding, headstrong, immutable, impervious, inflexible, ironfisted, refractory, resistant, steadfast, adamant

unglued

confused, unmoored, unhinged, unbalanced, unstable, unraveled, shaken, befuddled

unhinged
  unmoored, unglued, deranged, unstable, demented, disturbed, crazed, batty

unholy
  corrupt, depraved, base, unhallowed, profane, irreverent, dreadful, vile, immoral

unmoored
  unstable, unhinged, unglued, deranged, crazed, adrift, unanchored

unruffled
  placid, unflappable, composed, balanced, equanimous, cool-headed, poised, collected, calm

unsavory
  distasteful, obnoxious, offensive, repugnant, disreputable, seedy, questionable, shady, repulsive

unseemly
  indiscreet, tactless, crude, scandalous, tasteless, vulgar, distasteful, undignified

unsightly
  ugly, dull, hideous, repulsive, grotesque, drab, deformed, appalling

unsound
  perilous, hazardous, treacherous, uncertain, precarious

urbane
  polished, refined, suave, sophisticated, affable, elegant, poised

valiant
  gallant, fearless, unflinching, dauntless, heroic, intrepid, daring, undaunted

valorous
  gallant, fearless, dauntless, valiant, courageous

vehement
  forceful, intense, impassioned, fiery, passionate, resolute

vexing
  aggravating, bothersome, provoking, tiresome, disturbing, galling, exasperating, troubling, irksome, wearisome

vibrant
  robust, dynamic, hearty, spirited, vigorous, zestful

vigorous
  forceful, fierce, robust, dynamic, full-bodied, spirited, staunch, rugged, sturdy, vibrant, zestful, thriving, roaring, swarming, teeming

vile
  repugnant, abhorrent, atrocious, heinous, monstrous, vicious, wretched

virile
  potent, robust, manly, forceful, vigorous, energetic

vivacious
sparkling, effervescent, airy, breezy, exhilarating, frothy

whimsy, whimsical
charmed, dreamy, fanciful, romantic, playful, mischievous

wild
fierce, feral, delirious, deranged, frantic, uncontrollable, howling, raving, raging, savage, untamed

witless
dim-witted, foolish, inane, kooky, moronic, wacky, zany

wizardly
magical, bewitching, charismatic, enchanting, spellbinding, wondrous, mystical

wondrous
magical, enchanting, radiant, splendorous, glorious, brilliant

wretched
abominable, atrocious, contemptible, despairing, despicable, vile, dreadful, miserable, worthless, forlorn, repugnant, abhorrent

GENERAL APPEARANCE

ancient
age-old, primeval, antique, prehistoric, archaic, primordial, relic

antiquated
archaic, ancient, heirloom, dated, aged, obsolete

archaic
ancient, antiquated, prehistoric, obsolete, primitive

austere
stern, unapproachable, uninviting, staid, bare, clinical, grave, bleak, unadorned

bare
meager, gaunt, scant, spare, barren, empty, forsaken, void, blank, stripped

battered
crumbling, ravaged, dilapidated, decaying, rickety, aged, damaged, deteriorated, shattered, demolished

bedraggled
disheveled, unkempt, scruffy, untidy, mangy, shabby, scraggly, messy

besmirched
marked, patchy, tarnished, splotchy, blemished, smudged, tainted, frayed, spotty

blemished
tarnished, besmirched, blotched, debased, smudged, tainted, gashed, deformed

blighted
> ravaged, devastated, disintegrating, haggard, hollowed, plagued, wasted

blotched, blotchy
> marked, patchy, uneven, tarnished, besmirched, blemished, spotty, smudged, tainted, fragmented, frayed

craggy
> weathered, weather-beaten, rugged, rocky, stony, jagged

cruddy
> filthy, dirty, foul, grimy, grubby, grungy, polluted, soiled, squalid

crumbling
> battered, dilapidated, rickety, decaying, aged, deteriorated, eroded, disintegrating

decaying, decayed
> decrepit, rotting, deteriorated, rotten, spoiled, crumbling, eroding, deteriorating

decrepit
> decaying, rickety, battered, ramshackle, worn, degraded, tottering, crumbling, aged, dilapidated

deteriorated
> decayed, corroded, disintegrated, dilapidated, decrepit, decadent

dilapidated
> decrepit, shabby, rickety, battered, decaying, deteriorated, ruined, disheveled

disheveled
> bedraggled, unkempt, disarray, messy, sloppy, untidy, scruffy

disintegrating, disintegrated
> wasted, wrecked, ravaged, blighted, corrosive, devastated, haggard, plagued

disordered
> disarray, chaotic, havoc, jumbled, unsettled, ruffled, untidy

dreary
> desolate, forlorn, godforsaken, bleak, grim, colorless, ashen, pale, anemic, bland, faded, lifeless, pallid, sallow

drenched
> awash, covered, flooded, overflowing, submerged, doused, soaked

dusty
> sooty, grubby, grungy, gritty, crumbly, chalky, dirty

emaciated
> sunken, frail, gaunt, haggard, withered, barren, scrawny, wasted, stark

filthy
> dirty, cruddy, foul, grimy, grubby, grungy, odious, repugnant, squalid, polluted, soiled, vile

flooded
covered, overflowing, submerged, drenched, deluged, drowned, saturated, swamped, inundated, awash

grim
dreary, forlorn, bleak, forbidding, ghastly, grisly, gruesome, doomed

grimy
soiled, squalid, vile, filthy, dirty, repugnant, polluted, cruddy, odious, grubby, grungy, foul

grubby
foul, grimy, grungy, filthy, dirty, cruddy, polluted, soiled, squalid, sordid

grungy
soiled, squalid, filthy, dirty, grimy, grubby, cruddy, foul, polluted

hearty
robust, brawny, dynamic, full-bodied, rugged, sturdy, vibrant, vigorous, zestful

immaculate
unspoiled, untainted, spotless, flawless, unblemished, impeccable, untarnished, pristine

jowly
fleshy, mouthy, drooping

mangy
dingy, filthy, shabby, slovenly, unkempt, tattered, squalid, scruffy, shaggy

messy
bedraggled, bungling, careless, dilapidated, disheveled, sloppy, unkempt, untidy

meticulous
flawless, impeccable, scrupulous, precise, fastidious, painstaking, detailed, exact

muddy
sludgy, oozy, murky, cloudy, hazy, foggy, opaque, obscure, fuzzy, turbid, milky

overgrown
weedy, teeming, leggy, flourishing, dense, spreading

polluted
filthy, odious, repugnant, foul, soiled, contaminated, poisoned, tainted

primordial
ancient, age-old, primeval, prehistoric, archaic, relic, primal

primeval
pristine, ancient, age-old, primeval, prehistoric, archaic, primordial

pristine
flawless, immaculate, exquisite, meticulous, refined, purified, pure, clarified, crystalline, primal, unblemished

pure
refined, absolute, sterling, fresh, unblemished, unadorned, natural, spare

putrid
rotten, decayed, hideous, rancid, stench, sordid, spoiled, stinking, wretched

ramshackle
tottering, rickety, shifting, wobbly, flimsy, crumbling, decrepit, dilapidated, shabby

ratty
seedy, ragged, slipshod, squalid, tattered, filthy, unkempt

ravaged
blighted, corrosive, devastated, disintegrating, haggard, plagued, ruined, wasted, wrecked

rickety
dilapidated, decrepit, shabby, flimsy, brittle, breakable, battered, decaying, fragile, deteriorated, ruined, shaky, wobbly, tottering, ramshackle

robust
brawny, dynamic, full-bodied, hearty, muscular, sinewy, staunch, steely, rugged, sturdy, vibrant, vigorous, zestful, radiant

ruined, ruinous
blighted, devastated, battered, decaying, ravaged, deteriorated, irreparable, unsalvageable, disintegrating, wasted, wrecked

rustic
bucolic, rural, pastoral, woodsy, homespun, unrefined

scenic
picturesque, idyllic, ornate, charming, quaint, vivid, striking

scraggly
unkempt, scrawny, gawky, bedraggled, ragged, untidy, shoddy

scruffy
shabby, untidy, bedraggled, mangy, ragged, scraggly, disheveled

seedy
chintzy, cheap, ragged, ratty, slipshod, squalid, tattered, tawdry

severe
grave, sharp, austere, biting, drastic, harrowing, harsh, forbidding, stark

shabby
drab, dingy, dull, grungy, mangy, bedraggled, scraggly, ramshackle, scruffy, ratty, run-down

shoddy
bedraggled, degraded, dilapidated, frazzled, tattered, scraggly

slipshod
seedy, cheap, ragged, ratty, squalid, tattered, sloppy, dilapidated

sloppy
unkempt, untidy, messy, bungling, careless, clumsy, slovenly

slovenly
mangy, filthy, shabby, unkempt, tattered, squalid, ratty, dirty

sluggish
heavy, listless, dragging, dull, groggy, laggard, languid, lethargic, lifeless

smudged, smudgy
dusty, grubby, dingy, grimy, grungy, tarnished, blemished, sooty

sooty
dusty, grubby, dingy, grimy, grungy, smudgy, blackened

spare
scant, unadorned, stark, fine, precise, thin, confined, meager, bare, austere, gaunt

splattered
splashed, splotched, smudged, doused, sprinkled, spattered

spotty
scanty, sparse, diffuse, scarce, sporadic, patchy, uneven, erratic, thin

squalid, squalor
ratty, slipshod, mangy, filthy, shabby, slovenly, unkempt, tattered, seedy, cheap, ragged, run-down, grimy, ramshackle

stark
gaunt, barren, desolate, austere, bleak, severe, unadorned, spare, somber, distinct

straggly
disheveled, unkempt, grimy, grungy, sloppy, filthy, stained, foul

submerged
flooded, awash, overflowing, drenched, inundated, drowned

unadorned
unembellished, unvarnished, natural, stark, spare, pure, austere, undecorated, modest

unblemished
sterling, unspoiled, flawless, untarnished, unsullied, impeccable, pure

unkempt
disheveled, bedraggled, mangy, dingy, filthy, slovenly, tattered, squalid, messy, untidy, scraggly

unsightly
ugly, dull, hideous, repulsive, grotesque, unkempt, drab

untidy
bedraggled, disheveled, sloppy, unkempt, cluttered, disheveled, messy

weedy
reedy, scraggy, scrawny, puny, bony, gangly

withered
decaying, haggard, emaciated, drooping, withered, shrunken, gaunt

wobbly
faltering, bewildered, muddled, woozy, groggy, stunned, tottering, careening, toppling, bobbling, tumbling

wrecked
disintegrating, ravaged, blighted, corroded, devastated, plagued, ruined, wasted, demolished

VISION and SIGHT

apparition
illusion, ghost, delusion, phantom, hallucination, fallacy, figment

array
display, splendor, spectacle, extravagance, display, throng, pattern

behold
glimpse, discern, witness, glance, gaze, perceive, scan, spy, watch, observe

blatant
conspicuous, obvious, overt, unabashed, bald, flaunting, glaring, flagrant

blazon
blare, display, emblazon, broadcast, embellish, proclaim

bleary
blurry, foggy, drained, hazy, cloudy, unclear

blind
unseeing, sightless, oblivious, myopic, unaware

blindfold, blindfolded
curtain, blinder, cloak, mask, veil, blind

blind-side, blind-sided
blinded, hidden, unaware, unprepared, surprised, stampeded, blindspot

blink, blinking
flickering, glimmering, glinting, glittering, shimmering, twinkling, wink, flashing, sparkling

blurry
bleary, foggy, hazy, nebulous, cloudy, fuzzy, murky, opaque

See: Vision *and* Sight

camouflage
disguise, hide, veil, conceal, screen, façade, mask, masquerade, smokescreen

charade
masquerade, farce, sham, pantomime, pretense

clairvoyance
insight, perception, premonition, intuition, telepathy

clandestine
hidden, surreptitious, secretive, stealthy, concealed, veiled, cloaked

clear-eyed
unclouded, luminous, shining, perceptive, lucid

cloak, cloaked
hidden, concealed, veiled, shrouded, masked, obscured

cloudy, clouded
murky, foggy, hazy, opaque, muddy, obscure, fuzzy, turbid, shady, dreamy, milky, distorted, shadowy, nebulous, blurry, curtained

cogent
perceptive, sharp, discerning, vigilant, alert, penetrating, piercing, shrewd, keen

conceal, concealed
camouflage, disguise, hide, screen, mask, masquerade, shroud, cloak, obscure, veil

conspicuous
noticeable, overt, blatant, striking, apparent, obvious, marked, pronounced

covert
hidden, private, concealed, clandestine, camouflaged, disguised, furtive, stealthy, incognito, shrouded, surreptitious

cryptic
mysterious, secret, enigmatic, perplexing, puzzling, obscure

curtained
shady, clouded, shadowy, cloaked, lurking, undetected, occult, veiled, dark

decipher
unravel, untangle, decode, unscramble, translate, deduce, solve, disentangle

decoy
lure, snare, trap, entice, camouflage, deception, shill

delusion, delude
illusion, apparition, deception, phantom, mirage, fantasy, fallacy

detect
behold, glimpse, discern, perceive, scan, spy, view

discern
> envision, insight, perceive, detect, behold, ascertain

discerning
> sharp, perceptive, eagle-eyed, vigilant, astute, insightful, piercing, discriminating

disenchanted
> disillusioned, indifferent, disappointed, embittered, jaundiced, soured, bitter, cynical

disguise, disguised
> conceal, camouflage, hide, veil, screen, mask, masquerade

disillusioned
> disenchanted, soured, embittered, world-weary, cynical, shattered, bitter

elusive
> intangible, illusory, fleeting, mysterious, deceptive, evasive, ethereal, ghostly

enshrouded
> enclosed, cloaked, concealed, masked, hidden, shrouded, veiled, swathed

espy
> discern, view, detect, spot, discover, glimpse, observe

eye-catching
> stunning, spectacular, breathtaking, striking, arresting, dazzling, flashy, dashing, brazen, showy, splashy

façade
> hide, masquerade, camouflage, disguise, veneer, conceal, screen, mask, veil

faint
> indistinct, pale, thin, hazy, faded, fuzzy, shadowy

fathom
> discern, grasp, decipher, understand, decode, unravel, interpret, pinpoint, probe

figment
> illusion, ghost, delusion, phantom, hallucination, fallacy, vision, apparition, fantasy

fixated
> engrossed, obsessed, enamored, focused, infatuated, riveted, gripped, fanatical

flagrant
> overt, conspicuous, obvious, noticeable, blatant, pronounced, glaring

focus
> concentrate, focal point, pinpoint, fixate, sharpen

foggy
> cloudy, murky, opaque, muddy, obscured, fuzzy, bleary, blurry, illusory, dreamy, awry, distorted, imaginary, shadowy, nebulous, amorphous, hazy

See: Vision *and* Sight

foresee, foresight
anticipate, predict, envision, foretell, foreshadow, presage, vision, insight

furtive
hidden, surreptitious, secretive, clandestine, stealthy, concealed, veiled, cloaked

gape
gawk, gaze, ogle, stare, scrutinize, glare, peer, peek, search, pry, size up, probe

gawk
gape, gaze, goggle, stare, glare, peer, pry, probe

gaze
gawk, gape, stare, glare, glimpse, plumb, peek, search, pry, probe, seek, size up, scrutinize, peer, glance, behold

ghost, ghostly
apparition, illusion, delusion, phantom, hallucination, figment

glance
glimpse, discern, witness, peer, gaze, peek, squint

glare
glower, stare, gleam, peer, shine

glaring
flagrant, apparent, conspicuous, obvious, marked, noticeable, blatant, striking, pronounced, overt

glimpse
behold, discern, glance, peek, peer, gaze, squint, peep, flash, spot, view

hallucinatory, hallucinate
illusory, dreamy, distorted, imaginary, shadowy, mystical, unreal, deceptive

hawk-eyed
sharp, discerning, eagle-eyed, vigilant, clear-sighted, sharp-eyed, observant, perceptive

hazy
cloudy, misty, murky, foggy, obscured, fuzzy, bleary, nebulous, opaque, shadowy, blurry

hide, hidden
conceal, screen, masquerade, camouflage, clandestine, disguise, veil, façade, mask, secretive

hindsight
retrospect, recollection, vision

illusory
dreamy, foggy, cloudy, distorted, imaginary, shadowy, mystical, hallucinatory, unreal, deceptive

Thesaurus of the Senses

imaginary
 illusory, delusional, fantastic, mythic, shadowy, hallucinatory, dreamy, invented

imperceptible
 indiscernible, undetectable, unnoticed, inconspicuous, obscure, inconsequential, hidden, unseen

incognito
 camouflaged, disguised, masked, shrouded, stealthy, surreptitious, concealed, clandestine, secret

inconspicuous
 imperceptible, indiscernible, undetectable, unnoticed, concealed, obscure, inconsequential, unassuming

invisible
 imperceptible, intangible, hidden, veiled, concealed, unseen

keen
 perceptive, discerning, penetrating, piercing, shrewd, insightful, cogent, sharp

leer, leering
 ogle, glare, stare, peer, gawk, gaze, sneer, fixate, focus

mask, masked
 disguise, conceal, camouflage, hide, facade, guise, veneer, veil

masquerade
 camouflage, veil, disguise, hide, screen, mask, conceal

mirage
 illusion, delusion, hallucination, fallacy, figment, phantom

misty
 wispy, gauzy, foggy, vapory, humid, cloudy, murky, bleary

muddled
 jumbled, foggy, bewildered, fuzzy, confused, tottering, woozy, wobbly

murky
 cloudy, hazy, foggy, opaque, muddy, obscure, fuzzy, nebulous, blurry, shadowy, turbid

myopic
 short-sighted, narrow-minded, blind, unimaginative, biased, imperceptive

nebulous
 amorphous, blurry, cloudy, fuzzy, hazy, murky, opaque, shadowy, ambiguous, vague

obscure, obscured
 cloaked, hidden, concealed, veiled, shrouded, masked, cryptic, mysterious, vague, cloudy, shadowy

obstructed
jammed, blocked, impeded, barricaded, shrouded, occluded

ogle
leer, glare, stare, peer, fixate, focus, gawk, gape

opaque
nebulous, amorphous, blurry, cloudy, fuzzy, hazy, murky, shadowy, muddied

overt
conspicuous, obvious, marked, noticeable, blatant, striking, glaring, apparent, pronounced

pantomime
charade, imitate, gesture, mime, mimic, signal, mirror

patrol
watch, lookout, scan, stare, spy, focus, gaze, safeguard

peek
peer, gaze, search, pry, probe, size up, scrutinize, stare

peep
glimpse, peer, glance, squint, scan, blink

peer
gape, glare, gaze, plumb, peek, probe, search, pry, stare, squint

perceive
discern, detect, grasp, distinguish, observe, identify

perceptive
vigilant, alert, cogent, sharp, discerning, eagle-eyed, keen, shrewd, penetrating, piercing

phantom
specter, illusion, apparition, ghost, mirage, hallucination, delusion

prism
crystal, facet, spectrum, glass, viewpoint

probe, probing
peer, gaze, gape, glare, plumb, search, pry, seek, scrutinize, stare, prod

pry, prying
probe, scrutinize, stare, peer, gaze, gape, glare, snoop, meddle

reverie
daydream, musing, fantasy, trance

scan
patrol, lookout, stare, spy, focus, gaze, peer, browse, skim

screen
façade, masquerade, camouflage, disguise, veil, conceal, mask, smokescreen, blind

semblance
veneer, façade, guise, mask, pose, veil, aura

scrutinize, scrutinizing
scrupulous, meticulous, probing, unsparing, peering, searching, prying, precise

shadowy
illusory, dreamy, foggy, concealed, distorted, imaginary, nebulous, amorphous, blurry, fuzzy, hazy, murky, opaque, vague, cloudy

shady
clouded, curtained, shadowy, dark, shrouded, screened

sharp
perceptive, discerning, eagle-eyed, vigilant, piercing, penetrating, keen

short-sighted
narrow-minded, blind, biased, unthinking, myopic, unimaginative

shrewd
cogent, keen, penetrating, piercing, perceptive, sharp, discerning, vigilant, alert

shrouded
shadowy, curtained, clouded, cloaked, hidden, concealed, obscured, masked, veiled

smokescreen
disguise, hide, veil, conceal, screen, façade, mask, masquerade, camouflage

spectacle
array, display, splendor, extravagance, drama, parade, scene

spectrum
scope, span, scale, purview, sphere, continuum

squint
peer, scrutinize, scan, glance, peek, gape, glimpse

spy
detect, behold, discern, perceive, snoop, uncover, spot, sleuth, eyeball, scan

stare
gawk, gape, gaze, glare, peer, pry, probe, scrutinize, ogle, fixate, focus

surreptitious
stealthy, veiled, hidden, concealed, clandestine, disguised, furtive, skulking, shrouded, camouflaged, covert

unblinking
unabashed, undaunted, fearless, focused, bold, unflinching, fixed, unswerving

undetectable
imperceptible, indiscernible, unnoticed, inconspicuous, invisible, obscured, shadowy, unseen

SEE: VISION *and* SIGHT

undivided
focused, unswerving, intense, engrossed, unbroken, unflagging, concerted, intent, fixed

unflagging
undivided, unswerving, unbending, fixed, focused, unremitting

unnoticed
overlooked, unobtrusive, inconspicuous, obscure, disregarded, secret, unseen

unseen
hidden, undetected, unnoticeable, obscure, concealed, invisible, imperceptible, shrouded, veiled

unswerving
focused, determined, unfaltering, steady, undivided, unbroken, unflagging, intent, fixed

vantage
viewpoint, slant, outlook, angle, standpoint, position

veil, veiled
camouflage, disguise, screen, façade, masquerade, conceal, mask

vigilant
perceptive, watchful, sharp, discerning, eagle-eyed, circumspect, guarded, alert, mindful, observant

visionary
lofty, superlative, noble, grandiose, imaginative, starry-eyed

watch
patrol, lookout, scan, stare, spy, focus, gaze, peer

watchful
alert, cautious, circumspect, guarded, mindful, observant, vigilant

witness
behold, glimpse, discern, perceive, glance, gaze, attest

HEAR

If you have the ears to hear, the whole existence is just music.
—*Sadhguru Jaggi Vasudev, yogi and mystic*

VIBRATIONS *and* PERCUSSIONS - DISCORD *and* NOISE -
MUSIC *and* HARMONY - ONOMATOPOEIA -
SPEECH *and* UTTERANCES - MOVEMENT -
LISTENING - VOLUME

Silence is the seat of all sound. From formlessness, the sounds of the Big Bang emerged, first as a low groan and then a deep roar. Colossal waves of sound, containing all future sounds, rippled out of the nascent universe as an expanding hiss, their acoustic patterns unwinding and unfolding across the emerging cosmos. We carry the echoes of these primordial sounds within us, reverberations from the distant past.

The universe is mostly empty space—dark matter and vibrations to which we are largely deaf. Yet, in our narrow band of hearing, about 10 octaves, the world is a cacophony of sounds. It is a complex mixture of rhythms, tones, melodies, and percussions, from the barely perceptible ring to deafening booms—music, laughter, machines, wind and weather, birds and animals, waterfalls, streams, and oceans, traffic, planes, sirens, conversations, crowds. Even in silence, we can hear the hum of ambient noise.

Speech is our splendid sound currency. We speak in a myriad of languages and dialects. Our collective vocabulary tops billions of words that we richly arrange into innumerable patterns. In dialogue, we mimic each other, rearrange sounds, and invent new ways of communicating. Not even birds can match our vocal range of expression.

We are acutely receptive to a sound's quality, pitch, and timbre. From rhythmic cues, we hear the intention and cadence behind spoken words. Over our lifetimes, we build a vast aural library to identify and recognize sounds. We try to filter out distortions. Unfamiliar sounds surprise and sometimes deeply unsettle us.

From just a handful of core notes, we create music and harmonies of sublime quality. We sing, strike chords, and beat drums to express our deepest joys and sorrows. In song, we resonate with the transcendent emotion of music. We strive to be in tune with others and at the same time find our own voice. We play it by ear. At times, we find perfect pitch with the world.

Discordant sounds—screaming, scraping, grating, dripping—set our nerves on edge. We respond viscerally to shrillness, clamor, and ear-splitting volumes. We sense when something has a hollow ring or when others are tone deaf or strike a false note. Sometimes, we crave stillness and soundproofing.

Sounds orient us. With both ears, we hear in stereo. Faraway rumbles. Murmurs. Oncoming collisions. Whistling trajectories. Every sound we hear tells us something about itself—its form, its essence. And every form suggests its latent, hidden sound.

Finally, in our own private world, we are in continual dialogue with an inner voice, a constant guide who knows our hopes, doubts, and dreams. Turning inward, we can tap into the deep well of silence within us—a sanctuary of eternality that connects us to our origins.

In this section, lend your ears to the dynamic range of hearing words: vibrations and percussions, discord and noise, music and harmony, movement, speech and utterances, volume, and the delightful music that is onomatopoeia.

Vibrations *and* Percussions

backfire
  explode, bang, blast, burst, erupt, flare, boom, thunder, ricochet, backlash

bang
  batter, bat, beat, belt, deck, crash, detonate, hammer, rap, knock, smash, strike, slam, whack, explode, blast, thunder, thud, clash, rumble

bash
  bang, belt, clobber, deck, drub, knock, slam, smack, smash, thump, wallop, whack, bat

bell
  ring, clang, chime, toll, peal, resound, gong, ting, knell, alarm, buzz, siren

bellow
  roar, bawl, grunt, screech, sob, howl, gasp, growl, rave, rant, bark, shriek, boom, squawk, trumpet, thunder, wail, holler, bluster, bray

blare
  reverberate, ring, rumble, bellow, boom, clamor, echo, wail, thunder, trumpet, resound, blast, roar

blaring
  ringing, booming, wailing, thunderous, resounding, shrill, raucous, dissonant

blast
  boom, thunder, explode, backfire, bang, burst, erupt, flare

bluster
  blast, thunder, bellow, bombast, cacophony, commotion, uproar, clamor, melee, rumble, tumult, rant, roar

boom
  reverberate, resound, resonate, thunder, echo, pound, bellow, roar, explode, bang

booming
  deafening, ear-piercing, ringing, blaring, resounding, bellowing, roaring, crashing

brassy
  resounding, noisy, brash, blaring, boisterous, jarring, thunderous, tinny, clanging

clack
  clatter, rattle, clank, clang, clamor, clap, din, commotion, clink

clang
  ring, clink, chime, clank, jingle, peal, knell, ting, resound, jangle, gong, crash, clatter, clash, tinkling, ping, toll

clank
  chime, ding, jangle, peal, ring, ting, clink, clang, toll, jingle, knell, resound, rattle, din, clatter, ping

clap
> applaud, clash, clatter, commotion, knock, rumble, swat, thunderclap, thwack, wallop, whack, whomp, cheer, bang

clash
> commotion, brawl, collide, crash, discord, flap, quarrel, rumble, snarl, tussle, wrangle, bat, bang, batter, beat, belt, clobber, smash, hammer, knock, pummel, whack, jangle, clang

clatter
> rattle, clank, clang, clack, clamor, clap, din, commotion, ruckus, spout, clink, jangle, clash, jingle, peal, ping

click
> clink, clack, clop, clunk, flick, plunk, snap, tick, pop

clink
> clatter, clank, ping, ring, peal, tinkling, clang, jangle, clash, jingle, ding

clomp
> stomp, clop, trudge, smash, bang, knock, rap, thump, plod, thud

clop
> clunk, stomp, plunk, thud, clatter, rattle, clank, clang, clack, clap

crack
> crackle, sizzle, snap, blast, clap, pop, bang, smash

crackle
> crack, hiss, crash, buzz, fizz, snap

crash, crashing
> bang, boom, burst, jolt, knock, whack, batter, hammer, punch, smash, strike, beat

detonate
> bang, crash, hammer, knock, smash, strike, blast, explode

drone
> burble, gurgle, murmur, purr, whir, hum, rumble, whine, whistle, buzz, whir

drum
> beat, hammer, drone, hum, resound, thunder, thrum, boom, strum, throb, tap

echo
> resound, reverberate, thunder, explode, repercussion, ringing, chant

gong
> toll, bell, chime, clang, ting, knell, crash, alarm, cymbal

hammer
> thrash, wallop, whack, bang, pummel, batter, clobber, crash, knock, rap, smash, strike, beat

Hear: Vibrations *and* Percussions

high-pitched
reedy, shrill, shrieking, acute, piercing, sharp, cutting, falsetto

jangle, jangly
clang, clink, clatter, clash, jingle, peal, tinkling, ping, clank, rattle

jingle
clang, ring, clink, chime, toll, clank, ding, peal, knell, ting, resound, jangle

knell
clang, clink, chime, clank, jingle, peal, toll, ting, resound, summon, warning, ring

low-pitched
bass, drum, buzz, drone, rumble, muffled, echo, boom, thunder, hum

nuance
overtone, shade, hint, tinge, trace, distinction

peal
jangle, clang, clink, clatter, clash, jingle, tinkling, ping, bell, resound, chime, toll, ring

quiver, quivering
tremulous, shaky, trembling, vibrato, shuddering, jittery, quavering

reedy
thin, fragile, high-pitched, shrill, harsh, nasal, cutting

repercussion
echo, resound, reverberate, thunder, explode, ringing, booming

resonant
booming, consonant, harmonic, resounding, pulsating, pulsing, sonorous, echo, ringing, throbbing, thunderous, vibrating

resonate
chime, chant, sing, ring, clang, peal, toll, echo, resound

resound, resounding
bell, ring, clang, chime, toll, peal, resonate, boom, echo, thunder, ringing

reverberate, reverberating
boom, echo, rebound, rumble, sound, thunder, resound

ring
peal, toll, clang, jingle, tinkling, jingling, jangle, chime, ding, bell, knell, resound

roar
thunder, wail, whoop, bark, bellow, shout, burst, clamor, growl, rave, rant, bawl, boom, explode, holler, grunt, howl

roaring
resounding, thunderous, ringing, crashing, deafening, uproarious, boisterous, rowdy, pealing, piercing

rumble, rumbling
> thunder, resonant, hum, bellow, roar, resound, reverberate, echo, blast, boom, clap, drone, whir, clash, throb, jolt, shudder

shudder
> tremor, rumble, jolt, vibrato, shimmy, tremble, shiver, gyrate

sonic
> acoustic, sound, tune, chord, aural, vibration, reverberation, music, echo

thud
> clobber, bang, crash, hammer, knock, rap, smash, thrash, wallop, thump

thunder, thunderous, thundering
> rumble, wail, trumpet, echo, uproar, commotion, tumult, resound, blast, bellow, boom, clamor, crash, explode, rail, roar

thunderbolt, thunderclap
> rumble, blast, slap, boom, bang, roar

tinny
> thin, brassy, metallic, jingly, jangly, twangy

toll
> bell, chime, clang, gong, ting, knell, ring, signal, strike, summon, peal

tremble, trembling
> tremulous, quivering, shaky, vibrato, quiver, throb, shudder, quake

tremor
> rumble, jolt, shudder, vibrato, quake, quiver, ripple, shiver

tremulous
> quavering, quivering, trembling, vibrato, shaky, wobbly, warbling, wavering

undercurrent
> murmur, overtone, hint, tenor, vibe, riptide, undertow, tinge

undertone
> undercurrent, whisper, hint, murmur, buzz, nuance, tenor

vibrate
> whine, whistle, whir, hum, drone, chant, trill, purr, murmur, buzz, rumble, throb

vibrato
> tremor, rumble, vibration, quiver, warble, quaver, trill

DISCORD *and* NOISE

acrimonious, acrimony
> discordant, cacophonous, harsh, abrupt, biting, jarring, grating, gruff, raucous, screeching, shrill, clashing, cutting

atonal
dissonant, cacophony, discordant, off-key, sour, unmelodious, jangling, jarring

biting
harsh, abrupt, acrimonious, jarring, grating, raucous, discordant, piercing, shrill, screeching, cacophonous, clashing, cutting

bluster
blast, thunder, bellow, bombast, cacophony, commotion, uproar, clamor, melee, rumble, tumult, rant, roar

booming
deafening, ear-piercing, ringing, blaring, resounding, bellowing, roaring, crashing

cacophony
racket, clamor, discord, dissonance, discordance, uproar, raucous, screeching, din

caterwaul
scream, screech, howl, bawl, bay, bellow, squawk, wail, shriek, cry, yowl

clamor, clamorous
commotion, uproar, tumult, roar, ranting, raucous, raving, blaring, boisterous, brassy, cacophonous, jarring, deafening, clanging, racket, resounding, shrill, thunderous

commotion
clamor, uproar, tumult, roar, rant, racket, upheaval, turbulence

cutting
harsh, abrupt, acerbic, acrimonious, biting, jarring, grating, shrill, raucous, discordant, piercing, screeching, clashing

deafening
booming, ear-piercing, earthshaking, piercing, resounding, ringing, thundering, rattling

diatribe
tirade, denunciation, attack, screed, harangue, outburst, rant

din
racket, tumult, ruckus, commotion, clamor, roar, clang, clash, clatter, rattle, rumble

discord, discordant
cacophony, racket, clamor, uproar, acrimonious, biting, jarring, grating, raucous, screeching, shrill, clashing, din, cutting

dissonant
atonal, cacophony, discordant, off-key, sour, jangling, jarring, clashing

ear-piercing
deafening, booming, resounding, thundering, rattling, ear-splitting, ringing

ear-splitting

deafening, booming, ear-piercing, piercing, resounding, ringing, thundering, rattling

fracas

flap, tumult, strife, turmoil, uproar, racket, rumble, melee, scuffle, clash, tussle, brawl, riot, disturbance

frenzy, frenzied

ranting, clamorous, hysterical, raging, raucous, raving

furor

racket, agitation, cacophony, clamor, commotion, discord, uproar, turmoil, shrill, thunder

grating

piercing, jarring, biting, raucous, discordant, screeching, clashing, cacophonous, cutting, shrill

jarring

grating, shrill, raucous, raspy, dissonant, atonal, cacophony, sour, discordant, off-key, unmelodious, piercing, biting, screeching, clashing, cutting

melee

uproar, bluster, roar, brawl, clamor, commotion, embroil, rumble, thunder, tumult, furor

noisy

blaring, boisterous, brassy, cacophonous, clamorous, jarring, shrill, deafening, clanging, resounding, riotous, rip-roaring, thunderous

off-key

dissonant, atonal, cacophonous, discordant, sour, jangling, jarring, flat, tuneless, off-pitch, clashing

piercing

deafening, booming, earthshaking, resounding, ringing, rattling, thundering, thunderous, shrill

racket

agitation, cacophony, clamor, commotion, discord, furor, uproar, turmoil, thunder

raging

clamorous, hysterical, ranting, raucous, raving, stormy, seething, tempestuous, turbulent

raucous

agitated, clamorous, frenzied, hysterical, raging, ranting, raving, acrimonious, biting, jarring, grating, discordant, screeching, shrill, cacophonous, clashing, cutting

riot
>turmoil, uproar, commotion, racket, rumble, storm, anarchy, strife, rampage, revolt, melee, furor, brawl, clamor, fracas, clash, tussle, tumult

riotous, rioting
>unruly, uproarious, boisterous, tumultuous, brawling, chaotic, wild, turbulent

rip-roaring
>noisy, blaring, boisterous, brassy, cacophonous, clamorous, jarring, deafening, clanging, racket, resounding, riotous, rowdy, screaming, shrill, thunderous

ruckus
>clatter, rattle, clank, clang, clack, clamor, clap, din, commotion, upheaval, racket

screech, screeching
>cackle, squawk, whoop, yelp, scream, holler, yell, bellow, howl, bay, bawl, squeal, wail, bark, bleat

shriek
>blare, caterwaul, cry, holler, roar, screech, scream, squawk, wail, thunder, whoop, bawl, hail, moan, whine

shrill
>dissonant, ear-piercing, ear-splitting, grating, harsh, high-pitched, piercing, reedy, sharp, wailing, jarring, screeching

siren
>alarm, alert, buzzer, warning, bell, horn

stormy
>raging, clamorous, hysterical, ranting, raucous, raving, turbulent, tempestuous

tempestuous
>raging, clamorous, hysterical, ranting, raucous, raving, turbulent, stormy

tirade
>bawl, rant, attack, onslaught, blast, tongue-lashing, scream, harangue, wail, cry, rail, lament, shriek, diatribe

tumult, tumultuous
>clamor, commotion, uproar, roar, hysteria, raging, ranting, raving, raucous

turbulent
>raging, clamorous, hysterical, ranting, raucous, raving, stormy, tempestuous

turmoil
>racket, agitation, cacophony, clamor, commotion, discord, furor, uproar, thunder

uproar, uproarious
>roaring, raucous, deafening, clamorous, booming, boisterous, rowdy, rambunctious

vehement
>forceful, intense, impassioned, fiery, passionate, resolute, violent, powerful

vitriol, vitriolic
> biting, scathing, spiteful, venomous, vicious, cutting, withering, sharp

vociferous
> vehement, clamorous, blaring, clanging, boisterous, shrill, shouting, ranting, loud-mouthed, strident, shouting

MUSIC *and* HARMONY

acoustic, acoustical
> music, echo, reverberation, sound, tune, chord, aural, sonic

attuned
> receptive, tuned, harmonized, unified, integrated, matched

bugle
> trumpet, horn, pipe, whistle, clarion, cornet

cadence
> tone, rhythm, music, lilt, intone, accent, tempo, accent, inflection, intonation, meter, swing, measure

catchy
> memorable, musical, melodic, harmonious, tuneful, lyrical

chime, chiming
> chant, sing, resonate, clang, peal, toll, clink, jingle, gong, harmonic, mellifluous, harmonious, ring, melodious, ting

chord
> chorus, blend, harmony, tune, overtone, melody, chime, string, note

dulcet
> mellifluous, melodious, lyrical, musical, poetic, sonorous, tuneful, harmonious, harmonic, chiming, flowing

harmonious, harmonic, harmonized
> blended, tuneful, melodious, mellifluous, sonorous, chiming, attuned, lyrical

honeyed
> lyrical, musical, expressive, golden-tongued, melodic, sonorous, poetic, songful, mellifluous, tuneful, harmonious, harmonic

hum, humming
> drone, whine, whistle, whir, purr, murmur, buzz, vibrate, rumble, throb, chant, trill, thrum, strum

lyrical
> musical, expressive, golden-tongued, melodic, poetic, sonorous, songful, honeyed, mellifluous, tuneful, harmonious, harmonic, melodious, chiming, flowing

mellifluous

tuneful, harmonic, mellow, melodic, sweet-sounding, sonorous, chiming, dulcet, flowing, harmonious, melodious, musical, catchy, lyrical

melodious, melodic, melody

mellifluous, lyrical, musical, poetic, sonorous, tuneful, harmonious, harmonic, chiming, flowing

mingled

medley, chorus, blended, melded, mixed, harmonized

musical

lullaby, melody, tuneful, lyrical, expressive, poetic, sonorous, songful, chiming, harmonious, harmonic, melodious, mellifluous

nuance

overtone, undercurrent, mood, tenor, murmur, tone

octave

note, frequency, vibration, scale, tone, range, interval

overtone

undercurrent, mood, nuance, chord, tone

pitch

cadence, tone, frequency, harmonic, music, timbre

poetic

lyrical, musical, expressive, golden-tongued, melodic, sonorous, songful, flowing, honeyed, tuneful, harmonious, harmonic, melodious, mellifluous, chiming

resonating, resonant

booming, consonant, harmonic, resounding, pulsating, pulsing, sonorous, ringing, throbbing, thunderous, vibrating, full-throated, echoing

rhythm, rhythmic

cadence, intermittent, pulsating, oscillating, pulsing, throbbing, staccato, beat, undulating, tone, tempo

scale

octave, note, frequency, vibration, tone

songful

mellifluous, tuneful, harmonious, harmonic, melodious, lyrical, musical, poetic, expressive, golden-tongued, melodic, sonorous, honeyed, chiming

sonorous

reverberating, resonant, resounding, silver-tongued, melodious, round, vibrant, harmonious, tuneful, harmonic, lyrical, chiming, mellifluous, flowing, fluent, expressive, golden-tongued, honeyed, songful, rich

tempo

lilt, cadence, accent, inflection, meter, intone, rhythm, beat

tenor
> tone, mood, trend, drift, essence

timbre
> tone, resonance, voice, pitch, accent, inflection, intonation

tone, tonal
> timbre, resonance, pitch, accent, sound

tuneful
> harmonious, blending, harmonic, lyrical, melodious, mellifluous, chiming, fluent, flowing, sonorous

ONOMATOPOEIA (SOUND WORDS)

babble, babbling
> chatter, blather, ramble, blabber, murmur, gurgle, drivel, gibberish

blabber
> blather, chatter, ramble, yammer, murmur, gurgle, jabber, babble, gab, prattle

bubble, bubbling
> effervesce, foam, froth, fizz, gurgle, boil, percolate, gush, fizz

burble
> gurgle, bubble, rumble, blather, babble, murmur, purr, whir, drone, hum

buzz
> hum, drone, whine, whistle, whir, purr, murmur, vibrate, rumble, throb, trill

cackle
> snicker, snort, chuckle, bark, screech, squawk, whoop, chortle, smirk

caterwaul
> scream, screech, howl, bawl, bay, bellow, squawk, wail, shriek, yell, yowl

chatter
> jabber, gab, blather, chit-chat, babble, ramble, blabber, murmur, drivel, gibberish

cheep
> trill, burble, cluck, croon, gaggle, tweet, peep, chirp, chirrup

chirp, chirpy
> cluck, squawk, sing, trill, cheep, peep, chirrup, bellow, lilt, warble, quack, creak, trumpet, whistle

chirrup
> call, chitter, cluck, quack, chirp, cackle, hoot, tweet, clack, warble, crow, gobble, honk, whistle, trill, twitter

chitter
> quack, chirp, cackle, call, chirrup, cluck, clack, crow, gobble, honk, hoot, tweet, warble, whistle

chortle
hee-haw, roar, hoot, snicker, cackle, smirk, giggle, snort, chuckle, guffaw, crow

clack
clatter, rattle, clank, clang, clamor, clap, clunk, click, clink, crash, tap

clang
ring, clink, chime, toll, clank, ding, jingle, peal, knell, ting, resound, gong, crash, jangle, clatter, clash, tinkling, ping

clank
chime, ding, jangle, peal, ring, ting, clink, clang, toll, jingle, knell, resound, rattle, din, clatter, ping

clap
whack, clash, clatter, commotion, knock, rumble, swat, thunderclap, thwack, wallop, whomp, applaud, cheer, celebrate, bang

clash
commotion, brawl, collide, crash, discord, flap, quarrel, rumble, snarl, tussle, wrangle, hammer, knock, jangle, clang

clatter
rattle, clank, clang, clamor, clap, din, commotion, ruckus, jangle, clink, clack, clash, jingle, peal, ping

click
clink, clack, clop, clunk, flick, plunk, snap, tick, pop

clink
clatter, clank, ping, peal, tinkle, clang, jangle, clash, jingle, chime, ting, ring

clomp
stomp, clop, trudge, smash, bang, knock, rap, thump

clop
clunk, stomp, plunk, thud, clatter, rattle, clank, clang, clack, clap

cluck
chirp, clack, squawk, burble, cheep, croon, gaggle, tweet, peep, chirrup, trill

clunk
clatter, rattle, clank, clang, clack, clap, clink, clomp, plod, thump, tromp, clonk, thud

crackle
burn, clack, spark, sizzle, snap, crinkle, crack, fizz, hiss

creak
screech, squeak, squeal, wail, whine, whistle, groan, scrape, chirp, rasp, grind

crinkle
scrunch, rumple, crease, crimp, ripple, rustle, twist, wring, pucker, crumple

ding
> clang, ring, clink, chime, toll, clank, jingle, peal, knell, ting, resound

dribble
> drool, froth, gurgle, percolate, spit, sprinkle, drizzle, drip

drizzle
> percolate, seep, trickle, drip, dribble, leak, pour, spray, sprinkle

fizz, fizzle
> buzz, bubble, simmer, sparkle, sputter, effervesce, foam, froth, hiss

flick, flicker
> flip, flitter, pulse, tweak, click, snap, tick, tap

flutter
> flap, fly, jangle, whirl, wag, twirl, hover, beat, bat, wiggle, wave

gabble
> babble, chatter, drivel, gibberish, spout, sputter, jabber, rattle

gargle
> guzzle, swig, swill, gurgle, swish, gulp

gasp
> choke, pant, wheeze, shriek, squawk, grunt, screech, gulp, huff, puff

giggle
> chortle, hee-haw, roar, hoot, snicker, cackle, smirk, snort, chuckle

growl
> bark, hiss, howl, snarl, snort, gnarl, grunt, moan, bellow

gruff
> gravelly, husky, hoarse, guttural, testy, blunt, truculent, jarring, harsh, abrupt, biting, grating, raspy

gurgle, gurgling
> dribble, ripple, babble, bubble, splash, trickle, murmur, percolate, burble, rumble

guzzle
> gargle, swig, swill, gurgle, slosh, imbibe

hiss, hissing
> fizz, whistle, jeer, heckle, wheeze, sizzle, whine, bark, gnarl, snort, sneer

lisp
> drawl, nasal, snort, sniff, twang, sputter, spit, stutter

mumble
> murmur, whisper, mutter, babble, blather, chatter, ramble, blabber, gurgle, sigh

murmur
> whisper, mumble, mutter, sigh, babble, chatter, blather, ramble, blabber, gurgle, bellow, purr, vibrate, whir, rustle

Hear: Onomatopoeia

mutter
  mumble, murmur, whisper, blather, snort, splutter, stammer, babble, chatter, blabber, sigh

peep
  chirp, chirpy, sing, trill, cheep, warble, chirrup, coo, tweet, squeal, squeak

ping
  clink, clatter, clank, ring, peal, jangle, tinkling, clang, ting

plunk
  bang, crash, hammer, knock, strike, wallop, plop

prattle
  chatter, chat, jabber, blather, yammer, babble, blabber, rattle

purr
  burble, gurgle, murmur, whir, drone, hum, rumble, trill

raspy, rasping
  abrasive, throaty, scratchy, chafing, gravely, husky, gruff, hoarse, croaky

rattle
  clank, clatter, jingle, jangle, clink, joggle, ramble, bang, jolt, shatter, jounce, shake

rustle, rustling
  crinkle, crackle, swish, whistle, whisper, whish, whoosh, hum, murmur, whir

screech, screeching
  cackle, squawk, whoop, yelp, scream, holler, bellow, howl, squeal, bawl, wail, yell

seethe, seething
  bellow, boil, erupt, explode, fume, rant, rage, fume, flare

sizzle, sizzling
  boil, effervesce, fizzle, sear, seethe, burn, crackle, hiss, whistle

snap
  click, clink, clack, clop, flick, plunk, tick, crack, crackle, snarl, bark, pop

snarl
  growl, bark, hiss, howl, snort, gnarl, grumble, snap

sneer
  jeer, decry, hiss, heckle, snort, mock, scorn, deride, scoff, taunt, ridicule, revile

snicker
  chortle, hee-haw, roar, hoot, cackle, smirk, giggle, snort, chuckle

snort
  growl, bark, gnarl, hiss, howl, snarl, chortle, cackle, hoot, smirk, giggle, snicker, chuckle, lisp, drawl, sniff, twang, splutter, spit

spew
  billow, spit, gush, belch, burp, spittle, expel, heave

splash
> gurgle, gurgling, babble, bubble, dribble, ripple, trickle, percolate, sprinkle, spray

splat
> clash, crash, smash, plop, splatter, splash

splutter, spluttering
> spit, stammer, lisp, drawl, nasal, snort, sniff, cough, choke, spout, stammer

spout
> gush, spew, squirt, sputter, billow, spit, exude, surge, shoot, spray, belch

sputter
> fizzle, bubble, spit, spout, burst

squawk
> groan, moan, grouse, gripe, grumble, lament, shriek, snipe, whoop, wail, bark, bawl, screech, sob, bay, bellow, bleat, blare, caterwaul, howl, yell, yelp, cry

squeak
> creak, chirp, screech, squeal, wail, whine, whistle, grate

stomp
> clomp, clop, trudge, smash, bang, knock, rap, thump, trample

swoosh
> rush, ripple, undulate, flutter, flap, twirl, whirl, whorl, pivot, swirl

thrash
> smash, strike, bang, batter, chop, clobber, crash, hammer, knock, pummel, beat, punch, wallop

thump
> bang, biff, belt, clobber, deck, drub, crack, hammer, flog, knock, pelt, pound, pummel, slug, smack, slam, smash, rap, wallop, whack

ting
> clang, ring, clink, chime, clank, ding, jingle, peal, knell, resound, bell, gong, toll

tinkle, tinkling
> clink, clatter, clank, ping, ring, peal, jangle, clang, click, clack, clunk

trill
> burble, cheep, cluck, croon, gaggle, tweet, peep, warble, bellow, chant, chirp, drawl, lilt, murmur, trumpet, whistle, twitter

twang, twangy
> accent, nasal, tonal, lisp, drawl, snort, sniff

wail, wailing
> groan, howl, squeal, whimper, bellow, roar, bark, holler, rave, rant, shriek, sob, squawk, thunder, whoop, yelp, yell, bawl, screech, whine, snivel, weep, lament, blubber, moan

warble
> whistle, croon, chirrup, trill, bellow, chant, chirp, drawl, lilt, murmur, trumpet, twitter, sing, bray

whack
> bash, bang, beat, belt, clobber, deck, drub, knock, slam, smack, smash, thump, wallop, bonk, crack, hammer, flog, pelt, pound, pummel, slug, bat, biff, rap

wheeze
> breathy, hoarse, choke, quaver, tremulous, gasp, blow, pant, snort, whistle, puff, breathe, huff

whimper
> blubber, cry, moan, snivel, sob, weep, wail, whine

whir, whirring
> hum, fly, buzz, revolve, flutter, swish, vibrate, whistle

whirl, whirling
> flap, fly, flutter, jangle, wag, flurry, surge, twirl, whir

whish
> whistle, rustle, howl, whoosh, hum, warble, trill, whirl, murmur, buzz, vibrate

whisper, whispering
> murmur, sigh, babble, blather, gurgle, purr, vibrate, whir, breathe, coo, rustle, hush, subdued, muffled, muted

whistle, whistling
> rustle, howl, whish, whoosh, hum, warble, trill, whirl, murmur, buzz, vibrate, creak

whoop
> screech, sob, squawk, yelp, bark, bawl, bay, bellow, bleat, cackle, grunt

whoosh
> whistle, rustle, howl, whish, hum, warble, trill, whirl, murmur, vibrate, hum, buzz

yodel
> croon, ballad, chant, chirp, chorus, hum, lilt, serenade, sing, trill, warble, whistle

SPEECH *and* UTTERANCES

accent
> inflection, meter, intonation, timbre, tempo, modulate, twang, lisp, tone, drawl, articulation, cadence, beat

applaud
> clap, cheer, celebrate, laud, salute, hail, roar, shout

articulate
> eloquent, expressive, diction, enunciate, utter, fluent

babble

chatter, blather, ramble, blabber, murmur, gurgle, drivel, gibberish, jargon, clamor

ballad

croon, chant, chirp, chorus, hum, intone, lilt, serenade, sing, trill, warble, whistle, yodel

banter

quip, retort, wit, wise-cracking, repartee, chitchat, jest, mock

bark, barking

bawl, bay, bellow, bang, bleat, cackle, chant, grunt, screech, yell, squawk, whoop, yelp, howl, growl, wail, snarl, snort

bawl

whine, lament, shriek, wail, weep, bark, bay, bellow, bang, bleat, cackle, yell, rant, holler, squawk, chant, grunt, screech, sob, whoop, yelp, tirade, bemoan, snivel, whimper, sniffle

bay

screech, sob, squawk, bark, bawl, wail, howl, bellow, bleat, whoop, yelp, yell

beg

beseech, implore, plead, cajole, cry, insist, urge, appeal, pray

belch

burp, spew, spittle, spit, gush, emit, expel, erupt, hiccup

bellow

roar, bawl, grunt, screech, sob, howl, gasp, growl, rave, rant, wail, shriek, squawk, trumpet, thunder, bark

bemoan

weep, bawl, lament, wail, cry, mourn, grieve, whimper

benediction

blessing, eulogy, invocation, prayer, praise, gratitude

berate

scold, rebuke, chide, tongue-lash, vilify, besmirch, decry, denounce

beseech

implore, plead, beg, cry, pray, urge

besmirch

vilify, berate, decry, denounce, tongue-lash, defile, slander, slam

blab, blabber

blather, chatter, ramble, murmur, gurgle, jabber, babble, gab

blather

babble, blabber, chatter, ramble, murmur, gurgle, jabber, drivel, gab

Hear: Speech *and* Utterances

bleat
screech, wail squawk, bark, bawl, bay, grunt, hail, keen, bellow, cackle, chant, sob, murmur, whoop, yelp, yell, howl

blow
breathe, huff, expel, puff, gasp, wheeze, whistle, bluster, pant

blubber
whimper, cry, moan, snivel, sob, weep, wail, whine

blurt
blab, babble, diverge, leak, spout, ramble

boisterous
noisy, blaring, brassy, cacophonous, clamorous, jarring, deafening, clanging, racket, resounding, riotous, rip-roaring, screaming, shrill, thunderous, rowdy

bombast, bombastic
blabber, blather, boast, brag, drivel, prattle, rant, swagger, strut, bully, verbose, overblown

brawl
uproar, bluster, roar, clamor, commotion, quarrel, melee, rumble, tumult

bray
warble, bellow, chirp, drawl, murmur, trill, trumpet, whistle, neigh, lilt, whinny

breathe
huff, inhale, exhale, puff, pant, blow, gasp, wheeze, whisper, sigh, murmur, gulp, sniff, snore, snort

breathless
panting, gasping, wheezing, winded, gulping, choking

breathy
hoarse, gravelly, gruff, tremulous, guttural, husky, throaty

broadcast
announce, circulate, telegraph, blazon, blare, disseminate, relay, transmit

brusque
blunt, gruff, sharp, husky, raspy, gravelly, guttural, snippy, curt

burp
belch, spew, spittle, billow, spit, gush, hiccup

cackle
hee-haw, roar, hoot, snicker, smirk, giggle, snort, chuckle, chortle, guffaw, cluck

cajole
plead, beg, cry, insist, rally, implore, beseech, coax, wheedle, entice

call
signal, yell, shout, holler, crow, honk, hoot, tweet, whistle, plea, command

catchphrase
slogan, jingle, motto, watchword, saying

caterwaul
scream, screech, howl, bawl, bellow, squawk, wail, shriek, yowl, bay

catty
spiteful, snippy, biting, rancorous, backbiting

celebrate
applaud, clap, cheer, honor, laud, praise, revere

chant
call, sing, bay, bellow, chime, clang, hum, warble, chirp

chastise
criticize, rebuke, reprimand, berate, lambaste, scold, castigate, lash

chatter
jabber, blather, chit-chat, babble, ramble, blabber, murmur, gurgle, drivel, gab, gibberish

chatty
effusive, flip, gabby, gassy, gossipy, gushy, gregarious, long-winded, loquacious, verbose, windy, talkative, wordy

cheer
applaud, clap, celebrate, shout, roar, salute

chide
berate, scold, rebuke. lambaste, chastise, criticize

chortle
hee-haw, roar, hoot, snicker, cackle, smirk, giggle, snort, chuckle

chorus
croon, ballad, chant, chirp, hum, intone, lilt, serenade, sing, trill, warble, whistle, yodel, medley, blend

chuckle
chortle, cackle, hoot, smirk, giggle, snicker, snort, guffaw

close-lipped
tight-lipped, reticent, silent, taciturn, mute, terse, hushed, subdued, muffled, private, reserved, discreet

conniption
outburst, explosion, eruption, burst, tantrum, blowup, upheaval

coo
whisper, breathe, murmur, rustle, sigh, hush, cry

croaky
throaty, guttural, raspy, husky, gravelly, growling, scratchy

croon
ballad, chant, chirp, chorus, hum, lilt, serenade, sing, trill, warble, whistle, yodel

crow
chirrup, chitter, cluck, quack, chirp, warble, whistle, cackle, call, clack, gobble, honk, hoot, tweet

cry
groan, moan, grouse, gripe, grumble, lament, outcry, shriek, sob, squawk, tirade, wail, howl, blubber, whimper, snivel, weep

decry
ridicule, revile, vilify, deride, hiss, sneer, scoff, heckle, bark, gnarl, snort, mock, scorn, berate, besmirch, denounce, jeer

denounce
vilify, berate, besmirch, decry, tongue-lash, assail, revile, attack, rail, lambaste, condemn, rebuke

deride
mock, jeer, sneer, scorn, decry, scoff, taunt, mimic, ridicule, revile, insult

diatribe
tirade, denunciation, attack, screed, onslaught, harangue

drawl
lisp, crack, nasal, snort, sniff, twang, spit, splutter, warble, bellow, chirp, lilt, trill, murmur, trumpet, whistle

drivel
flummery, jabber, blather, dither, gibberish, dribble, ramble, rant, rubbish, spittle

dumbstruck
tongue-tied, speechless, stupefied, startled, dumbfounded, dazed, wordless, stammering

ebullient
exuberant, gushing, lavish, teeming, voluble, gossipy, gabby, windy, loquacious, verbose

effusive
abundant, ebullient, exuberant, gushing, lavish, teeming, voluble, gossipy, gabby, loquacious, verbose, windy, wordy, garrulous

elaborate (v)
embellish, amplify, magnify, clarify, energize, intensify, refine

elegy
lament, chant, hymn, march, dirge, requiem

eloquent
articulate, expressive, impassioned, passionate, ardent, outspoken, poignant, fluent

embellish
elaborate, amplify, magnify, exaggerate, intensify

enunciate
fluent, articulate, utter, express, vocalize, vent, affirm, proclaim

eulogy
accolade, homage, laudation, valediction, tribute, praise

exaggerate
embellish, hyperbole, puffery, hype, fabricate, distort, overstate, inflate

exhale
breathe, huff, inhale, puff, pant, blow, gasp, wheeze, emit, eject, expel

exhort
urge, implore, beg, plead, warn, admonish, caution

express
utter, articulate, vocalize, vent, enunciate, fluent, assert, convey

expressive
eloquent, articulate, impassioned, passionate, melodic, sonorous, melodious, fluent

extol
praise, acclaim, exalt, tout, applaud, commend, laud, glorify

exuberant
gushing, animated, lavish, vivacious, buoyant, energetic, profuse, ebullient

flout
taunt, disdain, deride, jeer, jest, quip, scoff, decry, ridicule, revile, scorn, spurn

fluent
articulate, enunciate, utter, lyrical, melodious, flowing, sonorous, eloquent

flummery
drivel, blather, dither, dribble, jabber, ramble, rant, rubbish, spittle, malarkey, poppycock, puffery

full-throated
bellowing, resonant, deep, resounding, loud-mouthed, vociferous

gab
blab, blabber, blather, chatter, cackle, flummery, jabber, rattle

gabby
loquacious, chatty, garrulous, gassy, long-winded, talkative, windy, verbose, wordy, effusive, gushy

garrulous
effusive, loquacious, verbose, windy, wordy, long-winded, babbling

gasp
choke, pant, wheeze, shriek, squawk, grunt, screech, huff, puff, gulp, sob

gassy
   verbose, chatty, gabby, gossipy, gushy, gregarious, long-winded, loquacious, flip, effusive, windy, garrulous

gibberish
   babble, drivel, jabber, blather, chatter, gobbledygook, malarkey, rant

gobbledygook
   babble, blather, gibberish, malarkey, drivel, rubbish

golden-tongued
   lyrical, musical, expressive, melodic, sonorous, eloquent, moving, mellifluous, tuneful, harmonious, melodious, stirring

gossipy
   chatty, effusive, flip, gabby, gassy, gushy, long-winded, loquacious, verbose, windy, blabber, garrulous

gravelly
   throaty, rasping, husky, gruff, hoarse, abrasive, scratchy, croaky, growling, raspy, guttural

gripe
   groan, moan, cry, grouse, grumble, lament, outcry, shriek, squawk, tirade, snipe, wail, mutter, grouch

groan
   wail, bawl, bellow, shriek, squeal, howl, moan, grouse, gripe, grumble, lament, outcry, squawk, tirade, cry, mourn

grouse
   quibble, nit-pick, grumble, groan, moan, gripe, lament, squawk, growl

growl
   bark, hiss, howl, snarl, snort, grunt, moan, gnarl

growling
   croaky, throaty, guttural, raspy, husky, grunting, snarling

grumble
   groan, moan, quibble, nit-pick, grouse, gripe, lament, squawk

grunt
   bellow, bleat, screech, bawl, bark, bay, squawk, whoop, yelp, growl, guttural, snarl

gushy, gushing
   chatty, effusive, flip, gabby, gassy, gossipy, gregarious, long-winded, loquacious, verbose, windy, spewing

guttural
   throaty, croaky, husky, gravelly, growling, breathy, hoarse, gasping, choked, raspy, quavering, tremulous, wheezing

hack
gasp, choke, pant, wheeze, wail, whoop, yelp, bark, huff, puff

hail
applaud, call, shout, salute, holler, signal

harangue
tirade, bawl, shriek, berate, onslaught, blast, tongue-lash, scream, wail, rant

hoarse
gruff, growling, husky, raspy, gravelly, guttural, raucous

holler
bawl, clamor, growl, roar, shout, yell, bellow, bark, gasp, rave, rant, shriek, sob, squawk, trumpet, thunder, wail, whoop, warble, yelp, bleat, screech

homage
eulogy, accolade, laudation, valediction, tribute, esteem, salutation

honk
quack, chirp, chirrup, chitter, cluck, clack, gobble, hoot, whistle, tweet, warble, crow

hoot
chortle, hee-haw, roar, snicker, cackle, smirk, giggle, snort, chuckle

howl, howling
hiss, snarl, snort, groan, squeal, wail, scream, screech, bellow, roar, bay, bleat, caterwaul, moan, holler, growl

huff
breathe, inhale, exhale, puff, pant, blow, gasp, wheeze

husky
croaky, throaty, guttural, raspy, gravelly, growling, gruff, hoarse

implore
beseech, plead, beg, cajole, cry, insist, rally, exhort, urge, appeal

incantation
chant, spell, invocation, enchantment, wizardry, sorcery

incoherent
inarticulate, unintelligible, stuttering, muffled, mumbling, garbled

ineffable
unutterable, unspoken, indescribable, inexpressible, unimaginable

inexpressible
indescribable, ineffable, unspoken, unutterable, unthinkable

inflection
lilt, cadence, accent, meter, intonation, rhythm, beat, tempo

inhale
breathe, huff, exhale, puff, pant, blow, gasp, wheeze, sniff

innuendo
tone, overtone, insinuation, implication, intimation, hint

insist
rally, implore, plead, beg, cajole, cry, beseech, urge

intimate (v)
allude, imply, hint, infer, insinuate, vent, signal, divulge

intone
lilt, cadence, chant, croon, sing, accent, inflection, rhythm

invocation
prayer, chant, devotion, appeal, command

jabber
drivel, blather, dither, dribble, flummery, ramble, rant, rubbish, spittle

jawbone
persuade, pressure, cajole, wheedle, pester, entice, tempt

jeer
decry, taunt, hiss, sneer, heckle, bark, gnarl, snort, mock, scorn, deride, scoff, ridicule, revile, boo

jest
jeer, mock, scoff, scorn, wit, wisecrack, banter, quip, crack, retort, tease, taunt, sneer, decry, ridicule, revile

jubilation
applaud, clap, cheer, celebrate, triumph, elation

laconic
terse, pithy, reticent, silent, taciturn, close-lipped, mute

lambaste
criticize, rebuke, reprimand, berate, chastise, scold

lament
groan, moan, grouse, gripe, grumble, outcry, shriek, squawk, wail, tirade, snipe, whine, weep

laudation
eulogy, accolade, homage, valediction, praise, acclaim

lilt
cadence, accent, inflection, meter, intone, rhythm, beat, tempo, sing, warble, trill, serenade, bellow, chant, chirp, drawl, murmur, trumpet, whistle

lisp
drawl, nasal, snort, sniff, twang, splutter, spit

long-winded

chatty, gregarious, verbose, windy, wordy, effusive, flip, gabby, gassy, gossipy, gushy, loquacious

loquacious

gassy, long-winded, talkative, chatty, garrulous, verbose, effusive, windy, wordy, gushy, gabby

loud-mouthed

full-throated, obnoxious, bellowing, vociferous, clamorous, crude, boisterous

lullaby

melody, song, tune, lull, croon, hum

malarkey

gobbledygook, babble, blather, gibberish, drivel

maunder

blather, mumble, ramble, babble, prattle, mutter, drivel

medley

chorus, blend, mingled, mash-up, mix

mimic

mock, parrot, parody, spoof, mirror

moan

groan, cry, grouse, gripe, grumble, lament, shriek, squawk, tirade, wail, howl

mock, mocking

jeer, sneer, scorn, decry, deride, scoff, taunt, mimic, ridicule, revile, lampoon

monotonous

banal, colorless, dreary, tiresome, tedious, wearying, repetitive, toneless, flat, dull

mouthy

wordy, chatty, effusive, gabby, gossipy, loquacious, gushy, windy, gregarious, long-winded, loud-mouthed

mumble

murmur, whisper, mutter, sigh, babble, blather, chatter, ramble, blabber, gurgle, grumble

mutter

mumble, murmur, whisper, sigh, snort, splutter, stammer, babble, chatter, blather, blabber

nasal, nasally

lisp, crack, drawl, snort, sniff, twang, splutter, spit

onslaught

tirade, bawl, rant, attack, blast, tongue-lashing, scream, harangue, wail, lament, cry, shriek

outburst
  explosion, eruption, tantrum, conniption, upheaval, outcry, outpouring, flare-up

outcry
  groan, moan, cry, grouse, gripe, grumble, lament, shriek, squawk, tirade, wail, protest, outburst, outpouring

pant
  breathless, gasp, wheeze, winded, blow, gulp, heave, huff, snort, puff, whiff, hiss

parrot
  mimic, mock, parody, spoof, mirror, lampoon

pitch, pitched
  tone, timbre, lingo, blather, prattle, drivel, chatter, parlance, saga, blurb

plead
  beg, cajole, cry, insist, rally, implore, beseech

prattle
  chatter, chat, jabber, blather, yammer, babble, blabber

puffery
  exaggeration, hype, praise, ballyhoo

quack
  chirp, cackle, call, chirrup, chitter, cluck, clack, crow, gobble, honk, hoot, tweet, warble, whistle

quaver, quavering
  breathy, tremulous, gasp, wheeze, tremble, shake, falter, warble, quiver, shudder, vibrate, oscillate, crack

quibble
  grouse, nit-pick, grumble, protest, niggle, moan, gripe

quip
  retort, chitchat, tease, crack, wit, jest, wisecrack, banter, repartee

rail
  protest, condemn, rage, denounce, blast, berate, attack, rant, scold, revile

rally
  plead, cajole, cry, insist, cheer, implore

ramble, rambling
  jabber, rattle, gurgle, babble, blabber, blather, chatter

rant, ranting
  shriek, wail, whoop, screech, tirade, clamorous, frenzied, hysterical, raging, raucous, raving

rasping, raspy
  abrasive, throaty, scratchy, chafing, gravely, husky, gruff, hoarse, croaky

rave, raving
holler, rant, rail, raucous, shriek, wail, clamorous, frenzied, hysterical, raging, extol

rebuff
reject, snub, spurn, repel, dismiss, rebuke, slight

rebuke
berate, scold, chide, tongue-lash, reprimand, rebuff, snub

repartee
wit, quip, jest, banter, wisecrack, gag

reticent
restrained, silent, taciturn, close-lipped, close-mouthed, terse, curt, mute

retort
quip, crack, wit, jest, wisecrack, chitchat, tease, banter

revile
condemn, denounce, berate, attack, lambaste, vilify, scold, castigate, blast, slam, slander

revelry
celebration, festivity, spree

ridicule
mock, jeer, sneer, scorn, decry, deride, scoff, taunt, revile

roister
carouse, celebrate, rollick, revel, romp, carouse, rejoice

scoff
taunt, annoy, deride, flout, jest, quip, mock, sneer, scorn, decry, ridicule, revile, jeer

scold
chide, denounce, rant, rebuke, berate, revile, admonish

scorn
decry, deride, scoff, mock, jeer, sneer, taunt, ridicule, revile

scream
holler, yell, bellow, screech, howl, tirade, bawl, squeal, rant, blast, wail, blare, shriek, racket

screech, screeching
cackle, squawk, whoop, shriek, scream, holler, bellow, howl, squeal

seethe
bellow, boil, erupt, explode, fume, rant, bristle, simmer, smolder

serenade
ballad, hymn, chorus, chant, melody, croon, dirge, lilt, trill, warble

sharp-tongued
harsh, biting, scathing, cutting, caustic, acid, shrill

shout
squawk, shriek, outcry, tirade, applaud, bark, bawl, wail, caterwaul, cackle, roar, chortle, clamor, holler, howl, scream, screech, squeal

shriek
blare, bugle, caterwaul, cry, holler, roar, screech, scream, squawk, wail, thunder, whoop, bawl, moan, whine

shrill
dissonant, ear-piercing, ear-splitting, grating, harsh, high-pitched, piercing, reedy, sharp, wailing, jarring, screeching

shush
quell, muffle, squelch, subdue, quash, stifle, hush, lull

sigh
murmur, whisper, mumble, babble, gurgle, mutter

signal
announce, echo, beacon, message, proclaim, beckon, call, holler

sing, song
lilt, cadence, accent, inflection, intone, rhythm, tempo, warble, trill, serenade, tune

smirk
laugh, chortle, cackle, hoot, giggle, snicker, snort, simper, chuckle

snarl
growl, bark, hiss, howl, snort, mutter

sneer
jeer, decry, hiss, heckle, snort, mock, scorn, deride, scoff, taunt, ridicule, revile

snicker
chortle, hee-haw, roar, hoot, cackle, smirk, giggle, snort, chuckle, guffaw

sniff, sniffle
lisp, crack, drawl, nasal, snort, twang, splutter, spit, snuff

snipe
jeer, attack, sneer, scoff, mock, deride

snivel
whimper, blubber, cry, moan, sob, weep, wail, bawl, gripe, groan, whine, sniffle

snore
snort, grunt, sniff, growl, hiss, lisp, huff, puff, wheeze

snort
growl, bark, gnarl, hiss, howl, snarl, chortle, cackle, hoot, smirk, giggle, snicker, chuckle, lisp, drawl, sniff, twang, splutter, stammer, spit

snuff

snort, sniff, snore, pant, puff, wheeze, sniffle

sob

whimper, snivel, weep, wail, bawl, blubber, moan, snort, whine, yelp, cry, screech

speechless

breathless, dazed, dumbfounded, shocked, tongue-tied, wordless, hushed, silent, subdued, tight-lipped, dumbstruck, mute

spit

lisp, drawl, snort, sniff, splutter, spittle, sputter

splutter

spit, stammer, lisp, drawl, nasal, snort, sniff, burst, explode, choke

squawk

caterwaul, groan, howl, screech, grouse, gripe, outcry, shriek, tirade, snipe, wail, whoop, bark, bawl, bellow, bleat, blare, yell

squeak

creak, chirp, screech, squeal, wail, whine, whistle, grate, peep

squeal

wail, bawl, bellow, cry, lament, groan, whine, screech, blare, blurt, gasp, hail, yelp, howl, shout, shrill, trumpet

squelch

stifle, quell, muffle, subdue, quash, hush, lull, crush, squash

stammer

mutter, mumble, murmur, sigh, snort, splutter, babble, chatter, blather, blabber

stifle

squash, shush, quell, muffle, quash, hush, lull, squelch, subdue

strident

grating, harsh, shrill, jarring, raucous, blaring, clashing

stutter

mutter, stammer, mumble, snort, splutter, babble, blather, blabber

summon

arouse, beckon, command, conjure, invoke, hail, rally

swagger

brag, boast, rant, strut, parade, bluster, crow

taciturn

laconic, reticent, close-lipped, mute, tight-lipped, unexpressive, silent, withdrawn

talkative

articulate, chatty, fluent, gabby, garrulous, gassy, gossipy, gushy, mouthy, wordy, outspoken, gregarious, talky, verbose, vocal

tantrum
tirade, conniption, outburst, explosion, eruption, burst, blowup, upheaval

taunt
annoy, deride, flout, mock, jest, quip, scoff, sneer, scorn, ridicule, decry, revile, jeer

telegraph
relay, broadcast, blazon, announce, circulate, blare, disseminate, transmit

testy
gruff, blunt, truculent, edgy, uptight, ill-tempered

throaty
raspy, gravelly, brassy, brazen, husky, hoarse, squawking, rasping, tremulous, croaky, abrasive, scratchy, gruff, growling

tight-lipped
reticent, restrained, close-mouthed, mute, taciturn

tirade
bawl, rant, attack, onslaught, blast, tongue-lash, scream, harangue, lament, cry, wail, shriek

tongue-tied
speechless, wordless, dumbstruck, lulled, hushed, garbled

tout
acclaim, praise, extol, trumpet, proclaim, herald, laud

trill
burble, cheep, cluck, croon, gaggle, tweet, peep, warble, bellow, chant, chirp, lilt, drawl, murmur, trumpet, whistle

truculent
gruff, testy, blunt, combative, quarrelsome, belligerent, bullying

trumpet
boom, explode, rant, thunder, wail, whoop, bugle, whistle, warble, bellow, chant, chirp, trill

twang, twangy
accent, nasal, lisp, tonal, drawl, snort, sniff

tweet
quack, chirp, cackle, call, chirrup, chitter, cluck, clack, crow, hoot, gobble, honk, warble, whistle

unexpressed
indescribable, inexpressible, ineffable, unutterable, unspoken

unexpressive
taciturn, close-lipped, mute, tight-lipped, reticent, emotionless

unintelligible
incoherent, unintelligible, stuttering, muffled, mumbling, garbled

unspeakable
unutterable, indescribable, inexpressible, inconceivable, ineffable

unspoken
ineffable, indescribable, inexpressible, unutterable, unexpressed

unutterable
inexpressible, ineffable, unthinkable, indescribable, unspeakable

uproar
bluster, tumult, brawl, clamor, commotion, embroil, melee, rumble, thunder, roar

utter
express, articulate, vocalize, vent, enunciate, blurt

vent
utter, express, articulate, vocalize, enunciate, voice

verbose
gushy, gregarious, long-winded, chatty, effusive, flowery, fluent, gabby, gossipy, loquacious, wordy, windy

vilify
berate, slander, slam, besmirch, decry, denounce, tongue-lash, condemn

vitriol, vitriolic
biting, scathing, spiteful, venomous, vicious, cutting, withering, sharp

vocalize
utter, express, articulate, vent, enunciate, fluent, chant, croon

voice
timbre, tone, resonance, lilt, express, utter, vent

voluble
ebullient, exuberant, gushing, teeming, gossipy, gabby, verbose, loquacious, windy, lavish

wail
groan, howl, squeal, whimper, shriek, squawk, yelp, bawl, bay, screech, sob, weep, lament, blubber, moan

weep
bawl, bemoan, lament, wail, whimper, blubber, moan, snivel, cry, sob

whine
bawl, bellow, gasp, lament, wail, howl, whistle, creak, gripe, grouse

whinny
cry, wail, shriek, whistle, neigh, bray, squawk, squeal

whisper
mutter, murmur, rustle, hiss, mumble, sigh, buzz, hum

winded
breathless, panting, gasping, wheezing, puffing

windy
garrulous, rambling, loquacious, verbose, wordy, long-winded

wordless
unspoken, quiet, hushed, silent, muted, whisper, tight-lipped, speechless, unsaid, subdued

wordy
chatty, effusive, flowery, fluent, gabby, gossipy, loquacious, gushy, gregarious, long-winded, windy

yell
bellow, scream, wail, growl, roar, thunder, cry, bawl, bark, bay, bleat, cackle, chant, grunt, hail, keen, screech, squawk, whoop

yelp
yowl, bark, bawl, bay, whimper, neigh, squeal, bellow, bleat, cackle, grunt, yell, screech, sob, squawk, whoop

yodel
croon, ballad, chant, chirp, chorus, hum, lilt, serenade, sing, trill, warble, whistle

Movement

bash
knock, slam, smack, bang, belt, clobber, deck, drub, smash, thump, wallop, bat, whack

bat
bang, batter, beat, belt, deck, drub, clobber, crash, knock, hammer, pummel, rap, smash, strike, thrash, wallop, smack, whack

batter
bang, beat, clobber, hammer, knock, pummel, rap, smash, strike, thrash, wallop, whack

billow
spew, spittle, spit, gush, burp, surge, pitch, ripple

blast
boom, thunder, explode, backfire, bang, burst, erupt, flare

burst
downpour, cascade, drench, monsoon, torrent, explode, blast, erupt, flare, surge, boom, thunder

Thesaurus of the Senses

cascade

downpour, burst, drench, monsoon, surge, torrent, avalanche, deluge, flood

chop

smash, strike, thrash, wallop, bang, batter, beat, clobber, crash, hammer, knock, pummel

collide

bang, smash, strike, crash, slam, shatter, clash, sideswipe, bump

downpour

burst, cascade, drench, monsoon, surge, torrent, deluge

drip

dribble, drizzle, leak, pour, percolate, trickle, drool, leach, sprinkle, gurgle, splash, seep

drum

beat, hammer, drone, hum, resound, thunder, thrum, strum, strike

effervesce

bubble, boil, fizzle, sizzle, foam, froth, fizz, lather

erupt

explode, backfire, bang, blast, burst, flare, smolder, thunder, boom

explode

backfire, bang, blast, burst, erupt, flare, boom, thunder

flap

fly, flutter, jangle, whirl, wag, flail, flop

flare

explode, backfire, blast, burst, erupt, smolder, boom, thunder

flick, flicker

flip, flitter, pulse, tweak, click, plunk, snap, tick, quiver, oscillate, wave

flutter

flap, fly, jangle, whirl, wag, hover, quiver, flit, flitter, dance, ripple

fracture

crack, snap, chisel, chip, fissure, rupture

hammer

thrash, wallop, whack, bang, pummel, batter, beat, clobber, knock, crash, rap, smash, strike

jolt

tremor, rumble, shudder, shock, blow, clash, collision, jar

knock

rap, bang, thump, slam, tap, hammer, strike, batter, beat, clobber, crash, smash, pummel, thrash, wallop

leach
trickle, drip, drizzle, percolate, seep, sprinkle, gurgle, dribble

pelt
slug, smack, slam, smash, wallop, whack, thump, bang, biff, belt, clobber, deck, drub, crack, hammer, flog, knock, pound, pummel

percolate
drip, dribble, drizzle, leak, pour, seep, trickle, sprinkle, leach

pound
boom, thunder, bellow, explode, bang, strike, hammer, thrash

pummel
strike, thrash, wallop, bang, batter, beat, clobber, crash, detonate, hammer, rap, knock, punch, smash

rail
thunder, blast, bellow, clamor, crash, explode, resound, rumble, wail, trumpet, echo, boom

rap
crash, detonate, hammer, whack, tap, pound, bang, batter, beat, clobber, knock, pummel, plunk, punch, smash, strike, thrash, wallop

rattle
clank, clatter, jingle, jangle, clink, joggle, ramble, jolt

ripple
crinkle, bristle, rustle, twist, wring, undulate, wave, flow, flutter, pulsate

seep
trickle, drip, drizzle, percolate, leach, sprinkle, gurgle, dribble, leak

shake, shaky
tremulous, quivering, trembling, quaking, jittery

slam
punch, smash, thump, hammer, strike, bang, batter, crash, deck, clobber, pummel, thrash, wallop, bash, bat, drub, smack, whack

smash
plunk, bang, beat, chop, clobber, crash, hammer, knock, pummel, punch, rap, strike, thrash, wallop, batter

spew
billow, spit, gush, belch, burp, spittle, heave, expel

splat
clash, crash, smash, splash, thud

spout
gush, spew, squirt, sputter, billow, spurt, expel

sprinkle
trickle, drip, drizzle, percolate, leach, seep, gurgle, dribble

stomp
clomp, clop, trudge, smash, bang, knock, rap, thump, trample

strike
bang, batter, beat, crash, hammer, knock, pummel, punch, smash, thrash, wallop,

strum
thrum, hum, rhythm, drum, beat, pluck

surge
burst, cascade, downpour, drench, monsoon, torrent, upsurge, gush, rush

tap
knock, drum, rap, strike, bump, flap, flick, pat, whack, thump

teem, teeming
gushing, abundant, ebullient, lavish, exuberant, swarming

thrash
smash, strike, bang, batter, chop, clobber, crash, hammer, knock, pummel, rap, punch, wallop, beat

throb, throbbing
pulsate, pound, purr, rumble, hum, drum, thud, thump

thump
bang, clobber, deck, drub, crack, hammer, flog, knock, pound, pelt, belt, slug, pummel, smack, slam, smash, rap, wallop, whack

thrum
strum, hum, rhythm, drum, purr, buzz, drawl, murmur, throb, trill

torrent
downpour, cascade, drench, surge, burst, monsoon, deluge

trickle
drip, drizzle, percolate, leach, seep, sprinkle, gurgle, dribble

wallop
smash, strike, thrash, bang, batter, beat, clobber, crash, hammer, knock, bash, pummel, punch, rap, thump, stomp

wrangle
clash, brawl, collide, quarrel, rumble, snarl, tussle, fracas, ruckus, flap

Listening

attuned
receptive, tuned, harmonized, aligned, integrated, connected

aural
acoustic, audio, phonic, audible, sonic

discern
perceive, detect, recognize, distinguish

eavesdrop
listen, snoop, hearken, heed, overhear, spy, tune in, monitor

heed
hearken, listen, eavesdrop, tune in, overhear

listen
eavesdrop, overhear, attend, snoop, heed, tune in

overhear
eavesdrop, hearken, heed, spy, tune in, monitor

VOLUME

amplify
magnify, crescendo, energize, elaborate, embellish, intensify, swell, boost

blare, blaring
ringing, booming, wailing, thunderous, resounding, shrill

booming
deafening, ear-piercing, ringing, blaring, resounding, bellowing, roaring

choke, choked
muffle, deaden, dampen, breathy, hoarse, quavering, tremulous, guttural, gasp, pant, stifle, squelch, wheeze, hack, mask, smother, deafen, hushed, muted

clipped
pithy, concise, compact, terse, succinct, blunt, curtailed, pointed, laconic, curt

close-lipped
tight-lipped, reticent, silent, taciturn, mute, terse, hushed, subdued, muffled, private, reserved

crescendo
amplify, magnify, energize, embellish, intensify, escalate, upsurge

dampen
muffle, deaden, muted, squelch, mask, choke, hushed, stifle

deaden
muffle, muted, dampen, squelch, mask, hush, subdue, stifle, quiet, blunt

deafening
booming, ear-piercing, earthshaking, piercing, resounding, ringing, thundering

decibel
loudness, volume, intensity, amplification

ear-piercing
deafening, booming, resounding, thundering, rattling, ear-splitting, ringing

ear-splitting
deafening, booming, ear-piercing, piercing, resounding, ringing, thundering, rattling

high-pitched
screaming, shrill, shrieking, acute, piercing, sharp

hush, hushed
subdued, muffled, murmur, muted, whisper, lull, tranquil, silent

inaudible
undetectable, imperceptible, muffled, hushed, muted, mumbled, soundless, silent, faint

incoherent
inarticulate, unintelligible, stuttering, muffled, mumbled, garbled

lull
soothe, calm, assuage, hush, quiet, silence, stillness, respite, quell, temper

magnify
intensify, amplify, crescendo, energize, embellish, elaborate, boost, surge, swell

mask
dampen, squelch, muffle, deaden, smother, choke, subdue, shield, stifle, mute

modulate
accent, inflection, rhythm, harmonize, attune, balance, temper, tweak, tune, adjust

muffle, muffled
deaden, mute, dampen, stifle, squelch, smother, choke, smother, hushed, subdued, whisper, drown, silence, mask

mute
laconic, reticent, silent, taciturn, close-lipped, terse, stifle, deaden, dampen, squelch, smother, hushed, subdued, muffled, whisper, choke, mask

piercing
deafening, booming, earthshaking, resounding, ringing, rattling, thundering, thunderous, shrill

pithy
clipped, concise, compact, terse, succinct, crisp, curt

quell
stifle, squash, shush, muffle, quash, hush, lull, squelch, subdue

quiet
hush, silent, muted, whisper, wordless, subdued, faint, tight-lipped, speechless, muffled, still

rip-roaring
noisy, blaring, boisterous, brassy, clamorous, jarring, deafening, clanging, rowdy, resounding, riotous, screaming, shrill, thunderous

roaring
resounding, thunderous, ringing, crashing, deafening, uproarious, boisterous, rowdy, clanging, piercing, rumbling

secret
clandestine, censored, close-mouthed, encrypted, unspoken, hushed, furtive

shrill
dissonant, ear-piercing, ear-splitting, grating, harsh, high-pitched, piercing, reedy, sharp, wailing, jarring, screeching

silent, silence
hushed, mute, reserved, restrained, still, tight-lipped, unspoken, wordless, mum, reticent, speechless, stillness

smother
muffle, deaden, muted, dampen, stifle, squelch, mask, choke, deafen, hushed, subdued, quash, snuff

squelch
muffle, deaden, dampen, stifle, mask, smother, choke, hush, mute, subdue, shush, suppress

stifle, stifled
assuage, censor, dampen, extinguish, hush, mute, suppress, muffle, deaden, squelch, smother, deafen, subdue

still, stillness
hush, silence, soundless, tranquil, calm, placid

subdue, subdued
hushed, muffled, murmur, muted, whisper, quell, overwhelm, suppress

terse
clipped, blunt, restrained, truncated, reticent, concise, brusque, pithy, curt

thready
feeble, thin, weak, reedy

tight-lipped
reticent, restrained, close-mouthed, muted

truncated
terse, clipped, blunt, pointed, restrained, reticent, abbreviated, curt, truncated

unsung

unexpressed, overlooked, unheralded, unacknowledged, nameless

uproarious

roaring, raucous, deafening, clamorous, booming, boisterous, rowdy, rambunctious

whisper

murmur, sigh, babble, blather, gurgle, purr, vibrate, whir, breathe, coo, rustle, hush, subdued, muffled, muted

TOUCH

The body says what words cannot.
—Martha Graham, dancer and choreographer

SKIN & BODY SENSATIONS *and* VISCERAL RESPONSES
TEXTURES *and* STRUCTURES
MOVEMENT, PRESSURE, *and* SPEED

Touch is our second set of eyes and ears through which we sense the world. In the absence of light, we can feel our way through darkness. Without hearing, we can intimately sense vibrations in our fingertips, bones, and skin. Touch even extends beyond our physical boundaries. We can kinesthetically get a "feel" for a place or situation. Or physically sense another person's gaze. Or our feelings can "go out" to someone in need.

The body remembers touch. Healing touch, revulsion, pain, pleasure all leave an indelible mark. Touch and our reactions to it communicate without words. *You are cherished. That gives me the creeps.* Deep-seated, blissful, gut-wrenching, profound.

We talk in the language of touch. When we are deeply moved, we say we are *touched.* When we are insulted, our *feelings* are hurt. Some people are *touchy, abrasive, out of touch,* or *tactless.* Others are *tactful, tactical,* or have a *light touch.*

We cannot completely shut off touch, though we can feel numb to it. We constantly float in a sea of sensations. We luxuriate in clothes and fabrics, breezes, water, movement and dance, the cuddle or caress of another. We feel the electric charge of arousal and the throbbing dagger of pain. We itch for something. Emotions burn and bubble within us. Essential for survival, touch is our blessing and curse—our reminder that we are alive, feeling every sensation.

In this section, we get a feel for tactile words describing various body and skin sensations and visceral responses, textures and forms, and words that convey movement, pressure, and speed.

SKIN & BODY SENSATIONS *and* VISCERAL RESPONSES

abhor, abhorrent
> repellent, atrocious, heinous, obnoxious, repugnant, contemptible, odious, vile, offensive, noxious, loathsome

absorbing
> immersing, engrossing, gripping, riveting, enthralling, arresting, spellbinding, consuming

aching
> throbbing, bruised, paining, panging, twinging, stabbing, shooting, stinging, tender, raw, nagging

acidic
> bracing, stinging, cutting, biting, sharp, acrid, caustic, astringent, bitter, sour

aflame
> fiery, blistering, burning, blazing, ablaze, flaring, searing, singeing, ignited

aggravating
> disturbing, exasperating, provoking, vexing, bothersome, galling, irksome

agitated
> roiled, flustered, ruffled, rattled, unsettled, aggravated, provoked, disquieted, shivering, shuddering, vexed

agitating
> aggravating, disturbing, galling, irksome, exasperating, provoking, vexing, bothersome

airless
> windless, stifling, choking, constrictive, oppressive, squelching, stuffy, strangling, suffocating

airy
> light, subtle, flowing, dreamy, languid, tranquil, breezy, buoyant, windy, feathery, fluffy, willowy, wispy, soft

Touch: Skin Sensations *and* Visceral Responses

anoint
  smooth, lubricate, daub, oil, smear, rub

antsy
  edgy, fretful, panicky, jittery, squirmy, touchy, uneasy, fidgety

apprehensive, apprehension
  trembling, disquieted, frightened, quivering, trepidation, shivering, uneasy, fearful, frozen

arduous
  grueling, backbreaking, irksome, tiresome, toilsome, onerous, wearying, laborious, crushing, back-breaking, rigorous, taxing, strenuous, wearisome

arid
  bone-dry, barren, dusty, parched, scorched, waterless, wilted, dehydrated, baked, desiccated, shriveled, withered

arousing, aroused
  stimulating, agitating, stirring, enlivening, provoking, thrilling, invigorating, startling, electrifying, alarming, vexing

assailed
  besieged, beleaguered, blockaded, stressed, surrounded, encircled, beset, harassed

assuage, assuaged
  soothe, allay, soften, appease, balm, comfort, hush, lull, smooth, quell, subdue, pacify, mollify, calm

astringent
  caustic, stinging, biting, constricting, cutting, sharp, bitter, harsh, acrid

aversion
  animosity, revulsion, hostility, abhorrence, antipathy, repulsion, disgust, distaste, reluctance, loathing

awash
  drenched, covered, flooded, overflowing, submerged, inundated, flushed

balm
  emollient, soothe, moisten, soften, lubricate, salve, solace, relief, comfort, restorative

balmy
  soothing, gentle, tranquil, temperate, pleasant, refreshing, mild

bare
  stark, plain, unadorned, unclothed, stripped, barren, harsh, naked, bald, primal, denuded, disrobed

bathe
  deluge, drown, dunk, imbue, infuse, inundate, saturate, submerge, permeate, pervade, drench, steep, instill, refresh, rinse, cleanse, douse

beset
assailed, beleaguered, besieged, surrounded, encircled, plagued, entangled, harassed

besieged
assailed, surrounded, encircled, beleaguered, harassed, stressed, beset, trapped

biting
acid, acerbic, brisk, bracing, bitter, cutting, edgy, stinging, sharp, acrid, caustic, astringent, intense, piercing, searing, scathing

bitter
astringent, cutting, caustic, stinging, biting, scathing, sharp

blanch, blanched
wince, pale, recoil, twitch, grimace, flinch, crouch, cringe, shrink, reel, retract, shudder, retreat, quiver, tremble, squirm

blazing
fiery, blistering, burning, flaring, searing, seething, aflame

blistering, blistered
bleeding, boiling, parched, heated, searing, seething, sizzling, sweltering, fiery, burning, torrid, feverish, flushed, inflamed, intense, fierce

blood-curdling
spine-chilling, creepy, spooky, bone-chilling, hair-raising, chilling, shocking, scary, terrifying, frightening, horrifying, spine-tingling

bloody, bloodied
bruised, wounded, blood-stained, gory, brutal, savage, ferocious

blush, blushed
warm, flushed, fiery, heated, radiant, reddened

blustery
windy, gusty, tumultuous, stormy, windswept, breezy, brisk, drafty, howling, turbulent

boiling
burning, torrid, searing, steamy, stifling, blistering, flushed, heated, feverish, seething, simmering, sultry, sizzling, sweltering, inflamed, fiery

bone-chilling
eerie, strange, creepy, freakish, spooky, spine-chilling, shocking, disturbing, scary

bothersome
irksome, provoking, tiresome, aggravating, disturbing, troubling, exasperating, galling, wearisome, vexing

bracing
chilly, crisp, exhilarating, invigorating, reviving, biting, nippy, brisk, bitter, cutting, stinging, caustic, astringent

Touch: Skin Sensations *and* Visceral Responses

breezy
airy, bubbly, buoyant, lively, spirited, windy, stormy, gusty, brisk, drafty

brisk
sharp, windy, biting, bracing, cutting, stinging, blustery, stormy, gusty, breezy, drafty

bristle, bristling
flare, ruffle, seethe, fume, rage, boil

bruised
aching, throbbing, welted, swollen, blackened, battered, marred, bloodied

buoyant
breezy, airy, bubbly, lively, spirited, windy, resilient

burn
ignite, fan, inflame, kindle, stoke, torch, scald, scorch

burning
blazing, blistering, simmering, fiery, boiling, seething, smoldering, impassioned, sweltering, torrid, ablaze, aflame, flaring, searing, stinging, parched

caress
embrace, nuzzle, stroke, touch, nudge, squeeze, cuddle

cathartic, catharsis
releasing, purifying, purging, cleansing, venting

caustic
acidic, acerbic, bitter, biting, cutting, piercing, stinging, astringent

chafe
rub, scrape, abrade, erode, graze, grate, chisel, scour, file, scratch, scuff, grind, corrode

charged
electric, electrify, thrilling, rousing, stirring, pervading, intense, fraught, tense, saturated

chilling
horrifying, blood-curling, spine-chilling, disturbing, shocking, hair-raising

chilly
shivering, frozen, brisk, bracing, frigid, exhilarating, invigorating, biting, nippy, reviving, icy, frosty, crisp

choking
stifling, constrictive, oppressive, squelching, stuffy, strangling, suffocating, windless, airless

choppy
jolting, agitating, bumpy, jarring, rough, turbulent, violent

clammy
> sweaty, damp, misty, moist, sticky, slithery, slimy, tacky, humid, muggy, steamy

cleanse
> freshen, purge, spruce, wash, bathe, refresh, lather, scrub, douse, swab, rinse

clench, clenching
> clasp, cling, clutch, grasp, grip, clamp, vise, grapple, constrict

congested
> stuffy, cramped, stifling, constricted, choked, clogged, grid-locked, jammed, blocked

constricted
> stifling, choking, oppressive, strangling, suffocating, squelching

contort, contorted
> wince, writhe, convulse, twitch, blanch, grimace, flinch, shudder, crouch, cringe, shrink, reel, retract, recoil, retreat, quiver, tremble, squirm, twist, mangle, warp, wring, wrench, flail

convulse, convulsing
> quake, bobble, fidget, flutter, heave, joggle, quiver, shake, tremble, twitch, waver, wobble

cower, cowering
> recoil, quake, cringe, tremble, shake, flinch, crouch, wince, shrink

cramped
> constricted, confined, congested, crowded, jammed

creepy
> bone-chilling, eerie, strange, freakish, spooky, scary, spine-chilling

cringe
> recoil, retract, shudder, retreat, quiver, swerve, tremble, squirm, flinch, wince, reel

crisp
> bracing, brisk, chilly, exhilarating, invigorating, reviving, nippy

cuddle
> nuzzle, touch, embrace, cling, clutch, cradle, grip, caress

cutting
> stinging, biting, sharp, acerbic, brisk, bracing, bitter, edgy, pointed, scathing, caustic, acid

damp
> moist, humid, muggy, clammy, misty, steamy, watery, drizzly, dank, dewy, rainy, sticky, swampy, tacky

dank
> damp, dewy, humid, moist, muggy, rainy, sticky, swampy, clammy, chilly

daub
smooth, lubricate, anoint, crown, oil, rub, massage

deadened
lifeless, numb, muffled, hardened, stifled

deluged
drenched, drowned, inundated, saturated, submerged, flooded, doused, soaked, swamped, overwhelmed

devastating, devastated
shattering, shocking, crushing, tormenting, mortifying, distressing, traumatic

dewy
muggy, rainy, damp, humid, moist, sticky, swampy, misty

discombobulated
flummoxed, bewildered, perplexed, confused, confounded, unsettled, baffled, disconcerted, rattled

disconcerting
unsettling, upsetting, disturbing, rattling, troubling, disquieting, perturbing, unnerving, shaken

disgust, disgusting
sickening, repulsive, shocking, revolting, detestable, repugnant, appalling

disquiet, disquieted, disquieting
flustered, agitated, ruffled, rattled, unsettled, befuddled, roiled, bewildered, shaken

disrobe, disrobed
bare, naked, primal, unclothed, stripped, stark, plain, undressed, unclad

distorted
scarred, blistered, defaced, disfigured, gashed, welted, gnarled, warped, twisted

distressing, distressed
alarming, shattering, disturbing, shocking, crushing, devastating, tormenting, stunning, mortifying, traumatic

douse
submerge, drench, bathe, deluge, drown, dunk, inundate, quench, saturate, soak

drafty
windy, blustery, windswept, gusty, breezy, brisk, airy, nippy, chilly

drenched
saturated, covered, flooded, overflowing, submerged, bathed, doused, drowned, imbued, infused, inundated, sopping, awash

drizzly
damp, moist, humid, muggy, clammy, misty, steamy, watery

edgy
> antsy, fretful, panicky, prickly, squirmy, touchy, uneasy, skittish, uptight, tense

eerie
> bone-chilling, strange, freakish, spooky, spine-chilling, creepy, scary

effervescent
> swishing, fizzling, bubbly, burbling, rustling, frothy, bouncy, foamy, sparkling, airy

electric, electrifying
> charged, thrilling, rousing, stirring, tingling, surging, arousing

embroiled
> entangled, ensnared, intertwined, entrenched, mired, enmeshed

emollient
> soothing, moistening, softening, balm, lubricating, pacifying, salve

encircled
> beleaguered, besieged, blockaded, stressed, assailed, surrounded, beset

engrossed, engrossing
> enticing, beguiling, magnetic, alluring, riveting, hypnotic, thrilling, gripping, enthralling, spellbinding, captivating, mesmerizing, arresting, enchanting

enliven, enlivening
> arouse, stimulate, stir, excite, thrill, invigorate, brighten, rejuvenate

enrapture, enraptured
> tantalize, attract, beckon, enthrall, stimulate, tempt, enamored, enchanted, mesmerized, charmed, fixated

enraged
> livid, seething, incensed, furious, infuriated, irate, outraged

entangled
> twisted, intertwined, tangled, snarled, embroiled, ensnared

enthrall, enthralling
> absorbing, immersing, engaged, riveting, hypnotic, thrilling, gripping, enticing, mesmerizing, engrossing, spellbinding, captivating, beguiling, magnetic, alluring, arresting, enchanting

entice, enticing
> engrossing, spellbinding, arresting, enchanting, captivating, hypnotic, gripping, enthralling, mesmerizing, alluring, beguiling, magnetic, tempting

entrenched
> ingrained, embedded, deep-seated, barricaded, blockaded, lodged, deep-rooted

exasperate, exasperated
> aggravated, inflamed, provoked, enraged, infuriated, incensed, maddened

Touch: Skin Sensations *and* Visceral Responses

excite
arouse, stimulate, stir, enliven, kindle, thrill, exhilarate, invigorate, energize, rouse, electrify

excruciating
agonizing, consuming, intense, piercing, shooting, tearing, acute, unbearable, racking, tormenting, stabbing

exhilarating
invigorating, electrifying, thrilling, breathtaking, bracing, rousing, stirring, intoxicating

fervent
impassioned, intense, passionate, vehement, ardent

feverish
flushed, burning, boiling, fervent, flaming, fiery, heated, seething, frenzied, frantic, overwrought

fidget, fidgety
quake, quiver, shake, tremble, twitch, waver, wobble, restless

fiery
burning, searing, boiling, flaming, heated, impassioned, seething, fierce, flushed, fervent, hot-headed, hot-tempered, vehement

fitful
restless, unsettled, erratic, jumpy, flighty, sporadic

flail, flailing
wave, flap, twist, writhe, thrash, flounder, lash

flaming
flushed, raging, feverish, boiling, fervent, heated, fiery, seething, sweltering, livid, burning, searing, scathing

flare, flaring
bursting, erupting, burning, blazing, seething, boiling, fuming

flighty
careening, dispersed, erratic, jumpy, sporadic, restless, twitchy, volatile, fitful, impulsive, scattered, capricious, fickle

flinch, flinching
crouch, recoil, shrink, wince, cringe, reel, retract, shudder, retreat, quiver, tremble, squirm, writhe, contort, twitch, grimace

flummoxed
bewildered, baffled, confused, confounded, discombobulated, perplexed, rattled

flushed
fiery, seething, blushing, boiling, heated, feverish, burning, searing, flaming

flustered
agitated, ruffled, rattled, unsettled, befuddled, bewildered, roiled, disquieted, shaken

frantic
frenetic, feverish, fraught, agitated, frenzied, agitated, distraught, hectic

frenetic
feverish, frantic, hectic, frenzied, raving, obsessive, maniacal, wild

frenzied
frenetic, hectic, feverish, frantic, raving, manic, crazed, hysterical, fraught, furious

freshen
cleanse, purge, scrub, spruce, wash, invigorate, refresh, revitalize, restore, clean

fretful
uneasy, fitful, panicky, squirmy, agitated, jittery, unsettled, anxious, antsy, fidgety, edgy

frightened
apprehensive, shivering, trembling, disquieted, fearful, startled, uneasy

frigid
chilly, bracing, freezing, shivering, frozen, brisk, numbing, frosty, biting, nippy

frosty, frosted
cold, chilly, brisk, biting, bracing, frozen, icy, shivering, freezing, numb, frigid

frozen
chilly, bracing, frigid, shivering, brisk, biting, nippy, frosted, numb, icy, impassive

gashed
scarred, blistered, defaced, disfigured, welted, gouged, slashed

gnawing
biting, consuming, gripping, piercing, shooting, tearing, alarming, harrowing, heart-rending, nerve-racking

grating
jarring, abrasive, biting, screeching, clashing, rasping, irksome

grimace, grimacing
flinch, cringe, reel, retract, tremble, twinge, pang, wince, writhe, contort, recoil, twitch, blanch, shudder, retreat, quiver, squirm

gripping
spellbinding, captivating, magnetic, riveting, hypnotic, thrilling, enthralling, mesmerizing, engrossing, arresting, enticing

grueling
arduous, backbreaking, irksome, tiresome, toilsome, strained, wearying, taxing, tortuous

TOUCH: SKIN SENSATIONS *and* VISCERAL RESPONSES

gusty
blustery, windy, tumultuous, stormy, windswept, breezy, brisk, drafty

gutsy
bold, unflinching, undaunted, valiant, unshrinking, fearless

gut-wrenching
stunning, distressing, alarming, startling, shocking, disquieting

hair-raising
spine-chilling, electrifying, creepy, spooky, bone-chilling, chilling, bloodcurdling, spine-tingling, shocking

harrowing
alarming, heartrending, gripping, terrifying, traumatic, nerve-racking, disturbing

harsh
biting, coarse, caustic, jarring, rugged, scraping, scratchy, grating

headstrong
unflinching, unyielding, adamant, ironfisted, steadfast, bullheaded

heart-rending
harrowing, alarming, gnawing, heartbreaking, nerve-racking, gripping, terrifying, tragic, piercing

heartsick
despairing, grieving, melancholy, despondent, disheartened

heated
fiery, passionate, intense, fierce, stormy, spirited, bitter, violent, acrimonious, vehement

high-strung
edgy, tense, temperamental, excitable, unstable, restless, neurotic

hot-headed
reckless, passionate, volatile, fiery, explosive, quick-tempered

humid
clammy, sweaty, damp, misty, moist, sticky, muggy, stifling, steamy, sweltering

icy
frozen, biting, bitter, detached, cutting, dispassionate, freezing, distant, frosted, impassive, numb, reticent, shivery, cold, stony

ignite
spark, kindle, energize, arouse, trigger, provoke

immersed
absorbed, enthralled, soaked, permeated, engrossed, spellbound

incendiary
provocative, inflammatory, combustible, inflaming, inciting

indignant
irate, aggravated, aggrieved, furious, livid, incensed

inflamed
feverish, boiling, fervent, heated, seething, aggravated, provoked, irked, flushed, burning, searing, fiery

infuriated
seething, livid, incensed, enraged, furious, outraged, indignant, irate

ingrained
entrenched, embedded, deep-seated, lodged, unshakable, deep-rooted, enduring

instilled
imbued, permeated, pervaded, bathed, steeped, drenched, doused, deluged, infused, inundated, saturated

instinctive
visceral, gut-feeling, deep-rooted, deep-seated, impulsive, reflexive, spontaneous

insufferable
unbearable, intolerable, unendurable, shattering, excruciating, gnawing, tormenting

intolerable
insufferable, unbearable, unendurable, shattering, excruciating, gnawing, tormenting

intrusive
meddling, invasive, prying, interfering, pushy, meddlesome, nosy, forward

invigorating
bracing, brisk, crisp, exhilarating, reviving, enlivening, revitalizing, refreshing, energizing

irate
incensed, enraged, furious, infuriated, outraged, livid, seething, raging, indignant

irksome
grueling, arduous, backbreaking, tiresome, toilsome, straining, wearying, bothersome, troubling

ironfisted
unflinching, unyielding, headstrong, stubborn, impervious, resistant, unbending, relentless, adamant

itchy, itching
ticklish, prickly, touchy, scratchy, tingling, crawling

jarring
harsh, biting, coarse, caustic, rugged, scraping, grating, jolting, bumpy, unsettling, cutting

jaundiced
disenchanted, disillusioned, indifferent, cynical, embittered, bitter, soured

jittery
trembling, uneasy, agitated, edgy, quivering, quaking, fidgety, shaky, twitchy, uptight, jumpy

jumpy
erratic, flighty, sporadic, restless, twitchy, fidgety, high-strung, skittish, spooked, edgy, fitful

labored
stilted, strained, forced, leaden, laborious, burdensome

laborious
arduous, grueling, taxing, strenuous, wearisome, cumbersome

languid
relaxed, lethargic, unhurried, sluggish, fatigued

lethargic
drowsy, languid, leaden, sluggish, stagnant, listless

lifeless
deadened, drab, torpid, listless, passive, lethargic, dull, lackluster, emotionless

listless
feeble, languid, moribund, sluggish, stagnant, lifeless, leaden, spiritless

livid
seething, incensed, enraged, furious, infuriated, irate, outraged, indignant

loathsome
deplorable, obnoxious, revolting, repugnant, abhorrent, detestable, execrable, vile

lubricate, lubricated
smooth, daub, emollient, soothe, anoint, oil, moisten, soften, balm

lull
soothe, calm, assuage, hush, quiet, silence, quell, temper

malaise
unease, distress, angst, disquiet, despair, affliction, discomfort

magnetic
arresting, enchanting, enticing, riveting, hypnotic, engrossing, thrilling, gripping, enthralling, alluring, spellbinding, beguiling, captivating, mesmerizing

misty
damp, moist, sticky, humid, muggy, foggy, bleary, steamy

moist
clammy, sweaty, damp, misty, humid, muggy, steamy

moisten
emollient, soothe, soften, balm, lubricate, dampen, saturate, soak

muggy
damp, humid, clammy, misty, moist, soggy, sticky, stuffy

naked
bare, bald, denuded, disrobed, primal, unclothed, stripped, stark, unadorned, exposed

needle, needling
goad, provoke, pester, irk, infuriate, taunt, badger, ruffle, prod, harass

nestle
burrow, cuddle, nuzzle, snuggle

nippy
chilly, bracing, brisk, exhilarating, invigorating, reviving, biting, frosty, crisp

numb, numbing
blunt, deadened, subdued, icy, frozen, detached, cold, impassive, stony, bewildered, stunned

nuzzle
caress, embrace, stroke, burrow, touch, cuddle, snuggle

off-putting
revolting, creepy, offensive, disagreeable, distasteful, repellent, vile, odious, unappealing, irritating

oil (v)
anoint, smooth, lubricate, daub, grease, smear, slather

oily
greasy, unctuous, slimy, slithery, lubricated, slippery, pomaded, smeary, slick

oppressive
stifling, choking, constrictive, airless, squelching, stuffy, strangling, suffocating, windless

pacify
placate, appease, console, soothe, calm, assuage, quell, comfort

pained
wounded, aggrieved, anguished, distressed, troubled, tormented, aggravated

painstaking
meticulous, scrupulous, exacting, tedious, diligent, rigorous, fussy, careful

palpable
tangible, apparent, conspicuous, detectable, evident, perceptible, distinct

palpitate, palpitation
trepidation, apprehension, shiver, tremble, disquiet, fright, quiver, unrest, unease

Touch: Skin Sensations *and* Visceral Responses

pang
> throb, tremble, twinge, grimace, pulse, vibrate, thump, ache, stab, spasm, wrench

panicky
> fretful, squirmy, antsy, touchy, uneasy, frenzied, startled, aghast, apprehensive, edgy

paralyzed
> startled, alarmed, crippled, frightened, perturbed, stunned, incapacitated, unnerved

parched
> shriveled, withered, thirsty, arid, dusty, waterless, dehydrated, wilted, desiccated, dried, scorched, dry

penetrating
> sharp, piercing, pointed, stinging, cutting, biting, puncturing, intense

perturbed
> startled, alarmed, stunned, unnerved, flustered, uneasy, troubled

piercing
> excruciating, gripping, pinching, scathing, scorching, puncturing, intense, sharp, skewering, stabbing, biting

pinched
> strained, tense, edgy, uneasy, winced, taut, drained, worn, fraught, distressed

placate
> soothe, mollify, pacify, appease, calm

pleasing
> delightful, pleasurable, gratifying, agreeable, engaging, satisfying, enchanting

pleasurable
> salubrious, pleasing, delightful, satisfying, sensuous, gratifying, sumptuous

pomaded
> oily, unctuous, lubricated, greasy, slick

provoking
> arousing, agitating, aggravating, stirring, vexing, rankling, irksome, needling, baiting, taunting, goading

punishing
> grueling, backbreaking, excruciating, strenuous, exhausting, crushing, tortuous, onerous, taxing, relentless, arduous

queasy
> squeamish, nauseated, faint, sickly, dizzy, woozy

quell
> soothe, soften, appease, assuage, calm, comfort, hush, lull, subdue

quiver

flinch, wince, jitter, teeter, totter, shiver, shudder, quaver, tremor, quake, bobble, convulse, fidget, flutter, joggle, shake, tremble, twitch

rankled

vexed, irked, annoyed, provoked, galled, tormented

rattled

unnerved, flustered, agitated, ruffled, unsettled, befuddled, shaken, bewildered, disquieted

recoil

retreat, tremble, waver, squirm, repulse, cringe, retract, shudder, quiver, flinch, swerve, wince, reel, balk, dodge

reel

recoil, shudder, quiver, flinch, wince, squirm, tremble, cringe

refresh, refreshing

invigorate, freshen, rejuvenate, revitalize, cleanse, revive, enliven

relish

revel, savor, bask, indulge, enjoy, delight in, cherish, luxuriate in

repose

rest, calm, stillness, ease, peace, serenity, poise

repulse, repulsive

recoil, balk, dodge, qualm, retreat, tremble, waver, wince, cringe, retract, squirm, shudder, quiver, flinch, swerve, reel

restless

fitful, erratic, edgy, uneasy, flighty, jumpy, twitchy, fidgety, agitated, unsettled

revel

savor, relish, bask, indulge, enjoy, delight in, cherish, wallow

riveting

enchanting, hypnotic, thrilling, gripping, enthralling, mesmerizing, engrossing, spellbinding, captivating, beguiling, magnetic, alluring

rousing

electric, charged, thrilling, stirring, spirited, arresting

salacious

vulgar, suggestive, lewd, crude, obscene, lascivious, risque

salubrious

pleasing, delightful, healthful, pleasurable, agreeable, salutary, invigorating, revitalizing

salutary

healing, salubrious, nourishing, beneficial, restorative

Touch: Skin Sensations *and* Visceral Responses

scald, scalding
seared, burning, scorched, parched, smoldering, singed, charred, stinging

scar, scarred, scarring
blistered, defaced, disfigured, distorted, welted, pockmarked, pitted, gashed

scathing
caustic, searing, stinging, scalding, withering, cutting, blistering, fierce, biting, devastating

scintillating
dazzling, effervescent, flickering, gleaming, glimmering, radiant, sparkling

scorching, scorched
searing, scalding, singed, blackened, burned, parched, smoldering, steaming

searing
blistering, scorching, scalding, singeing, seething, burning, sizzling, parched, sweltering, stinging, withering, fiery

seethe, seething
flaring, roiled, stewing, fuming, smoldering, simmering, boiling, livid, infuriated

sensation
tingling, tremor, undercurrent, rush, charge

sensuous, sensual
luscious, voluptuous, luxurious, pleasurable, arousing, stimulating, pleasing, lush, sumptuous

serene
tranquil, soothing, peaceful, calm, placid, restful, still, undisturbed

shaky
jittery, wobbly, twitchy, unsteady, quivering, giddy, dizzy, woozy, insecure

shattering
shocking, crushing, devastating, tormenting, stunning

shiver, shivering
tremble, quiver, shudder, quake, quaver, tremor, twitch, twinge, shake

shocking
stunning, distressing, alarming, startling, gut-wrenching, disgusting, horrifying

shooting
excruciating, biting, gripping, piercing, cutting, stabbing, agonizing

shrill
sharp, piercing, penetrating, stinging, cutting, biting, earsplitting

shrink
flinch, crouch, cringe, recoil, wince, reel, retract, shudder, retreat, quiver, wilt, tremble, squirm

shudder, shuddering
shiver, tremble, quiver, quake, quaver, tremor, twitch, cringe, reel, recoil, retract, flinch, wince, swerve, squirm

sickening
disgusting, shocking, revolting, detestable, appalling, repulsive, repugnant

simmer, simmering
sizzling, burning, sweltering, parched, flushed, searing, singeing

singed, singeing
blistering, burning, flaring, blazing, ablaze, aflame, fiery, searing, smoldering

sizzling
blistering, boiling, flushed, heated, feverish, seething, sweltering, burning, searing, singeing

skittish
antsy, fretful, panicky, jumpy uneasy, uptight, tense, edgy, fearful, jittery, anxious, excitable

sluggish
fatigued, languid, lethargic, listless, sluggardly, leaden, stagnant

slumberous
languid, tranquil, lethargic, listless, sedated

smolder, smoldering
simmering, sizzling, sweltering, blazing, sultry, blistering, burning, searing, fiery, singeing

snuggle
nestle, burrow, cuddle, nuzzle, caress

soft, soften
fuzzy, furry, squishy, doughy, pliable, emollient, soothe, moisten, balm, lubricate

soggy
drenched, saturated, sopping, soaked, waterlogged, damp, sodden

solace
comfort, soothe, calm, relief

soothe
soften, appease, assuage, balm, calm, comfort, hush, lull, quell, smooth, subdue

soothing
tranquil, comforting, calming, consoling, pacifying, warming, peaceful

sopping
drenched, saturated, soggy, soaked, sodden, waterlogged, dripping, drowned

spasm
shudder, twitch, tremor, outburst, frenzy, convulsion, eruption, shiver, shake

spine-chilling
eerie, freakish, spooky, scary, bone-chilling, hair-raising, chilling, blood-curdling, creepy, spine-tingling

spruce
cleanse, clean, freshen, purge, scrub, wash, tidy

spurn
rebuff, reject, scorn, snub, repulse, slight, jilt

squeamish
nauseated, queasy, faint, uneasy, sickly, shaky, disgusted

squirm, squirmy
cringe, reel, recoil, retract, shudder, retreat, quiver, flinch, wince, uneasy, tremble

startled
stunned, astonished, astounded, stupefied, dazed, flabbergasted, shocked, aghast, dumbfounded, dumbstruck, thunderstruck

steamy
feverish, boiling, flaming, heated, seething, sweltering, parched, flushed, sizzling, burning, searing, singeing, sultry, fiery

steely
steadfast, unflinching, unswerving, unwavering, stony, inflexible, unyielding, gritty

stifling
windless, choking, constrictive, oppressive, squelching, sweltering, suffocating, airless

stilted
awkward, clumsy, stodgy, leaden, unwieldy, wooden

stinging
acrid, caustic, biting, bitter, acid, cutting, sharp, scathing

stirring
thrilling, rousing, electrifying, lightning, charged, energizing, exhilarating, gripping, provocative, electric

stony
detached, cold, cutting, dispassionate, distant, frosted, impassive, numb, reticent

stormy
windswept, breezy, blustery, windy, gusty, tumultuous, passionate

strained
uneasy, pinched, winced, tense, edgy, distressed, forced, awkward

strenuous
laborious, arduous, crushing, grueling, hefty, jaw-breaking, taxing, rigorous, wearisome

stuffy

musty, stale, congested, stifling, suffocating, oppressive, stagnant

stunned

astonished, astounded, staggered, stupefied, dazed, flabbergasted, shocked, aghast, dumbfounded, dumbstruck, thunderstruck

stunning

startling, alarming, arousing, frightening, unnerving, devastating, bewildering, amazing, shocking

stunted

hampered, hindered, restricted, impeded, stymied

suffocated, suffocating

stifling, choking, constrictive, oppressive, squelching, strangling, stuffy

sultry

fiery, sizzling, burning, searing, scorching, humid, sensual, sticky, smoldering, steamy

swab

refresh, lather, scrub, douse, cleanse, wipe, scrub, daub

swampy

dank, damp, dewy, humid, moist, muggy, rainy, sticky

sweaty

clammy, damp, moist, sticky, slithery, slimy, humid, muggy

sweltering

stifling, sultry, blistering, burning, fiery, melting, roasting, scalding, scorching, sizzling, boiling, parched, flushed, feverish, seething, searing, singeing

swoon, swooning

faint, tremble, quiver, shaky, dizzy, ecstatic, collapse, weak, giddy, unsteady, wobbly

tactful

gracious, polished, sensitive, perceptive, poised, deft, delicate, discreet

tactile

tangible, palpable, discernible, perceptible

tactless

crude, blunt, gauche, thoughtless, boorish, blundering, clumsy, gruff, crass

tangible

palpable, distinct, tactile, concrete, perceptible, conspicuous

tantalizing

alluring, attractive, beckoning, charming, enrapturing, enthralling, provoking, seducing, stimulating, tempting

Touch: Skin Sensations *and* Visceral Responses

taxing
  laborious, crushing, grueling, rigorous, strenuous, wearisome, arduous

tedious
  dreary, dull, lifeless, repetitive, tiresome, wearisome, monotonous, irksome

temperate
  balmy, soothing, gentle, tranquil, pleasant, steady

tense
  charged, rigid, stern, stiff, taut, strained, clutched, pinched

tepid
  lukewarm, cool, feeble, muted, weak, dull, lifeless, languid

thrill, thrilling
  arouse, enthrall, excite, rush, surge, electrify, stimulate, enliven, kindle, charged, rousing, stirring, riveting, gripping, arresting, mesmerizing, engrossing, spellbinding, enticing

throb, throbbing
  tremble, twinge, pang, grimace, pulse, vibrate, thump, aching, stabbing, piercing, pulsate

thunderstruck
  startled, stunned, astonished, astounded, stupefied, flabbergasted, shocked, aghast, dumbfounded, dumbstruck, dazed

tickle, ticklish
  tingle, itchy, arouse, excite, touch, tease, prickly, scratchy

tinge
  touch, smattering, sprinkling, dash, pinch

tingle, tingling
  burn, shiver, tremor, twinge, itch, sting, throb, prickly, quiver, rush

tiresome
  grueling, arduous, toilsome, strained, wearying, wearisome, exasperating, irksome

toilsome
  grueling, arduous, backbreaking, irksome, tiresome, strained, wearying

tormenting
  excruciating, biting, gnawing, intense, piercing, unbearable

torpid
  lethargic, dull, numb, sluggish, languid, lackadaisical

torrid
  blistering, boiling, feverish, fiery, flushed, heated, searing, stifling, simmering, sultry, steamy, hot, sweltering

touchy
> prickly, squirmy, uneasy, antsy, fretful, uptight, volatile, sensitive, testy, edgy

toxic
> venomous, bitter, caustic, poisonous, deadly, noxious, lethal

tranquil
> soothing, temperate, composed, calm, placid, serene, undisturbed, balmy

tremble, trembling
> quiver, quake, fidget, shake, twitch, waver, wobble, cringe, flinch, wince, jitter, shiver, reel, recoil, shudder, squirm

tremor
> shiver, tremble, quiver, shudder, quake, quaver, twitch, rattle, jerk, bobble, jolt, jostle, quake, shake, throb, tic, tingle, vibrate

tremulous
> quivering, jittery, wobbly, tottering, teetering, twitchy, shivering, trembling, shaky

trepidation
> apprehension, shiver, tremble, disquiet, fright, palpitation, quiver, unrest, unease

twinge
> twitch, grimace, tweak, gnaw, throb, tremble, pang, pulse, spasm, prick, stab, jab

twitch, twitchy
> fitful, flighty, jumpy, sporadic, restless, quake, fidgety, quiver, shake, tremble, tremor

unbearable
> intolerable, unendurable, insufferable, shattering, excruciating, gnawing, tormenting

undercurrent
> hint, tenor, vibe, riptide, undertow, tinge, murmur, overtone

uneasy, unease
> edgy, antsy, fretful, panicky, prickly, squirmy, touchy, fitful, jittery, unsettled, unstable

unendurable
> unbearable, intolerable, insufferable, shattering, excruciating, gnawing, tormenting

unflappable
> immovable, flinty, unyielding, hardened, unbending, unflinching, unruffled, cool-headed, steely

unflinching
> unyielding, adamant, headstrong, inflexible, refractory, resistant, steadfast, steely

unnerved
> flustered, rattled, perturbed, stunned, agitated, ruffled, dismayed, disquieted

unnerving
rattling, agitating, perturbing, stunning, disquieting, disconcerting, unsettling

unruffled
calm, unflappable, composed, balanced, equanimous, placid, poised, collected, cool-headed, serene

unswerving
steadfast, unflinching, unwavering, undaunted, gutsy, determined, focused, gritty

unwavering
steadfast, unflinching, unswerving, intense, resolute, undaunted, unyielding

venomous
bitter, caustic, cutting, toxic, poisonous, noxious, vile, hostile

vexing
agitating, aggravating, rankling, irksome, provoking

vigor
brute, robustness, exuberance, hardiness, vitality, zeal, intensity

visceral
gut, instinctive, deep-rooted, deep-seated, ingrained

vitality
vigor, brute, robustness, exuberance, hardiness, zeal

vivacious
lively, breezy, ebullient, buoyant, sparkling, playful, effervescent, bubbly

volatile
capricious, fickle, mercurial, explosive, erratic, unstable, turbulent, unpredictable

wallow, wallowing
revel, luxuriate, roll, wade, tumble, splash, delight, indulge, lurch, plunge

wearisome, wearying
tiresome, exasperating, pestering, toilsome, aggravating, bothersome, vexing, disturbing, provoking, troubling, laborious, arduous, grueling, taxing, irksome

welt
scar, blister, wound, gash, bruise, swelling, pockmark

wince
writhe, contort, twitch, blanch, grimace, flinch, crouch, cringe, recoil, shrink, retract, shudder, retreat, quiver, tremble, squirm, reel

windless
stifling, choking, constricting, airless, stuffy, suffocating, still

windswept
windy, breezy, brisk, drafty, blustery, stormy, gusty

windy
> gusty, breezy, blustery, stormy, windswept, brisk, drafty

wrenching
> gut-wrenching, distressing, alarming, startling, shocking, jarring, agonizing

writhe
> contort, recoil, twitch, wince, quiver, tremble, squirm, blanch, grimace, flinch, cringe, reel, retract, shudder, convulse

yearn
> hunger, itch, pine, crave, ache, lust, thirst

TEXTURES *and* STRUCTURES

airy
> light, subtle, flowing, languid, breezy, buoyant, windy, feathery, fluffy, willowy, wispy, soft

arid
> bone-dry, barren, dusty, parched, dry, scorched, baked, waterless, dehydrated, desiccated, shriveled, wilted, withered

armored
> unbreakable, impervious, resistant, unyielding, indestructible, shatterproof, durable

baked
> desiccated, shriveled, wilted, crisp, withered, parched, scorched, arid, dusty, dry, waterless, dehydrated

barbed
> spiny, bony, thorny, pronged, spiky, bristly, prickly, sharp, pointed

bare
> stark, unadorned, barren, naked, bald, denuded, primal, unclothed, stripped, plain

barren
> stripped, stark, plain, unadorned, sapless, bare, naked, bald, harsh, denuded

bearded
> furry, hairy, fuzzy, shaggy, feathery, downy, fluffy, woolly

bendable
> supple, flexible, lithe, willowy, rubbery, springy, limber, resilient, agile

blubbery
> thick, chunky, meaty, plump, stout, burly, heavy, doughy, fatty

blunt
> dull, rounded, abrupt, stark, worn, stubby

Touch: Textures *and* Structures

bone-dry
barren, dried, dusty, parched, seared, scorched, desiccated, arid, baked

bony
spiny, barbed, thorny, pronged, bristly, prickly, sharp, pointed, spiky

bouncy
springy, buoyant, elastic, flexible, lithe, stretchy, willowy

braided
textured, lattice, meshed, lacy, weaved, interlaced, twisted

brambly
thorny, prickly, spiky, pointed, stinging, tangled, bristly, barbed, knotty

brawny
sinewy, fleshy, muscular, rugged, buffed, ropy

bristly
coarse, rough, bumpy, scratchy, prickly, ragged, spiny, brambly, thorny, spiky, harsh

brittle
delicate, crumbly, fragile, breakable, crisp

buffed
polished, silken, satiny, sleek, smooth, shiny, glossy

bulletproof
impenetrable, impervious, indestructible, resistant, unyielding, dense

bumpy
coarse, bristly, rough, scratchy, prickly, ragged, choppy, lumpy

burly
plump, stout, thick, chunky, meaty, blubbery, heavy, doughy

bushy
woody, scrubby, shaggy, bristly, furry, prickly, woolly, fuzzy

busty
voluptuous, buxom, plump, ample, curvy

buxom
busty, voluptuous, curvy, plump

caked
lumpy, chunky, clotted, congealed, curdled, jelled, encrusted, bumpy

calloused
leathery, rugged, wrinkled, weather-beaten, sinewy, ropy, tough, hardened

chalky
dusty, crumbling, gritty, flaky, scaly, sooty, powdery

chunky
lumpy, bumpy, caked, clotted, congealed, curdled, jelled, meaty, plump, burly, blubbery, doughy

clayey
earthy, coarse, muddy, sandy, sticky

clingy
gluey, sticky, gooey, gummy, tacky

clotted
caked, chunky, lumpy, bumpy, congealed, curdled, jelled

coarse
rough, bumpy, harsh, scratchy, bristly, prickly, ragged, textured, rugged

congealed
lumpy, bumpy, caked, chunky, clotted, jelled, curdled

corroded
rusted, tarnished, disintegrating, abraded, scratched, scraped

cottony
fuzzy, soft, gauzy, silky, satiny, velvety, gossamer, plush, smooth

cozy
plush, snug, luxurious, frilly, posh, cushy, comforting

craggy
rugged, harsh, rough, coarse, jagged, pitted, weather-beaten

creased
wrinkled, withered, shriveled, furrowed, grooved, aged, crinkled, ruffled, worn, leathery

crinkled
ruffled, crumpled, tousled, tangled, disheveled, rumpled, wrinkled, scrunched

crisp
smooth, starched, clean, brittle

crumbly
flaky, sooty, dried, dusty, shriveled, wilted, withered, brittle

curdled
lumpy, bumpy, caked, congealed, jelled, chunky, clotted

dainty
airy, wispy, lacy, delicate, fragile, fine

denuded
stripped, exposed, barren, bare

desiccated
dry, parched, scorched, arid, dusty, dehydrated, wilted, shriveled, withered

disfigured
mangled, crippled, lacerated, shredded, torn, scarred, defaced, distorted, gashed

disheveled
ruffled, crinkled, crumpled, tousled, tangled, rumpled, bedraggled, slipshod, wrinkled, unkempt

distorted
blistered, defaced, disfigured, gashed, welted, gnarled, crooked, warped, askew, scarred

doughy
soft, squishy, mushy, spongy, thick, chunky, meaty, plump, stout, burly, blubbery, heavy

downy
feathery, fluffy, fuzzy, furry, velvety, woolly, fleece, shaggy, silky

dried
bone-dry, dusty, parched, desiccated, shriveled, arid

droopy
dangling, flapping, draped, slumped, sagging, crumpled, wilted, limp, flaccid, flimsy, wobbly, floppy, bent, flabby, slouching

dry
parched, baked, dusty, waterless, dehydrated, desiccated, shriveled, wilted, crisp, withered, arid

dull
blunt, worn, flat

durable
rigid, immobile, steely, strong, stiff, solid, resistant, shatterproof, indestructible

dusty
arid, chalky, crumbly, sooty, dried, parched, waterless, dehydrated, desiccated, powdery

earthy
clayey, coarse, muddy, sandy, gritty, grainy

elastic
flexible, malleable, supple, springy, bouncy, buoyant, stretchy, pliant

embedded
entrenched, ingrained, deep-seated, lodged, rooted

feathery
downy, flossy, fluffy, fuzzy, furry, velvety, woolly, fleecy, shaggy, airy

feeble
flaccid, limp, weak, frail, flimsy, fragile, debilitated

fibrous
>stringy, thready, pulpy, sinewy, woody, ropy

filthy
>dirty, grimy, sticky, muddy, sooty, smudgy, grungy, soiled, cruddy, mucky

firm
>taut, stretched, tense, tight, rigid, stiff, sturdy

flabby
>droopy, flaccid, languid, flimsy, floppy, lax, baggy, limp, sagging

flaccid
>limp, droopy, flimsy, fragile, wobbly, shaky, floppy, slack

flaky
>dusty, chalky, crumbly, scaly, peeling

fleecy
>feathery, woolly, downy, fluffy, furry, shaggy

fleshy
>meaty, blubbery, rotund, plump, pudgy, stout, chunky, portly, heavyset

flexible
>pliant, elastic, malleable, supple, springy, lithe, spongy, stretchy, bendable

flimsy
>fragile, brittle, wobbly, rickety, wispy, shaky, floppy, willowy

floppy
>flimsy, wobbly, shaky, limp, willowy, slack, loose, sagging

flossy
>feathery, downy, fluffy, fuzzy, furry, velvety, woolly

fluffy
>fleecy, woolly, fuzzy, furry, downy, shaggy, hairy, feathery, velvety

fluid
>liquid, juicy, watery, flowing, runny, molten

foamy
>bubbly, frothy, velvety, soapy, fizzy, lathering

fossilized
>rigid, stiff, ossified, bony, calcified, hardened, petrified, solidified

fragile
>rickety, delicate, shaky, flimsy, brittle, wobbly, frail

frail
>withered, wilted, feeble, flimsy, delicate, brittle, tenuous, weak

frilly
>luxurious, posh, plush, trimmed, lacy, ornate, gauzy, filigree

Touch: Textures *and* Structures

frothy
> bubbly, fizzy, foamy, soapy, lathering, sudsy

furrowed
> wrinkled, grooved, crinkled, ruffled, creased, crumpled, fluted

furry
> fuzzy, bearded, shaggy, feathery, downy, fluffy, woolly, cottony, hairy, whiskered

fuzzy
> furry, woolly, shaggy, feathery, downy, fluffy, hairy

gauzy
> flimsy, thin, sheer, wispy, lacy, gossamer, papery, slinky, silken, silky

glossy
> satiny, smooth, sleek, slick, shiny, shining, gleaming, lustrous, silky, glassy

gluey
> sticky, gooey, gummy, tacky, clingy, viscous

gooey
> sticky, gummy, jellied, gluey, clingy, tacky, syrupy, viscous

gossamer
> lacy, airy, gauzy, wispy, flimsy, fine, silky, fibrous

greasy
> slippery, slimy, gunky, oily, slithery, lubricated, slick, smeared

grimy
> muddy, filthy, sooty, dingy, dirty, smudgy, grungy, soiled, mucky

gritty
> sandy, earthy, clayey, coarse, gravelly, muddy, powdery, granular

grungy
> grimy, dingy, dirty, muddy, filthy, sooty, smudgy, unkempt, greasy, gunky

gummy
> gluey, clingy, sticky, gooey, gelled, tacky, syrupy, viscous, gunky

gunky
> slimy, clammy, grungy, gluey, gooey, sticky, slithery, tacky, grimy

hairy
> furry, feathery, downy, fluffy, fuzzy, bearded, shaggy, woolly

hardy
> vigorous, muscular, vital, robust, firm, hearty, rugged

heavy
> thick, chunky, plump, stout, burly, blubbery, bulky, hefty, unwieldy, weighty

immobile
> rigid, stern, stiff, stationary, motionless, frozen, stagnant

impervious
impermeable, airtight, impenetrable, unyielding, immutable, inflexible, refractory, resistant

indestructible
shatterproof, unbreakable, impervious, resistant, unyielding, armored, durable

inflexible
taut, rigid, dense, unyielding, immutable, impervious, refractory, resistant

infused
drenched, permeated, instilled, doused, drowned, inundated, saturated, bathed

itchy
prickly, scratchy, tingling, rough, grating

jagged
rough, coarse, cutting, scratchy, sharp, notched, irregular, pointed, spiked, serrated, ragged

jelled, jellied
gummy, gooey, gluey, clingy, sticky, tacky, syrupy, viscous

juicy
liquid, fluid, watery, flowing, moist, oozy, oily, slippery

jumbled
tangled, disordered, twisted, knotted, matted, coiled, muddled, knotty, garbled

knotted
tangled, gnarled, twisted, matted, coiled, muddled, jumbled

knotty
tangled, convoluted, jumbled, intricate, knotted, gnarled, thorny, twisted

lacy
airy, gauzy, gossamer, papery, slinky, wispy, frilly, meshed

leaden
wooden, heavy, plodding, weighty, dense

leathery
rugged, wrinkled, weather-beaten, sinewy, ropy, fibrous, tough

limber
supple, flexible, lithe, willowy, rubbery, springy, resilient, bendable, agile

limp
flimsy, floppy, droopy, flimsy, flaccid, feeble

liquid
fluid, juicy, watery, flowing, smooth, molten, moist, melted

lithe
springy, bouncy, buoyant, elastic, flexible, stretchy, willowy

TOUCH: TEXTURES *and* STRUCTURES

loose
slack, limp, flabby, saggy, droopy, flaccid, flimsy, floppy

lubricated
smooth, oily, wet, greasy, moistened, slippery, smooth

lumpy
bumpy, caked, chunky, clotted, congealed, curdled, jelled

luscious
lush, voluptuous, luxurious, sumptuous, luxurious, smooth

lustrous
silky, satiny, smooth, sleek, slick, velvety, glossy

luxurious
cozy, frilly, posh, plush, sensual, voluptuous, lush

malleable
flexible, pliant, elastic, supple, willowy, rubbery, springy, bendable

marshy
boggy, swampy, dank, damp, dewy, humid, moist, muggy, rainy

matted
tangled, snarled, twisted, knotted, coiled, muddled, jumbled

meaty
stout, burly, blubbery, thick, chunky, heavy, plump

moistened
wet, lubricated, dampened, humid, misted

moldy
mildew, sooty, fusty, rotting, decaying

mucky
sticky, tacky, gooey, gummy, gunky, clammy, oozy

mucous
viscous, sticky, tacky, thick, gummy, gooey, oozy, slimy, mucky

muddy
earthy, clayey, sandy, grimy, dirty, filthy, sooty, smudgy, grungy, gritty

muscular
sinewy, brawny, rugged, strapping, burly

mushy
squishy, doughy, spongy, sloshy, sludgy, slushy, oozy

netted
woven, braided, lattice, laced, weaved, webbed, interwoven, lacy, meshed

oily
slimy, greasy, gooey, sticky, slithery, pomaded

ooze, oozing
   drain, effuse, leach, seep, trickle, exude, emit, secrete, drip

oozy
   slimy, sludgy, oily, slithery, slushy, muddy

ossified
   rigid, stiff, fossilized, bony, calcified, hardened, solidified

papery
   lacy, airy, gauzy, gossamer, slinky, wispy, paper-thin, flimsy

parched
   seared, shriveled, singed, withered, dry, dusty, waterless, crispy, dehydrated, arid, baked, desiccated, dried

pliant, pliable
   flexible, elastic, malleable, supple, springy

plump
   thick, chunky, meaty, stout, burly, blubbery, heavy, doughy

plush
   luxurious, frilly, posh, sensual, voluptuous, silken, silky, cottony, satiny, velvety, cozy

pockmarked
   scarred, blistered, defaced, disfigured, distorted, welted, gashed

pointed, pointy
   barbed, cutting, edged, stinging, sharp, piercing, thorny, spiked, pronged

porous
   spongy, absorbent, permeable, squishy

posh
   luxurious, cozy, frilly, plush, sensual, voluptuous

prickly
   thorny, spiky, pointed, stinging, tangled, brambly, barbed, knotty, bristly, spiny

pronged
   spiny, bony, barbed, thorny, spiky, bristly, prickly, sharp, pointed

protrude, protruding
   bulge, jut, overhang, extend, project, poke

ragged
   coarse, bristly, rough, bumpy, harsh, scratchy, tattered

razor-edged
   sharp, piercing, cutting, biting, razor-sharp

refractory
   inflexible, resistant, unyielding, immutable, impervious

TOUCH: TEXTURES *and* STRUCTURES

resilient
supple, flexible, pliable, agile, durable, sturdy, buoyant, bendable

resistant
protected, immutable, unyielding, impervious, inflexible, repellent, refractory

rickety
flimsy, fragile, wobbly, shaky, floppy, brittle, tottering, teetering, ramshackle, dilapidated, unsound

rigid
steely, stern, stiff, tense, wooden, taut, sturdy, durable, immobile

robust
hardy, rugged, brawny, tough, exuberant, hearty, muscular, strong, sturdy

ropy
thready, stringy, leathery, fibrous, sinewy, pulpy, coarse

rough
coarse, cutting, scratchy, jagged, rugged, textured, bumpy, ridged, ruffled, irregular

rubbery
flexible, lithe, willowy, springy, bendable, elastic, pliable

ruffled
crinkled, crumpled, tousled, disheveled, rumpled, frilly, disordered

rugged
harsh, rough, coarse, jagged, pitted, muscular, craggy, weathered, durable, rocky, leathery

rumpled
ruffled, crinkled, crumpled, tousled, tangled, disheveled, crimped, creased

sagging, saggy
floppy, slumping, droopy, crumpled, dangling, shrinking, wilted, flabby, flaccid, flimsy

sandy
earthy, clayey, coarse, gravelly, muddy, gritty, powdery

sapless
arid, bone-dry, dried, dusty, parched, baked, sapped, shriveled, withered

sappy
sticky, tacky, gooey, syrupy, oozy, runny

satiny
smooth, sleek, slick, velvety, shiny, glossy, gleaming, lustrous, silky

saturated
doused, drenched, bathed, deluged, imbued, infused, inundated, submerged

scaly

dry, flaky, flaking, peeling, rough

scarred

scratched, blistered, ripped, torn, pockmarked, disfigured, pitted, blemished, defaced

scratchy

raspy, abrasive, scraping, chafing, gravelly, ragged, coarse, jagged, itchy

scruffy

tattered, ragged, disheveled, raggedy, ratty, unkempt, mangy, shaggy, worn

shaggy

fleecy, feathery, woolly, downy, fluffy, furry, hairy

sharp

piercing, razor-edged, pointy, penetrating, pointed, stinging, cutting, razor-sharp

shatterproof

unbreakable, impervious, indestructible, durable, unyielding, armored

sheer

thin, wispy, gauzy, translucent, gossamer, papery, lacy, flimsy

shriveled

desiccated, wilted, withered, shrunken, deflated, sunken

silken, silky

buffed, cottony, satiny, velvety, gossamer, plush, sleek, smooth

sinew, sinewy

fleshy, muscular, brawny, leathery, rugged, ropy

slack

loose, limp, flabby, sagging, flaccid, floppy, baggy, flimsy

sleek

slick, shiny, satiny, smooth, lustrous, silky, glassy, polished

slick

velvety, shiny, satiny, glossy, shining, gleaming, lustrous, silky, slippery, sleek

slimy

slippery, clammy, gummy, gunky, slithery, slobbery, sloshy, slushy, squishy, greasy, slick, gooey, oozy, oily

slinky

gauzy, gossamer, papery, wispy, lacy, airy, willowy

slippery

silky, glassy, oily, slithery, lubricated, slick, greasy, soapy

slithery

clammy, viscous, gooey, ropy, stringy, slippery, glossy, oily, sleek, soapy

Touch: Textures *and* Structures

slobbery
slimy, slippery, gunky, oily, slithery, sloshy, slushy, squishy, sticky, greasy, slick, sludgy, drooling, spitting, frothy

sloppy
careless, fumbling, gawky, clumsy, blundering, muddy, messy

sloshy
slimy, slippery, slithery, slushy, squishy, sludgy, slick, splashing, splattering, sticky

sludgy
squishy, mushy, sloshy, spongy, slimy, slippery, slithery, slobbery, slushy, oozy

slushy
slimy, slippery, slobbery, sloshy, squishy, clammy, mucky, oozy, sludgy

smooth
polished, lubricated, satiny, sleek, silky, velvety, silken, buffed, creamy, glossy

smudgy, smudged
grimy, dingy, dirty, muddy, filthy, sooty, grungy, smeary, streaky

soggy
drenched, saturated, sopping, soaked, water-logged, sodden

sooty
chalky, muddy, dusty, grimy, dingy, filthy, smudgy, grungy

sopping
drenched, saturated, water-logged, sodden, soggy, soaked, flooded, drowned

spiky
prickly, bristly, thorny, ticklish, pointed, spiny, bony, barbed, sharp, pronged, sharp, pointy

spiny
barbed, thorny, pronged, spiky, bristly, prickly, sharp, edgy, pointed

spongy
absorbing, porous, permeable, springy, elastic, resilient

springy
bouncy, buoyant, elastic, flexible, lithe, stretchy, willowy, rubbery

squishy
mushy, spongy, cushiony, squelchy, soft

stark
bare, bald, stripped, plain, barren, harsh, blunt

static
stagnant, inert, fixed, frozen, immobile, motionless, rigid

steely
rigid, durable, immobile, stern, stiff, taut, firm

sticky
gluey, gooey, tacky, gummy, mucky, sappy, syrupy, viscous, mucous

stiff
wooden, leaden, stodgy, stilted, awkward, clumsy, rigid, immobile, stern, tense, constrictive, turgid

stout
blubbery, heavy, thick, chunky, meaty, plump, burly, doughy, portly, stocky

stretchy
elastic, elongated, springy, bouncy, buoyant, flexible, extended, lithe, willowy

stringy
ropy, straggly, wiry, lanky, gangly, bony, fibrous, sinewy, spindly

sturdy
tough, solid, hefty, robust, durable, resilient, stiff

supple
flexible, lithe, willowy, springy, agile, limber, resilient, bendable, nimble, pliant

syrupy
gooey, viscous, jellied, sticky, tacky, sappy, sugary, clingy, gummy

tacky
sticky, gooey, gummy, gluey, viscous

tangled
twisted, knotted, matted, coiled, muddled, jumbled

tattered
ripped, shredded, threadbare, torn, frayed, worn, ragged

taut
firm, stretched, tense, tight, rigid, stiff, flexed, strained

tender
soft, delicate, fragile, frail, gentle

texture, textured
braided, fabric, lattice, meshed, lacy, netting, weaved, rough

thick, thickened
chunky, meaty, plump, stout, burly, blubbery, heavy, doughy, stocky, gooey

thin
flimsy, fragile, brittle, sheer, wispy, willowy, delicate, narrow, sparse, thinning

thorny
prickly, spiky, pointy, stinging, tangled, bristly, brambly, barbed, knotty

thready
ropy, stringy, leathery, fibrous, sinewy, stranded

Touch: Textures *and* Structures

turgid
swollen, bloated, distended, puffy, bulging

uncoiled
unraveled, unearthed, untangled, unfurled, disentangled, flattened, unfolded, unwound

unwieldy
stilted, awkward, clumsy, leaden, wooden, cumbersome, ungainly, hefty, bulky

unyielding
immutable, impervious, inflexible, unflinching, adamant, resistant, headstrong, ironfisted, refractory, shatterproof

velvety
feathery, downy, fluffy, silken, silky, cottony, satiny, plush, sleek, creamy

viscous
sticky, tacky, thick, mucous, gummy, gooey, gluey, syrupy

voluptuous
curvy, curvaceous, shapely, buxom, alluring

waterless
parched, scorched, arid, dusty, dehydrated, desiccated, shriveled, bone-dry, dry, wilted, withered

watery
damp, moist, humid, muggy, misty, steamy, drizzly, liquid, fluid, juicy, flowing

weighty
wooden, plodding, leaden, cumbersome, heavy

well-trodden
worn, threadbare, tattered, frayed, ragged

whiskered
woolly, furry, fuzzy, feathery, fluffy, hairy, shaggy, downy, bristly, velvety, fleecy

willowy
wispy, lanky, lithe, supple, graceful, agile, elastic, springy

wilted
withered, shriveled, wrinkled, shrunken, droopy, sagging

wiry
sinewy, burly, lean, stringy, skinny, supple, ropy

wispy
airy, dainty, flimsy, gauzy, lacy, papery, sheer, willowy

withered
shriveled, faded, emaciated, wilted, wrinkled, shrunken, droopy, dehydrated, desiccated, sunken

wobbly
> flimsy, rickety, floppy, teetering, tottering, unsteady, unstable, shaky, ramshackle

wooden
> plodding, leaden, stiff, stilted, awkward, rigid, weighty

woody
> bushy, scrubby, stiff, fibrous, sinewy, stringy, stalky, pulpy

woolly
> furry, fuzzy, feathery, fluffy, hairy, shaggy, whiskered, downy, velvety, fleecy

worn
> threadbare, tattered, ragged, shabby, dull, frayed

wrinkled
> withered, shriveled, furrowed, ridged, crinkled, worn, creased

MOVEMENT, PRESSURE, and SPEED

abrade
> erode, scratch, scrape, grind, corrode, chafe, scuff, graze, grate, disintegrate, rub, wear away

adept
> deft, skillful, agile, savvy, nimble, dexterous, masterful

agile
> deft, adept, nimble, dexterous, light-footed, flexible, lithe

amble
> totter, trudge, idle, saunter, meander, loiter, mosey, lurch, sidle, toddle, shimmy, gyrate, sashay

anchor
> clamp, brace, clasp, clench, clutch, shackle, tether, strap, yoke, fasten

annihilate
> obliterate, destroy, decimate, shatter, crush, demolish

backfire
> backlash, repercussion, ricochet, explosion, boomerang

backlash
> blowback, repercussion, backfire, boomerang, retaliation

bait
> ensnare, trap, entangle, enmesh, embroil, snare, entrap, snag, lure, hook

balk
> recoil, resist, flinch, shirk, reject

Touch: Movement, Pressure, *and* Speed

barricade, barricaded
obstruct, impede, blockade, defend, fortify

bash
punch, smash, strike, clobber, bang, blast, trounce, whack, wallop

bat, batter
smack, slap, swat, thump, whack, wallop, drub, bang, bash, beat, pelt, jab, pummel

batten
clamp, fasten, fix, secure, tighten

beckon
gesture, flag, mime, wave, charm, tempt, entice, signal, lure, coax, summon

befall
ensue, transpire, materialize, emanate, arise, emerge

belabor
thrash, pound, thump, hammer, overwork, dwell on, overdo

bind
fetter, bridle, encumber, entangle, impede, hobble, restrain, saddle, tether, tie, yoke

blast
clobber, bang, bash, bonk, punch, smash, strike, trounce, whack

blend
churn, emulsify, stew, whisk, fuse, merge, meld, mingle, unite

blockade, blockaded
barricade, surround, besiege, isolate, seal, close off

blowback
backlash, repercussion, backfire, boomerang, retaliation

blunder, blundering
bungle, grabble, stumble, fumbling, flounder, botch, bobble, misstep, clumsy, cloddish, sloppy, uncouth, groping

bobble
blunder, fumble, bungle, botch, stumble

bolt
scurry, hasten, burst, scuttle, gallop, hustle, scramble, dash, rush, scamper, scoot, sprint, trot

boomerang
ricochet, backfire, backlash, recoil, rebound, deflect

botch
fumble, blunder, bungle, grabble, stagger, stumble, flounder

brace
clamp, anchor, clasp, clench, clutch, grasp, grip, vise

bridle
fetter, bind, encumber, impede, hobble, restrain, saddle, tether, tie, yoke

browbeat
bully, harass, coerce, hound, bulldoze, pressure

brunt
impact, force, shock, clash, onslaught, repercussion

bubble
foam, froth, fizzle, burble, swish, effervesce, simmer, gurgle, overflow

bungle
fumble, blunder, grabble, stagger, stumble, grope, flounder, botch

burden
strain, load, weight, drag, encumbrance, impose, hinder, impede

burrow
nestle, cuddle, nuzzle, snuggle

burst, bursting
spew, cascade, erupt, flare-up, outbreak, heave, pour, spit, surge, squirt, spurt

bustle, bustling
swarm, stream, spill, flit, scurry, flutter, scamper, rush

calibrate
fine-tune, adjust, align, connect, sharpen, balance, correct, fiddle with

capture
grab, grasp, grip, seize, snatch, snag, snare, entrap, lasso, harpoon, trap, hook, rope

careen, careening
hurtle, bolt, dash, crash, lurch, sway, pitch, tilt

caress
embrace, nuzzle, stroke, touch, nudge, cuddle, fondle, snuggle, squeeze

carve
chisel, engrave, mold, sculpt, shave, hew, trim

cast
fling, heave, lob, sling, hurl, pitch, toss

catapult
fling, propel, launch, blast, spur, cast, pitch, sling

chafe
rub, scrape, abrade, erode, graze, grate, chisel, scour, file, scratch, scuff, grind

chain
shackle, yoke, saddle, fetter, tether, anchor, bridle, batten, hamper, harness, leash, muzzle, restrain, bind, encumber, impede, entangle

chisel
   carve, engrave, mold, sculpt, shave, scrape, scuff, knead, weld, hew, shape

churn
   agitate, blend, emulsify, ferment, stew, whisk, ripple, flutter, swirl, roll, ruffle

clamp
   anchor, brace, clasp, clench, clutch, grasp, grip, vise, fasten, batten

clasp
   clamp, clutch, envelop, grasp, grip, pin, clench

claw
   chip, grasp, puncture, rip, scuff, stab, tear, scratch, dig, scrape

clench
   clasp, cling, clutch, grasp, grip, clamp

cling
   clutch, grasp, grip, clench, clasp, cradle, adhere, cuddle, linger, embrace

clobber
   bang, blast, bonk, punch, smash, strike, trounce, whack, wallop

cloister
   seclude, protect, seal, shelter, confine, enclose

clop
   stomp, clump, stamp, shuffle, trot, tramp, trudge, plod

cluster
   bundle, huddle, flock, gather, crowd, bunch

clutch
   clench, clasp, cling, grasp, grip, clamp, anchor, brace

coalesce
   fuse, unite, merge, blend, integrate, join

coast
   glide, drift, hover, sail, skate, skim, float, waft, buoy, soar, flit, dart, flutter, dance, flicker, flurry, fly, wave

collapse
   crumble, fail, shatter, topple, disintegrate, cave in, buckle, slump, faint, fold, sag

constrain
   strap, yoke, cloister, impede, shackle, fetter, anchor, tether, hem in, hinder, leash, muzzle, hobble, hamper, cripple

contort
   wince, writhe, convulse, recoil, twitch, blanch, grimace, flinch, crouch, cringe, shrink, reel, retract, shudder, retreat, quiver, flail, tremble, squirm, twist, mangle, warp, wring, wrench

convulse

> quake, bobble, fidget, flutter, heave, joggle, quiver, shake, tremble, twitch, waver, wobble

cower

> recoil, quake, cringe, tremble, grovel, flinch, wince, shrink, hide, crouch

cradle

> rock, support, shelter, steady, embrace, cling, clutch, cuddle, grip, caress, nuzzle, encircle

crawl

> limp, amble, stagger, totter, trudge, inch, squirm, creep, drag, plod

creep, creeping

> crouching, prowling, lurching, inching, worming, slithering, groveling, skulking, wriggling, crawling, sneaking

cringe

> recoil, retract, shudder, retreat, quiver, tremble, squirm, flinch, wince, reel

cripple

> debilitate, sabotage, shackle, rattle, unnerve, mangle, hinder, impede, hobble, hamper

crouch

> flinch, cringe, shrink, wince, reel, recoil, retract, shudder, retreat, quiver, tremble, squirm

crown

> adorn, festoon, enthrone, coronate, endow, honor, anoint

crumble

> churn, crush, erode, grind, pulverize, pound, grate, smash, mash

crumple

> crinkle, rumple, crush, squash, smash, scrunch, crease

crush

> crumble, erode, squish, grind, pulverize, squash, trample, mash, crunch

cuddle

> nuzzle, touch, embrace, cling, clutch, cradle, grip, caress

dance

> twirl, whirl, flap, frolic, shimmy, gyrate, twist, trot, sashay, saunter, flit, prance, waltz, strut, swing

dangle

> bobble, flap, flaunt, drape, droop, flutter, unfold, toss, wag

dapple

> splatter, splash, shower, speckle, slosh, sprinkle, flick, streak, fleck, speck

Touch: Movement, Pressure, *and* Speed

dart
flit, flutter, dance, flicker, float, flurry, skate, waft, skim, soar, glide, bolt, fly

dash
scurry, hasten, bolt, burst, scuttle, gallop, hustle, scramble, rush, scamper, scoot, sprint, trot, dart, pell-mell

debilitate
cripple, sabotage, shackle, rattle, unnerve, paralyze, immobilize

decimate
destroy, obliterate, shatter, explode, ruin

deface
scar, blister, disfigure, distort, gash, welt, mar, mangle, sully

deft, deftness
adept, nimble, dexterous, proficient, skillful

delve
pry, dig, poke, wedge, root, ferret, wrench, wring, squeeze, extract, wrest, fish, rummage

dexterous
skilled, proficient, agile, deft, artful, masterful, adept, nimble, smooth, facile

diffuse (v)
spread, pour, scatter, disperse, strew, dissipate

disengage
unravel, extract, extricate, uncoil, untangle, detach, unfasten, untie, loosen

disentangle
extricate, extract, unravel, disengage, release, untangle, detach, unwind

disfigure, disfigured
mangled, misshaped, scarred, defaced, distorted, gashed, marred, maimed, deformed

dispel
quell, ease, allay, banish, dismiss

disperse, dispersed
spread, scatter, diffuse, unleash, fling, dissipate

dissipate
scatter, strew, unleash, fling, disperse

dither, dithering
falter, hesitate, vacillate, waver, stumble, stammer, oscillate, waffle, seesaw, fluctuate

dodge
balk, hedge, waver, wince, cringe, retract, quiver, flinch, swerve, bolt, lunge

dogged

tenacious, unflagging, determined, unyielding, persistent, firm, stubborn, hard-nosed, persevering

douse

submerge, wash, lather, drench, bathe, deluge, drown, dunk, swab, inundate, saturate, scrub, rinse, cleanse, splash

drag

tug, haul, heave, lug, yank, hitch, pull, tow

drain

ooze, drip, leach, seep, trickle, exude, emanate, emit, surge, siphon

drape

dangle, flap, flaunt, droop, flutter, unfold, toss, cloak, cover, wrap, swathe, adorn, envelope

drench

saturate, awash, cover, flood, overflow, submerge, bathe, deluge, douse, drown, dunk, imbue, infuse, inundate

dribble

percolate, gurgle, seep, trickle, drip, leak, sprinkle, ooze, squirt, spout

drift

float, waft, buoy, hover, sail, skim, glide, flit, dart, flutter, dance, flicker, flurry, skate, flap, soar

drip

ooze, drain, effuse, trickle, exude, emanate, emit, leach, secrete, dribble, leak, percolate, sprinkle, seep

droop

dangle, flap, drape, slump, sag, crumple, wilt, flop, wither, shrivel, shrink

drown

dunk, infuse, drench, deluge, douse, inundate, saturate, submerge

drub

pummel, bang, flail, flap, hammer, lash, patter, pound, thump, wallop

drudgery

toil, labor, monotony, sweat, chore, grind, struggle

drum

pulsate, flutter, hammer, patter, throb, thump, vibrate

dunk

douse, drown, drench, bathe, deluge, inundate, saturate, submerge

dwindle

wilt, wither, shrivel, shrink, droop, taper, wane, ebb, subside

effervesce
simmer, swish, fizzle, bubble, burble, rustle, froth, foam, lather

effuse
exude, emanate, emit, ooze, seep, discharge, gush, radiate, flow

elongate
stretch, strain, pull, lengthen, extend, elastic, spring, protract

emanate
exude, effuse, emit, leach, ooze, secrete, spread, radiate

embody
merge, breathe, encircle, embrace, meld, express, integrate

embolden
invigorate, spur, energize, rouse, stimulate, inspire

embrace
cling, encompass, cradle, cuddle, grip, caress, nuzzle, stroke, encircle, clutch

embroil
ensnare, trap, bait, entangle, enmesh, snare, entrap, snag

emergent
appearing, surfacing, developing, fledgling, budding, emanating, nascent, rising

emulsify
churn, blend, ferment, ripple, stew, whisk, soften

encompass
enclose, encircle, surround, corral, beset, envelop, cling, clutch, grip, confine

encumber
impede, hobble, restrain, fetter, bind, bridle, entangle, saddle, tie, tether, burden, strain

engrave
chisel, carve, mold, sculpt, shave, chip

enlarge
swell, expand, inflate, burst, bloat, balloon, distend

enmesh
trap, bait, entangle, ensnare, embroil, snare, entrap, snag

ensnare
enmesh, embroil, trap, entrap, bait, entangle, snare, snag

entangle
tether, tie, ensnare, trap, bait, enmesh, snag, fetter, bind, bridle, encumber, impede, embroil, snare, entrap, hobble, restrain, saddle

entrap
entangle, enmesh, snare, snag, ensnare, trap, bait, embroil

Thesaurus of the Senses

envelop
> enclose, encircle, engulf, swathe, encompass, shroud

erode
> crumble, crush, grind, pulverize, chafe, rub, scrape, abrade, graze

erupt
> spew, burst, cascade, eject, flare-up, outbreak, heave, pour, explode, surge, squirt, spurt, spit

etch
> imprint, impress, stamp, mark, trace, emboss, inscribe, brand

expand
> swell, inflate, burst, bloat, balloon, enlarge, distend

explode, explosive
> burst, shatter, blast, erupt, detonate, rupture, volatile, incendiary, fiery, charged, combustible, escalating

extract
> unravel, disengage, plumb, uncoil, unearth, extricate, untangle

extricate
> disentangle, extract, liberate, disengage, release

exude
> effuse, emanate, emit, leach, ooze, secrete, radiate, flow

evoke
> excite, stimulate, arouse, elicit, awaken, rouse, provoke

facile
> effortless, deft, flowing, smooth, proficient, dexterous

falter
> stumble, hesitate, reel, hedge, waver, shudder, vacillate, swerve, fluctuate, wobble, stammer

ferment
> churn, agitate, stew, fester, foam, brew, bubble, foment, froth, simmer, provoke

fetter
> bind, bridle, encumber, entangle, impede, restrain, saddle, tether, tie, shackle, constrain, hem in, hinder, leash, muzzle, yoke, hamper

fiddle
> tinker, dabble, fidget, finger, meddle, manipulate, twiddle

fidget
> fiddle, fret, twitch, jitter, wiggle, squirm, shuffle, wriggle, spasm

fish
> rummage, hunt, root, sift, cast, troll, bait, grope, fumble, ferret

Touch: Movement, Pressure, *and* Speed

fizz, fizzing
bubbling, burbling, effervesce, simmering, swishing, frothing

flag
gesture, beckon, wave, mime, signal, undulate, flap, salute, motion, hail, warn

flail, flailing
wave, thrash, pummel, drub, flap, lash, thump, wallop, twist, flog, writhe

flap, flapping
twirl, whirl, flick, shimmy, twist, dangle, bobble, drape, droop, flutter, unfold, toss, wag, sway

flaunt
dangle, parade, flourish, flap, drape, flutter, broadcast, boast

flick
twirl, swish, flap, jerk, pluck, whisk, snap, tap

flicker
flit, dart, flutter, dance, float, flurry, skate, hover, shimmer

flinch
crouch, recoil, shrink, wince, cringe, reel, retract, shudder, retreat, quiver, tremble, squirm, writhe, contort, twitch, grimace

fling
cast, heave, lob, sling, hurl, pitch, scatter, strew, unleash, disperse, catapult, launch, heave

flit
dart, flutter, dance, flicker, flurry, flap, wag, hover, whiz, hover, dash

float
waft, hover, sail, skim, soar, buoy, drift, glide, flit, dart, flutter, dance, flicker, flurry, skate

flood, flooded
drenched, awash, overflowing, submerged, teeming, soaked

flop
slump, droop, sag, crumple, dangle, flutter, tumble, flap

flounce
stomp, march, stamp, barge, clomp, clop, lurch, tramp, trudge, bounce

flounder
fumble, blunder, bungle, grabble, stagger, stumble, grope, thrash, struggle, muddle

flow, flowing
surge, cascade, stream, exude, gurgle, ebb, gush, rush, ooze, seep, course, trickle, spring, flood

fluctuate

shake, agitate, vibrate, oscillate, seesaw, veer, waver, undulate, vacillate, sway

flurry

flit, flutter, dance, flicker, float, skate, burst, whirl, swirl

flutter

flit, waft, buoy, drift, hover, sail, soar, glide, dart, dance, flicker, float, dangle, bobble, flap, unfold, toss, wag

fly

glide, soar, sail, breeze, hover, flutter, flap, wave, circle, drift, float, swoop, zip, zoom, whoosh

fondle

pet, cuddle, caress, grope, nuzzle, nestle, stroke, snuggle, paw

frolic

dance, twirl, whirl, shimmy, gyrate, twist, trot, sashay, saunter, prance, rollick

fry

scorch, sear, scald, singe, seethe, burn, broil, flare, parch, smolder

fumble, fumbling

blunder, bungle, grabble, stagger, stumble, grope, flounder, botch

fuse

coalesce, unite, merge, blend, mingle, weld

gallop

scurry, hasten, bolt, burst, scuttle, hustle, scramble, dash, rush, scamper, scoot, sprint, trot

gesture

beckon, flag, mime, nudge, wave, motion, nod, signal, bow, shrug, wink, sign

glance, glancing

ricochet, rebound, deflect, graze, skim, brush, scrape, sideswipe

glide

coast, drift, hover, sail, skate, soar, skim, float, waft, buoy, flit, dart, flutter, dance, flurry, fly

glom

stick, adhere, attach, grip, clinch, hook, snatch

goad

incite, provoke, prod, badger, tease, arouse, needle, spur

gouge

lacerate, scoop, chisel, dig, scrape, gash, burrow, claw

grab

capture, grasp, grip, seize, snatch, snag, yank, pluck, wrest

Touch: Movement, Pressure, *and* Speed

grapple
wrestle, struggle, tackle, confront, grab, grasp, clash, tackle, seize

grasp
grab, capture, grip, seize, snatch, snag, wrestle, clasp, hook

grate
scrape, shred, chisel, scour, scratch, scuff, lacerate, file, chafe, rub, abrade, grind, graze

graze
chafe, scrape, scratch, brush, abrade, shave, scuff, skim, glance, rub

grimace
flinch, cringe, shrink, reel, retract, tremble, twinge, pang, wince, writhe, contort, recoil, twitch, blanch, shudder, retreat, quiver, squirm

grind
crumble, crush, erode, squash, pulverize, abrade, scratch, scrape, mince, smash, grate, pound

grip
clamp, anchor, brace, clasp, clench, clutch, grasp, vise, embrace, snag, snatch, squeeze

grope
fumble, blunder, bungle, grabble, stagger, stumble, flounder, poke, pry, fish, finger

grovel, groveling
kneel, crawl, cower, snivel, cringe, stoop, slither, skulk, wriggle, crouch, creep

gyrate
dance, twirl, whirl, flap, flick, frolic, shimmy, twist, trot, sashay, saunter, spiral, spin, pirouette

hammer
pummel, drum, thump, pound, drub, bang, strike, trounce, whack

hamper
shackle, fetter, constrain, hem in, hinder, muzzle, strap, impede, hobble, cripple, saddle, leash

harness
mobilize, tame, yoke, channel, curb

harpoon
snare, capture, entrap, lasso, lure, rope, hook, ensnare, trap, bait, entangle, snag, enmesh, embroil

haul
drag, heave, lug, hitch, tow, load, hoist

headlong

steep, precipitous, hasty, abrupt, breakneck, rushing, heedless

heave

lug, haul, fling, surge, lob, hurl, hoist, drag, yank, hitch, cast, sling, pitch

hedge

dodge, shield, cushion, sidestep, waffle, shuffle, stall, vacillate, quibble

hem in

yoke, impede, hobble, hamper, shackle, fetter, constrain, tether, hinder, leash, muzzle, strap

hew

chop, sculpt, chisel, knead, carve, shape, engrave, mold, cleave, hack, weld

hinder

impede, hobble, hamper, shackle, fetter, anchor, tether, constrain, hem in, leash, muzzle, strap, cripple, thwart

hitch

tow, drag, tug, haul, lug, tether, harness, fasten, moor, chain, yoke

hobble

fetter, bind, bridle, encumber, entangle, restrain, saddle, shackle, tether, cripple, constrain, hinder, impede, hamper

hoist

boost, hike, lob, lift, heave, elevate

hook

lasso, lure, rope, harpoon, ensnare, bait, entangle, enmesh, snag, embroil, entrap, snare, capture

hover

float, waft, buoy, drift, sail, skim, glide, flit, dart, flutter, dance, flurry, skate, flicker, soar

hurl

fling, cast, heave, lob, sling, pitch, propel

impale

skewer, pierce, puncture, stab, spear, spike

impede

fetter, bind, bridle, encumber, entangle, hobble, restrain, saddle, shackle, tether, constrain, hinder, muzzle, hamper, cripple

impinge

intrude, encroach, invade, infringe, trespass, meddle

imprint

impression, stamp, mark, trace, emboss, etch, brand, emblem

Touch: Movement, Pressure, *and* Speed

improvise
invent, concoct, ad-lib, unscripted, makeshift

incinerate
burn, scorch, torch, cremate, destroy, ignite, combust

inert
stagnant, dormant, still, motionless, immobile

inexorable
relentless, incessant, unrelenting, unremitting, persistent, ceaseless, implacable, inflexible

inundate
drench, deluge, douse, drown, saturate, flood, engulf, overwhelm

jab
smack, slap, swat, thump, whack, stab, bat, wallop, drub, poke, lunge, nudge, thrust

jerk
tug, jolt, heave, yank, wrest, shake, lurch

jiggle
shake, agitate, vibrate, fluctuate, rattle, sway, shimmy, twitch, bob, bounce

jittery
trembling, quivering, quaking, convulsing, fidgety, shaking, twitchy, flinching, wincing

joggle
waver, wobble, bobble, jerk, shake, twitch, squirm, jiggle, jostle, rattle, jolt

jolt, jolting
tremor, shiver, tremble, quiver, shudder, quake, quaver, shock, twitch, rattle, agitate, electrify

jostle
rattle, shake, joggle, scramble, elbow, jab, press, push, nudge, knock

kindle
arouse, stimulate, stir, enliven, excite, ignite, stoke, torch, fan

knead
sculpt, squeeze, weld, twist, press, shape, ply, mold, rub

knock
whack, thump, bang, bash, clash, clobber, punch, wallop

lacerate
mangle, disfigure, shred, tear, scrape, slash, gash, lance, stab, cut, puncture, rip

lap, lapping
splashing, swishing, sloshing, licking, swallowing, rolling, rippling, slapping

lash
pummel, drub, flail, flap, hammer, pound, thump, wallop, whip, thrash

lasso
snare, capture, entrap, lure, rope, trap, hook, harpoon, ensnare, bait, entangle, enmesh, snag

lather
froth, foam, soap, scrub, douse, swab, cleanse

leach
exude, effuse, emanate, emit, ooze, secrete, infuse, drain, seep, percolate

leak
trickle, dribble, drip, percolate, seep, sprinkle

leash
shackle, fetter, anchor, tether, constrain, hem in, muzzle, strap, bridle, rein, restrain, yoke

limp
amble, crawl, stagger, totter, trudge, hobble, stumble, teeter

lob
fling, cast, heave, sling, hurl, pitch, flip, propel, launch

lug
drag, tug, haul, heave, yank, hitch, pull, tow, strain

lumber, lumbering
stumble, fumble, trudge, slog, plod, shuffle, lurch, tromp, stomp

lunge
pounce, spring, swoop, dive, descend, sweep, nosedive, thrust, jab, charge, surge

lurch
stumble, stagger, totter, pitch, careen, fumble, bumble, heave, seesaw, wobble, slide, sway

lure
bait, entangle, enmesh, embroil, snag, snare, capture, entrap, lasso, rope, trap, hook, harpoon, ensnare

maneuver
navigate, guide, finagle, jockey, pilot, wield, steer

mangle, mangled
cripple, disfigure, shred, rip, twist, contort, warp, wring, wrench, writhe, tear

maraud, marauding
loot, pillage, plunder, ransack, ravage, raid

maunder, maundering
roam, drift, stray, wander, amble, meander

Touch: Movement, Pressure, *and* Speed

meander, meandering
saunter, amble, idle, mosey, sidle, toddle, frolic, maunder, stroll, ramble, drift, traipse

meddle, meddling
pry, encroach, impose, intrude, invade, snoop, tamper

meld
merge, encircle, embrace, fuse, blend, mix, integrate, mingle

merge
meld, mingle, fuse, embrace, embody, encircle, unite, converge

mesh
tangle, knit, connect, engage, harmonize, lock

mime
beckon, flag, gesture, nudge, wave, mimic, imitate

mired
entangled, embroiled, ensnared, tangled, floundering, impeded, trapped

misstep
gaffe, blunder, stumble, miscue, topple, slip, bungle, faux pas

mold
chisel, carve, engrave, sculpt, knead, press, cast

muss
ruffle, crinkle, crumple, tousle, tangle, dishevel, rumple, churn, jumble, muddle

mutilate
shred, grind, mangle, pulverize, shave, split, tear, lacerate, maim, disfigure, rip

muzzle
shackle, fetter, anchor, tether, constrain, stifle, hinder, leash, strap, yoke, gag

needle
goad, badger, irk, taunt, bait, pester, nettle

nestle
burrow, cuddle, nuzzle, snuggle

nettle
rankle, vex, irk, provoke, gall, goad, pester, ruffle, rile

nimble
adept, agile, deft, dexterous, lithe, limber, graceful

nudge
gesture, nag, press, prod, touch, elbow, flag, nestle, jab

nuzzle
caress, embrace, stroke, burrow, cuddle, snuggle

obliterate
> destroy, decimate, shatter, explode, annihilate, eradicate, expunge

onslaught
> brunt, impact, force, shock, clash, attack

oscillate
> pulsate, drum, fluctuate, seesaw, teeter, throb, thump, vibrate

outstretched
> spreading, radiating, lengthened, extended, expanded, reaching

overflow, overflowing
> drenched, awash, flooded, submerged, teeming, swarming, spilling

pang
> throb, tremble, twinge, grimace, vibrate, thump, ache, stab

pantomime
> charade, imitate, gesture, mime, nod, salute, signal, shrug, wink

paralyze
> startle, petrify, cripple, frighten, perturb, stun, unnerve, demolish, incapacitate

patter
> scurry, flutter, tiptoe, tap, scuttle, trip, scamper

pell-mell
> rushed, headlong, swirling, recklessly, haphazardly, hastily, chaotic

penetrate
> pierce, stab, probe, puncture, spike, prick, suffuse, perforate

percolate
> bubble, dribble, gurgle, leach, seep, trickle, drip, ooze, leak

perfunctory
> mechanical, cursory, offhand, slipshod, indifferent, disengaged, halfhearted, automatic, superficial

permeate
> soak, diffuse, drench, infuse, inundate, saturate, immerse, pervade, steep, penetrate

pervade
> imbue, permeate, drench, steep, instill, infuse, inundate, saturate

pierce
> puncture, stab, skewer, impale, penetrate, spike, perforate, cut

pitch
> fling, cast, heave, lob, sling, hurl, toss, launch, propel

pivot
> twist, twirl, wring, swivel, spin, wriggle, dance, whirl, revolve

TOUCH: MOVEMENT, PRESSURE, *and* SPEED

plod, plodding
slog, amble, trample, trudge, drag, lumber, stomp, tread

pluck
flick, grab, joggle, wrest, yank, snatch, capture, seize, clutch, grip, grasp, snag

plunge
swoop, dive, descend, sweep, nosedive, lunge, plummet, tumble, hurtle, sink

poke
prod, prick, probe, pry, stab, jab, dig, nudge, thrust

pounce
lunge, leap, dive, attack, strike, surge, spring

pound
pummel, bang, drub, hammer, lash, patter, thump, wallop, bash

press
nudge, nag, prod, knead, push, squeeze, squash, jam, crush, clasp

prick
poke, pierce, probe, pry, stab, pierce, puncture, drill, perforate

probe
poke, prick, pry, penetrate, pierce, dig, prod, sift

prod
press, push, nudge, nag, jab, rouse, goad, poke, dig, elbow, butt

propel
catapult, fling, launch, blast, spur, cast, shoot, thrust, throw, hurl, project

pry
delve, dig, poke, wedge, twist, wrench, wring, squeeze, extract, wrest

prying
invasive, snooping, intrusive, meddling, pushy, nosy

pulsate
quiver, fluctuate, heave, oscillate, throb, thump, vibrate, pulse, drum, beat, heave, surge

pulse
throb, tremble, twinge, bang, vibrate, thump, quiver, twitch, surge, thud, pound

pulverize
smash, grind, shatter, crush, crumble, pound, pulp, mash, mince

pummel
drub, hammer, lash, pound, thump, wallop, batter, thrash, flog, pelt, trounce

punch
whack, thump, bang, bash, clobber, knock, wallop, blast, bonk, smash, strike, trounce

puncture

claw, rip, stab, tear, poke, skewer, pierce, deflate, prick, rupture, lance, nick, slit, perforate, slash

purge

cleanse, expel, freshen, scrub, spruce, purify, eradicate, expunge, oust

purify

cleanse, distill, filter, refine, clarify, purge

pushy

overbearing, prying, intrusive, meddling, aggressive, bumptious, forceful, offensive, domineering

quail

flinch, recoil, cower, cringe, tremble, shake, shrink, shudder, wince, quake

quake

bobble, convulse, fidget, quiver, shake, tremble, twitch, tremor, shiver, shudder, sway, wobble, recoil

quaver

tremble, quiver, shudder, quake, tremor, twitch, rattle, oscillate, wobble, sway, shake

quicken

arouse, excite, awaken, kindle, enliven, electrify, invigorate, revitalize, revive, stimulate, stir

quiver

shiver, shudder, quaver, tremor, quake, shake, tremble, twitch

rankle

vex, irk, annoy, provoke, gall, harass, inflame, nettle

rattle

unnerve, fluster, agitate, ruffle, unsettle, befuddle, bewilder, roil, disquiet, shake, spasm, sway, shudder, vibrate, shiver, jiggle

recoil

balk, dodge, retreat, tremble, waver, wince, repulse, cringe, retract, shudder, quiver, flinch, swerve, squirm, reel

reel

cringe, recoil, retract, retreat, quiver, flinch, wince, swerve, squirm, tremble, shudder

restrain

fetter, bind, bridle, encumber, impede, hobble, saddle, tether, tie, subdue, stifle, shackle

retract

retreat, recede, shrink, recoil, ebb, withdraw, wane

retreat
recoil, shrink, retract, reel, recoil, relinquish, recede, vacate

ricochet
boomerang, backfire, backlash, recoil, rebound, deflect, bounce, glance

rip
shred, tear, wring, claw, poke, puncture, stab, split, wrench

ripple
churn, flutter, swirl, roll, blend, ruffle, whisk, wrinkle, splash, sway, swell, surge, undulate, wave

rock
sway, pitch, reel, totter, wobble, lurch, careen, falter, jiggle, seesaw, shake

roil
rattle, unsettle, agitate, ruffle, shake, vex, disturb

roll
ripple, churn, flutter, swirl, ruffle, whisk, revolve, circle, rock, undulate, unfold, spin

rollick, rollicking
prance, caper, frolic, romp, lively, spirited, exuberant, playful

rummage
root, fish, hunt, sift, rifle, poke, comb, scour, delve, ferret, ransack

rush
scurry, hasten, burst, scuttle, gallop, hustle, scramble, dash, sprint, bolt, trot, surge

sabotage
cripple, debilitate, wreck, ruin, hamper, torpedo, subvert

saddle
fetter, bind, bridle, encumber, entangle, impede, hobble, restrain, tether, tie

sail
float, waft, buoy, drift, hover, skim, soar, glide, dart, flutter, dance, flurry, skate, fly, breeze, flap, wave

salvage
recover, rescue, reclaim, preserve, recoup

sashay
dance, twirl, whirl, frolic, shimmy, gyrate, twist, saunter, sway, glide, prance

saunter
amble, meander, mosey, sidle, toddle, whirl, shimmy, gyrate, trot, sashay, stroll

scamper
bolt, burst, scuttle, gallop, scurry, hasten, hustle, scramble, dash, rush, trot, scoot

scatter
strew, unleash, fling, disperse, dissipate, spread, disband, scramble

scoot
bolt, gallop, dash, scuttle, scramble, rush, scamper, scurry, hasten, hustle, burst, sprint, trot

scour
rub, scrape, buff, polish, rummage, root, comb, ransack, rummage, ferret out

scramble
bolt, hustle, scoot, burst, rush, scamper, scuttle, gallop, scurry, hasten, sprint, dash

scrape
grate, chisel, scour, file, scuff, abrade, scratch, grind, chafe, rub, graze

scratch
gouge, scuff, scrape, chafe, graze, abrade, grind, corrode, rub

scrawl
scribble, doodle, scratch, squiggle, jot

scribble
scratch, squiggle, scrawl, doodle

scrub
wash, bathe, refresh, lather, douse, rinse, cleanse, wipe, freshen, purge, spruce, swab

scuff
scratch, grind, rub, graze, chip, scrape, grate, chisel, scour, file, chafe, abrade

sculpt
chisel, knead, weld, hew, carve, shape, engrave, mold, shave, cast

scurry
gallop, hustle, scramble, hasten, burst, scuttle, dash, rush, scamper, scoot, sprint, trot, bolt

scuttle
scoot, sprint, scurry, hasten, bolt, burst, gallop, hustle, scramble, dash, rush, scamper

seep
ooze, leach, trickle, effuse, secrete, dribble, bleed, drip, sweat, soak, bubble

seize
grab, grasp, snatch, pounce, clutch, nab, grip, clasp, pluck

shackle
fetter, anchor, tether, constrain, hinder, leash, muzzle, hobble, hamper, cripple, yoke, chain

Touch: Movement, Pressure, *and* Speed

shake
agitate, vibrate, fluctuate, jiggle, shiver, shudder, rattle, sway, rock

shave
chisel, carve, engrave, mold, sculpt, trim, shear, graze, strip

shelter
cradle, shield, harbor, enclose, guard, screen, cushion, insulate, ward

shimmy
dance, twirl, whirl, gyrate, twist, amble, sashay, saunter, wobble

shower
splatter, splash, dapple, slosh, sprinkle, inundate, pour, spray, mist, swamp, deluge, flood

shred
grind, mangle, rip, pulverize, shave, split, tear, mutilate, lacerate, fray, strip, tatter

shudder
shiver, tremble, quiver, quake, quaver, tremor, twitch, cringe, reel, recoil, retract, flinch, wince, swerve, squirm

shuffle
amble, clop, hobble, lumber, lurch, scuffle, stagger, trudge, scrape, jumble

sidle
saunter, creep, sneak, slink, inch, edge, amble

sift
root, strain, rummage, comb, probe, winnow, sieve, trawl, filter, fish

skate
flit, dart, flutter, dance, float, flurry, glide, coast, drift, hover, sail, soar, skim

skewer
pierce, puncture, impale, stab, prick, cut, bore, slash

skim
float, waft, buoy, drift, hover, soar, glide, flit, dart, flutter, flicker, flurry, skate, sail

skulk, skulking
creep, prowl, slink, snoop, crouch, lurk, roam, sneak

slap
whack, bat, wallop, smack, swat, thump, jab, drub

slather
smear, spread, daub, rub, wipe, smooth, coat

slump
flop, droop, sag, crumple, shrink, plummet, slide, slouch, tumble, topple, wilt, collapse

smack

slap, swat, thump, whack, bat, wallop, jab, drub, swipe

smash

clobber, bang, bash, blast, bonk, punch, strike, trounce, whack

snag

rip, entangle, enmesh, ensnare, trap, bait, embroil, snare, entrap, hook, tear

snare

entrap, lasso, enmesh, rope, trap, hook, harpoon, ensnare, bait, snag, entangle, capture, lure, embroil

snatch

capture, grab, seize, clutch, pluck, grasp, grip, snag, wrest, yank, nab

snuggle

nestle, burrow, cuddle, nuzzle, caress

soar, soaring

float, waft, buoy, drift, hover, skim, glide, flutter, dance, skate, sail, spiral

spasm

shudder, twitch, tremor, outburst, frenzy, convulsion, eruption, shiver, shake

spatter

spray, splash, splatter, slosh, sprinkle, flick, douse

spew, spewing

burst, cascade, eject, erupt, flare-up, outbreak, heave, pour, spit, surge, squirt, spurt

spill

flood, overflow, swarm, stream, teem, splash, slosh, dribble, pour, splatter, squirt

spin

twist, wring, swivel, pivot, whirl, twirl, whorl, whisk, flutter

splash

dapple, shower, speckle, sprinkle, splatter, flick, douse, spatter, slosh, strew, slosh

splatter

splash, dapple, shower, speckle, sprinkle, flick, spatter, douse, spray, slosh

sprinkle

splatter, splash, dapple, shower, speckle, slosh, flick, pepper, spray, strew, mist, scatter

sprint

scurry, hasten, bolt, burst, scuttle, gallop, hustle, scramble, dash, rush, scamper, scoot, trot

spruce

cleanse, clean, freshen, purge, scrub, tidy, primp

spurt
surge, squirt, spew, burst, cascade, eject, erupt, heave, pour, spit

squiggle
scrawl, scribble, doodle, scratch, wiggle, curl

squirm
cringe, reel, recoil, retract, shudder, retreat, quiver, flinch, wince, swerve, uneasy, tremble

stab
puncture, poke, claw, chip, pierce, jab, prick, spike, spear

stagger
fumble, careen, lurch, stumble, teeter, sway, zigzag, waver, wobble, totter

startle
alarm, arouse, paralyze, frighten, perturb, stun, unnerve, shock, jolt

stave
avert, fend off, prevent, foil, thwart, ward, hinder, stymie, forestall

steady
brace, quell, subdue, balance, secure, bolster, buttress, gird, prop

steep
infuse, inundate, saturate, permeate, imbue, pervade, instill, douse, diffuse, soak, drench, absorb, immerse

stew
churn, agitate, blend, emulsify, ferment, ripple, whisk

still
dormant, fixed, undisturbed, immobile

stimulate
excite, kindle, arouse, stir, enliven, provoke, thrill, spark, trigger, electrify

sting
tingle, jab, prick, bite, pierce, stab, poke, burn

stir
arouse, stimulate, enliven, excite, kindle, provoke, thrill, vex, rustle, agitate, spur, propel

stomp
amble, barge, clump, clop, flounce, scuffle, shuffle, stagger, tramp, trudge

strap
shackle, fetter, anchor, tether, leash, muzzle, harness, yoke

strew, strewn
scatter, unleash, fling, disperse, dissipate, litter, toss, sprinkle

strike

clobber, bang, punch, smash, trounce, whack, lash, collide, knock, pummel, hammer, pound

stroke

caress, embrace, nuzzle, soothe, pet, comfort, brush, paw, fondle

struggle

grapple, fiddle, wrestle, tackle, fumble, blunder, bungle, flounder, botch

stumble

bungle, stagger, flounder, wrestle, grapple, fiddle, tackle, blunder, botch, fumble

stun

startle, alarm, arouse, frighten, perturb, unnerve, shock, paralyze, daze, overpower daze

stunt, stunted

hamper, hinder, restrict, impede, curb, thwart, bridle, constrain

stupor

trance, rapture, musing, reverie, daze, bewilderment, swoon

stymie

obstruct, hinder, hamper, thwart, crimp, confound, foil, constrain, restrain

submerge

drench, bathe, deluge, douse, drown, inundate, saturate, cover, flood, dunk

surge

erupt, spew, burst, cascade, eject, flare-up, outbreak, heave, pour, spurt, rush

swaddle, swaddled

swathe, cover, wrap, sheathe, bind

swat

smack, slap, thump, whack, bat, wallop, jab, drub, slug, knock, paw, crush

swathe, swathed

swaddle, wrap, cover, bind, drape, sheathe

sway

shake, swing, vibrate, fluctuate, jiggle, shiver, shudder, rattle, roll, wobble, lurch

swell

expand, inflate, burst, bloat, balloon, enlarge, distend, bulge, surge, fatten, billow, intensify, puff

swerve

veer, lurch, weave, careen, totter, stray, sidestep, zigzag

swirl

ripple, churn, flutter, blend, whisk, eddy, billow, spiral, revolve, flow, spin, twirl, whirl, snake

Touch: Movement, Pressure, *and* Speed

swish
effervesce, rustle, bubble, burble, hiss, whistle, rush

swivel
twist, contort, twirl, wring, spin, pivot, wiggle, whirl, flail, revolve, swing

swoon
faint, tremble, quiver, collapse, weaken, fade

swoop
plunge, dive, descend, sweep, nosedive, lunge, pitch, slide

tackle
grapple, wrestle, grab, seize, block, halt

tamp
ram, cram, wedge, jam, shove, squeeze, crush, squash

tear
claw, puncture, rip, stab, mangle, lacerate, shred, sever, slash, cut

teem, teeming
abound, bristle, bustle, flood, overflow, swarm, stream, spill

teeter, teetering
shaky, flapping, quivering, jittery, tottering, wobbly, twitchy

tether
anchor, bridle, chain, harness, leash, restrain, shackle, yoke, fetter, bind, saddle, tie

thrash
pound, thump, hammer, writhe, jerk, flail, trounce, pummel, batter

thump
pulsate, drum, hammer, oscillate, patter, throb, vibrate, pound, thrash

thwart
obstruct, hinder, hamper, stymie, dodge, impede, curb

toddle
saunter, amble, idle, meander, mosey, sidle, teeter, totter

toss
dangle, bobble, flap, flaunt, drape, droop, flutter, unfold, wag, fling, lob, pitch, hurl

totter, tottering
limp, amble, stagger, trudge, teeter, lurch, careen, stammer, sway, zigzag, weave

tousle
ruffle, crinkle, crumple, muss, tangle, dishevel, rumple

traipse
amble, stroll, roam, trudge, trek, plod, wander, shuffle

trammel

    barricade, impede, shackle, fetter, obstruct, constrain, hamper, bridle, entrap

trap

    enmesh, embroil, ensnare, bait, entangle, snare, entrap, snag, hook, ambush, entangle

trickle

    dribble, drip, leak, percolate, seep, sprinkle, ooze

trigger

    provoke, activate, precipitate, launch, instigate, stir

trot

    frolic, shimmy, gyrate, twist, sashay, saunter, scamper, scurry, scuttle

trounce

    clobber, bang, bash, blast, bonk, punch, smash, strike, whack, drub, whip, thrash

trudge

    limp, amble, crawl, stagger, totter, prod, slog, stumble, tromp, wade

twiddle

    doodle, fiddle, twist, jiggle, twirl, fidget, putter, tinker

twirl

    gyrate, twist, swirl, whirl, wind, wring, swivel, spin, pivot, wriggle, squirm, flap, dance, flail

twist

    contort, mangle, twirl, warp, wring, swivel, spin, pivot, wriggle, squirm, wrench, whirl, flail, writhe

upsurge

    gush, outpouring, surge, groundswell, escalation, upswing, torrent, cascade, burst, rush

unfaltering

    unswerving, steady, undivided, unbroken, unflagging, focused, intent, determined, unwavering, tireless, unfailing

unflagging

    unbroken, unswerving, unbending, direct, focused, inexhaustible, unceasing, unrelenting, tireless

unfold

    flap, flutter, spread, unfurl, unravel, uncurl, unwind, fan out

unfurl

    unfold, unravel, unwind, flap, spread

unleash

    scatter, strew, fling, disperse, dissipate, vent, discharge, unchain

unnerve
cripple, debilitate, sabotage, shackle, rattle, startle, arouse, flinch, perturb, stun

unravel
disengage, extract, plumb, uncoil, unearth, untangle, unwind, disentangle, unsnarl

unswerving
undivided, unbroken, unflagging, focused, unwavering, determined, unfaltering, steady, intent

untangle
extricate, extract, unravel, disengage, untwist, disentangle, unknot, uncoil, untie

unwavering
unswerving, unfaltering, unshaken, steadfast, unflappable, sustained, unyielding, constant

vibrate
pulsate, drum, flutter, hammer, oscillate, throb, thump, tremble, twinge, pulse

vise
clamp, anchor, clasp, clench, clutch, grasp, grip

waffle
waver, dither, falter, wobble, vacillate, oscillate, hem and haw

waft
flutter, flit, drift, hover, sail, skim, puff, glide, dance, flicker, float, flap

wag
dangle, flap, drape, flutter, unfold, toss, fly, jangle, whirl, flop

wallop
hammer, pummel, bang, drub, pound, thump, punch, belt, slam

wandering
meandering, roving, nomadic, winding, roaming, drifting, wayfaring, vagabond, straying, vagrant

warp, warped
twist, contort, mangle, wring, wrench, writhe, distort, deform

waver, wavering
quake, fidget, falter, quiver, shake, tremble, twitch, wobble, waffle, vacillate, hedge, teeter

wayfaring
meandering, roving, nomadic, winding, drifting

whack
thump, bang, bash, clash, clobber, knock, punch, wallop

whip
lash, thrash, goad, provoke, flog, rouse, agitate

whir, whirring
hum, fly, buzz, revolve, flutter, swish, vibrate

whirl, whirling
twirl, spin, flap, ripple, dart, whorl, whisk, flutter, swirl, pivot, revolve, circle, surge, whir, bustle

whirlwind
tornado, hurricane, vortex, cyclone, twister, lightning, whirlwind, eddy

whisk
churn, dart, whip, flick, sweep, hurtle, snatch, pluck, bolt, race, gallop, zoom, scuttle, scurry, zip

wiggle
squirm, twitch, twist, writhe, wriggle, jiggle, flail

wince
writhe, contort, twitch, blanch, grimace, flinch, crouch, cringe, recoil, shrink, retract, shudder, retreat, quiver, tremble, squirm, reel

wobble
shake, flop, teeter, sway, totter, rock, sway, seesaw, quiver, careen, tremble, waver

wrench
twist, wring, jerk, tug, yank, rip, wrest, dislodge, heave

wrestle
grapple, fiddle, struggle, tackle, fumble, scuffle, tangle, stumble, tussle, grab

wriggle
twist, twirl, wring, swivel, pivot, squirm, wiggle, writhe, flail, slither

wring
twist, tear, claw, rip, wrench, squeeze, scrunch, knead, wrest

writhe
contort, recoil, twitch, wince, blanch, grimace, flinch, cringe, reel, retract, shudder, retreat, quiver, tremble, squirm

yank
pluck, flick, grab, joggle, wrest, snatch, wrench, seize

yoke
shackle, fetter, anchor, tether, constrain, hem in, hinder, leash, muzzle, strap

TASTE

An apple is an excellent thing — until you have tried a peach.
—George du Maurier, illustrator and novelist

FLAVORS - MOUTHFEEL *and* TEXTURE -
EATING, CHEWING, *and* FOOD

Taste is strongly connected to our instincts and emotions—our innermost pleasures, desires, and dislikes. Taste words, such as *bittersweet, spicy, sour, juicy,* can describe our experiences and memories in flavorful terms. We may find some situations *unpalatable* or *distasteful,* or they leave a *bad taste* in our mouths or have a peculiar *aftertaste,* while we find other experiences delicious or intoxicating. We may hunger for excitement or relish adventure—and salivate in anticipation.

Taste is a blend of flavors, textures, temperatures, smells, and even ambiance. This explains why some things taste better with the right mood or tempting aroma. The five basic tastes—*sweet, sour, salty, bitter, savory*—combine into an astonishing array of flavors of varying intensity, from *floral* to *acrid* to *tangy,* to entice our palates. The texture and mouthfeel of food—whether something is *creamy, rubbery, runny,* or *crispy*—profoundly affect our taste and enjoyment of food. Smell also intensifies and colors our experience of taste, so much so that taste is inextricably tied to smell.

Curiously, sense of taste is also connected to personal aesthetics and decorum. We call some things *tasteful,* when we find them pleasing and stylish, or *tasteless, unsavory,* or *in bad taste* when they insult our sensibilities. We may think someone has *good taste* in selecting cars or belt buckles, or *poor taste* in their choice of lampshades or lawn ornaments—a highly subjective assessment or perhaps an *acquired taste.*

The taste words in this book are divided into subcategories to help readers reflect on different facets of this intriguing sense: the range and subtleties of flavors; the mouthfeel and textures of foods; and the many words to describe eating, drinking, and chewing. Bon appétit!

FLAVORS

acerbic
sour, bitter, sharp, biting, caustic, astringent, tart, acrid

acidic
sour, sharp, burning, caustic, vinegary

acrid
acidic, bitter, sharp, tart, sour, biting, pungent, stinging, burning, harsh

aftertaste
finish, sensation, impression, zing, punch

aged
mellow, rich, flavorful, softened, ripe, soft, rounded, smooth

almond
nutty, toasted, sweet, delicate

apple
fruity, sweet, tart, berry, plummy, bright, sour, mellow

astringent
harsh, sharp, acerbic, acid, dry, cutting, biting, bitter

banana
fruity, sweet, tropical, starchy, luscious

beefy
meaty, gamy, fleshy, savory, hearty, pungent, salty

berry
sweet, fruity, plummy, sugary, mellow, rich, tart

bitter
acerbic, pungent, sharp, harsh, acrid

Taste: Flavors

bittersweet
bitter, rich, coffee, burnt, sweet, chocolate

blackened
seared, scalded, burnt, crispy, scorched

bland
flavorless, tasteless, flat, dull, insipid, mushy, weak, watery

bouquet
floral, perfumy, fruity, flowery, spicy

brackish
salty, briny, piquant, saline, salted

bright
lively, flavorful, zesty, sparkling, effervescent, bubbly, intense

briny
salty, brackish, seaweed, saline, kelp, dulse

brisk
refreshing, fresh, crisp, lively, bracing, invigorating, stimulating

burnt
crispy, blackened, toasted, scorched, seared, charred, scalded, singed

butterscotch
buttery, creamy, sweet, caramel, toffee, candied, sugary, luscious

buttery
creamy, smooth, luscious, caramel, smooth, rich, milky, velvety, gooey, fluffy

candied
sweet, honey, syrupy, sugary, sticky, grainy, sugar-coated

caramel
candied, buttery, creamy, honey, syrupy, sweet, toffee, bonbon

caustic
acidic, biting, burning, scalding, cutting, pungent, tart, corrosive, acrid

cheesy
creamy, melting, sharp, rich, buttery, gooey, luscious, nutty, salty

cherry
berry, juicy, sweet, sour, perfumy, fruity

chocolaty
cocoa, sweet, rich, buttery, creamy, bitter, milky, bittersweet

cinnamon
spicy, apple, sweet, allspice, aromatic

citrus, citrusy
> lemony, acidic, sour, citron, orange, bergamot, zesty, pungent, tangerine, lively, crisp, bright

cloying
> sugary, syrupy, oversweet, nauseating, gooey, honey, sappy

cocoa
> sweet, rich, bitter, bittersweet, mocha, chocolate

coffee
> bitter, burnt, toasted, mocha, chocolate, espresso

creamy
> buttery, smooth, silky, luscious, whipped, velvety, milky

crisp
> fresh, cool, refreshing, invigorating, bracing, brisk, citrus

delectable
> delicious, luscious, mouth-watering, tasty, succulent, scrumptious, sumptuous, toothsome

delicate
> soft, subtle, exquisite, silky, tender, mild, smooth

delicious
> delectable, flavorful, scrumptious, mouth-watering, lip-smacking, enticing, luscious, tempting

dirt
> sandy, muddy, gritty, grainy, earthy, clayey

dull
> bland, insipid, flat, stale, muddy, plain, flavorless

earthy
> grassy, mineral, muddy, dirt, mossy, robust, rustic, savory

eggy
> creamy, velvety, rich, buttery, fluffy

enticing
> delicious, luscious, tempting, delectable, flavorful, scrumptious, mouth-watering, lip-smacking

exotic
> spicy, flavorful, fiery, zesty, piquant, tangy, enticing

exquisite
> delicate, luxurious, intense, rich, subtle

fatty
> greasy, oily, buttery, slippery, gristly, lardy, unctuous

fermented
sour, alcoholic, fizzy, hoppy, salty, briny, overripe

fetid
rotten, rancid, rank, putrid, stinking, fusty, repulsive, revolting, rotting, foul

fiery
spicy, hot, burning, scorching, biting, sharp, piercing

fishy
meaty, gamy, fleshy, seaweed, kelp

flat
dull, bland, flavorless, stale, weak

flavorful, flavorous
lively, zesty, pleasing, spicy, rich, tasty, savory, delectable, luscious, tempting, pungent, zingy

flavorless
dull, flat, bland, insipid, tasteless

fleshy
meaty, gamy, plump, beefy, savory

floral
flowery, perfumy, grassy, bouquet

flowery
floral, perfumy, fruity, bouquet

fresh
cool, crisp, brisk, invigorating, raw, lively, ripened, flavorful

fruity
sweet, tropical, berry, plum, citrus, apple, cherry

full-bodied
rich, robust, flavorful, hearty, concentrated, heady, heavy, potent, bold

fusty
musty, stale, dusty, moldy, damp, mildewy, fetid

gamy
meaty, beefy, fleshy, pungent, strong, tainted

garlicky
oniony, savory, pungent, sharp

gingery
peppery, candied, sugary, bold, sharp

glazed
candied, sugary, syrupy, gooey, honey, confectionery

grassy
herbal, oniony, mossy, earthy, botanical

gristle, gristly
fatty, oily, fleshy, meaty, fibrous, sinewy, tough

heady
intoxicating, stimulating, alcoholic, potent, powerful, robust

hearty
robust, rich, flavorful, satisfying, filling

herbal, herbaceous
zesty, spicy, peppery, tangy, grassy, floral

honey, honeyed
sweet, candied, syrupy, sugary, toffee, caramel

hot
fiery, spicy, scalding, scorching, burning, zesty, seasoned

insipid
bland, dull, flavorless, flat, tasteless, stale, watery

intoxicating
heady, potent, alcoholic, strong, bracing

invigorating
crisp, fresh, refreshing, quench, lively, sparkling

jammy
fruity, floral, bouquet, plummy, berry, sweet

jejune
dry, unnourishing, dull, insipid, meager, bland

juicy, juiciness
mouth-watering, succulent, ripe, moist, syrupy, pulpy

lemony
sour, citrus, citron, piquant, sharp

licorice
anise, fennel, spicy, aromatic, candied

lip-smacking
delectable, flavorful, scrumptious, mouth-watering, delicious, sumptuous, enticing

liquor
stiff, bracing, smooth, alcoholic, malty, whiskey, elixir

lively
bright, sparkling, refreshing, crisp, bracing, fresh, invigorating, zesty

luscious
creamy, buttery, silky, smooth, delectable, sumptuous, toothsome, succulent, appetizing

malty
alcoholic, fizzy, hoppy, yeasty, sudsy, foamy

meaty
fleshy, thick, plump, robust, savory, hearty, beefy, pungent

medicinal
menthol, metallic, plastic, off-flavor, aftertaste, bitter, artificial

mellow
rich, smooth, soft, soothing, aged, full, round

melting
creamy, smooth, velvety, silky, buttery

menthol
cool, minty, crisp, invigorating, wintergreen, peppermint, fresh

metallic
metal, copper, mineral, medicinal

mildewy
stale, damp, dusty, moldy, musty, funky, rotten, fusty

milky
creamy, thick, buttery, rich, velvety

mineral
complex, salty, earthy, coppery, rich, smooth

minty
cool, crisp, invigorating, menthol, wintergreen, peppermint

mocha
coffee, bitter, burnt, toasted, chocolate, espresso, cocoa

moldy
mildewy, musty, stale, damp

mouth-watering
delectable, juicy, scrumptious, succulent, luscious, savory, tempting

muddy
earthy, gritty, sandy, dirty, grainy, soggy, swampy

mushroom
rich, earthy, muddy, savory, umami, pungent, meaty

mustard
pungent, sharp, spicy, oniony, garlicky, sour, bitter, zippy

musty
stale, fusty, damp, moldy, skunky, dusty, mildewy

nectar
sap, honey, tonic, juice, elixir, ambrosia

nutty
crunchy, almondy, toasted, buttery, crispy, sweet

oaky
woodsy, woody, smoky, complex, rich, bitter

off-flavor
stale, contaminated, rotten, funky, unpleasant, tainted, musty

oily
greasy, fatty, unctuous, buttery, creamy

oniony
garlicky, savory, pungent, sour

overpowering
pungent, spicy, intense, acrid, robust, potent

overripe
astringent, rotten, spoiled, rotting, sour, rancid

oyster
briny, salty, savory, umami, meaty, clam, shrimp, seaweed, fishy

palatable
tasty, flavorful, pleasing, agreeable, appetizing, enticing, tempting, edible

penetrating
stiff, sharp, biting, piercing, potent, intense, bracing

peppermint
menthol, cool, minty, crisp, invigorating, wintergreen, fresh

peppery
spicy, savory, fiery, gingery, pungent, zesty, hot, stinging

perfumed, perfumy
floral, bouquet, flowery, fragrant

pickled
salty, spicy, fermented, cured, vinegary, briny

piney
wintergreen, grassy, floral, perfumy, rosemary, sharp

piquant
spicy, tangy, savory, zesty, rich, sharp, peppery

plummy
fruity, floral, raisiny, wine, bouquet, jammy

potent
heady, intoxicating, pungent, intense, penetrating

pungent
bitter, piquant, sharp, spicy, overpowering, peppery, stinging, tangy, zesty

putrefied
rotten, decayed, decomposed, stinking, festering, spoiled

putrid
rotten, rancid, rank, fetid, foul, rotting

rancid
fetid, spoiled, putrid, rank, moldy, rotting, curdled, sour

rank
rotten, rancid, putrid, fetid, noxious, sour, tainted, foul

raw
fresh, uncooked, unrefined, natural, lively, energizing, robust

refreshing
lively, brisk, bracing, invigorating, quenching, sharp, sparkling, bright, crisp

rich
flavorful, velvety, robust, juicy, savory, succulent, full-bodied, nourishing

ripe
sweet, succulent, luscious, moist, tender, juicy

robust
bold, flavorful, rich, full-bodied, potent

rotten
putrid, rancid, rank, fetid, rotting, moldy, foul, sour

saccharine
sugary, cloying, oversweet, artificial, medicinal, syrupy, sappy

salty
piquant, spicy, savory, zesty, briny, pungent

sapid
delectable, ambrosial, pleasing, engaging, tasty, zesty, palatable, enticing

sapor
flavor, taste, essence, zest, extract, savor, tang, zing

savory
piquant, succulent, zingy, tangy, umami, pleasing, pungent, spicy, zesty, enticing

scrumptious
delicious, luscious, mouth-watering, tasty, succulent, delectable, tempting, enticing

seared
burnt, charred, crispy, blackened, toasted, scorched

seasoned
flavorful, rich, zesty, spicy, savory, tasty

seaweed
fishy, piscine, briny, kelp, salty, saline

sharp
tart, tangy, astringent, sour, pungent, intense

silky
creamy, smooth, velvety, buttery, delicate, silken

skunky
musty, swampy, bitter, mossy, moldy, dank, musty, perfumy, tainted

soapy
sudsy, bubbly, tallow, waxy, foamy, frothy

soft
chewy, delicate, doughy, buttery, fluffy, velvety, mellow

sour
acerbic, lemony, vinegary, tart, sharp, puckering, rotten

sparkling
effervescent, lively, bright, invigorating, refreshing, crisp

spicy
fiery, hot, exotic, tangy, rich, pungent, peppery, savory, piquant, zesty, stinging, seasoned

stale
dry, musty, rancid, fusty, flat, moldy, sour

succulent
tender, delectable, delicious, luscious, mouth-watering, toothsome, juicy

sugary
sweet, syrupy, candied, honey, gooey, sticky, grainy, toffee, caramel, oversweet, confectionery

sulfur
rotten egg, metallic, skunky, rubber

sumptuous
luscious, delectable, succulent, rich, appetizing, exquisite

swampy
mossy, spongy, damp, marshy, muddy, skunky, moldy

sweet
sugary, syrupy, honey, gooey, candied, caramel, toffee

Taste: Flavors

syrupy
sugary, sweet, sticky, gooey, honey, gummy, sappy

tallow
waxy, soapy, sudsy, fatty

tangy
spicy, piquant, rich, sharp, pungent, peppery, zesty, salty, seasoned, tart

tart
sharp, lemony, vinegary, sour, biting, acidic

tasteless
flavorless, flat, dull, insipid, bland, weak, watery, stale

tasty
delicious, luscious, mouth-watering, delectable, succulent, flavorful, enticing, tempting

tempting
enticing, delicious, luscious, delectable, flavorful, scrumptious, mouth-watering, tasty, lip-smacking

tender
succulent, ripe, juicy, moist, delicate, soft

toasted, toasty
buttery, crusty, yeasty, crispy, nutty, roasted

toffee
buttery, creamy, sweet, caramel, butterscotch

tonic
refreshing, restorative, soothing, juice, nectar, stimulant, elixir, remedy, nourishing

toothsome
succulent, delectable, delicious, luscious, mouth-watering, savory, palatable, rich, scrumptious, tempting

turpentine
lacquer, metallic, synthetic, chemical, pungent, sharp, burning, caustic, fuming

umami
savory, salty, piquant, tangy, mushroom, pungent

unappetizing
unappealing, undesirable, insipid, unpalatable, vapid, unsavory, repulsive

vanilla
sweet, fragrant, creamy, buttery, toffee, caramel

vapid
insipid, jejune, tasteless, flavorless, flat, dull, bland, weak, empty

velvety
creamy, smooth, buttery, silky, luscious, whipped, rich, silken

vinegary
sour, acidic, sharp, briny, pickled, fermented

wine
sweet, dry, fruity, liquor, alcoholic, bouquet, oaky, intoxicating

wintergreen
cool, minty, crisp, invigorating, menthol, peppermint, piney

woody
grassy, earthy, mossy, stringy, oaky

yeasty
hoppy, fermented, frothy, fizzy

zesty
zingy, tangy, spicy, pungent, flavorful, peppery, fiery, zippy

zingy
zesty, flavorful, rich, tangy, spicy, peppery, lively

zippy
flavorful, tangy, spicy, bright, flavorful

MOUTHFEEL *and* TEXTURE

astringent
dry, drying, sharp, bitter, acrid, biting, harsh

baked
soft, doughy, roasted, crusty, stewed

biting
acerbic, stinging, caustic, acidic, cutting, fiery, sharp

boiling
scorching, scalding, burning, hot, seared, sizzling, stinging

bracing
cold, icy, refreshing, biting, frosty, invigorating, crisp, lively

bubbly
frothy, effervescent, fizzy, sudsy, sparkling, lathery

burning
scorching, scalding, boiling, acidic, caustic, fiery, tingling, searing

caustic
acidic, biting, burning, scalding, abrasive, pungent, acrid

Taste: Mouthfeel *and* Texture

chalky
gritty, powdery, granular, grainy, mealy, sandy

chewy
doughy, soft, crusty, crispy, crumbly, fibrous

chilled
cool, cold, frosty, icy, frosted

coarse
crunchy, scratchy, rough, grainy, lumpy, bumpy, rough

cold
icy, bracing, chilled, frosty, crisp, cool

congealed
lumpy, curled, thick, bumpy, clotted, gelled, glob, coagulated

cool
crisp, minty, chilled, icy, numbing, menthol, refreshing, stimulating

creamy
buttery, smooth, silky, luscious, whipped, velvety, milky, silken

crisp
fresh, cool, refreshing, invigorating, bracing, tart, tangy

crispy
crunchy, crusty, flaky, brittle, crumbly, dry

crumbly
crispy, flaky, brittle, crusty, powdery, crunchy

crunchy
crispy, crusty, nutty, crumbly, brittle

crusty
flaky, crispy, brittle, dry, crunchy

curled
congealed, lumpy, thick, bumpy, clotted, blobby, gelled

delicate
soft, subtle, exquisite, silky, tender

desiccated
dry, parched, baked, scorched, dusty, shriveled

dry
desiccated, parched, gritty, chalky, astringent, crumbly

effervescent
frothy, bubbly, sparkling, fizzy, foamy, carbonated

fatty
greasy, oily, heavy, gristly, blubbery, unctuous

fizzy
 bubbly, effervescent, frothy, foamy, sudsy, sparkling, lathery

flaky
 crispy, crusty, pastry, crumbly, brittle

fleshy
 meaty, gamy, beefy, plump, blobby

foamy
 frothy, whipped, sudsy, whisked, fizzy, bubbly, lathery

frothy
 foamy, fizzy, whipped, bubbly, effervescent, sudsy, lathery

full
 satisfying, round, thick, rich, smooth, full-bodied, robust

gelatinous
 jellied, congealed, sticky, viscous, glutinous, clotted, gelled

gooey
 sticky, gummy, syrupy, tacky, sugary, slimy, gluey

greasy
 oily, fatty, slimy, buttery, slimy, gristly

gristle, gristly
 fatty, oily, fleshy, greasy, fibrous, tough, chewy

gritty
 sandy, chalky, mealy, powdery, grainy, granular

gummy
 sticky, gooey, syrupy, tacky, gluey

heady
 potent, alcoholic, exhilarating, intense, strong, intoxicating

heavy
 fatty, greasy, oily, full, ample, laden

hot
 fiery, spicy, scalding, scorching, burning, biting, peppery, stinging

icy
 cold, bracing, frosty, frozen, crisp, numbing

juicy
 mouth-watering, succulent, ripe, moist, watery

lukewarm
 tepid, cool, flat, dull

lumpy
 congealed, curled, thick, bumpy, mushy, clotted, gelled, blobby

mashed
creamy, soft, pureed, smooth, pulpy, pasty, crushed, minced

mealy
dry, powdery, gritty, chalky, crumbly, grainy

meaty
fleshy, thick, gamy, beefy, rich, full, savory

mellow
rich, smooth, soft, delicate

melting
creamy, smooth, velvety, silky, buttery, silken

milky
creamy, thick, buttery, silky, velvety

minced
mashed, pureed, diced, ground, crushed

moist
juicy, succulent, tender, watery

muddy
earthy, gritty, sandy, mealy, grainy, spongy, swampy

mushy
sloppy, lumpy, runny, soft, squishy, pulpy, mashed, slushy, spongy, doughy

nourishing
refreshing, restorative, soothing, stimulating, energizing, tonic

numbing
icy, biting, bracing, cool, frozen

oily
greasy, fatty, unctuous, buttery, slippery, smeary, slimy, creamy

parched
desiccated, dry, baked, scorched, shriveled, dried

pasty
gummy, gluey, chalky, sticky, doughy, gooey, starchy

powdery
chalky, mealy, gritty, grainy, sandy, granular, crumbly

plump
meaty, round, full, fleshy, beefy

prickly, prickling
stinging, tingling, burning, piercing, tickling

puckering
sour, acidic, vinegar, astringent, tart

pulpy
  mushy, stringy, sloppy, lumpy, runny, slushy

quenching
  invigorating, refreshing, satiating, moistening, cooling, appeasing, satisfying

refreshing
  lively, brisk, bracing, invigorating, quenching, sparkling, satisfying, crisp

rubbery
  chewy, tough, leathery, spongy, squishy, pulpy

runny
  watery, thin, soupy, slurpy, slushy, soggy, tasteless, weak, sloppy, dripping

sandy
  gritty, crumbly, powdery, grainy, powdery

scalding
  boiling, burning, scorching, blistering, piping, steaming, sizzling, fiery, stinging

scorched
  seared, blackened, charred, scalded, singed, burnt

scorching
  boiling, scalding, blistering, sizzling, burning, stinging, charred, fiery

silky
  creamy, smooth, velvety, buttery, melted, silken

slimy
  slobbery, slippery, greasy, gooey, slick, oozy, mucous

slippery
  slimy, greasy, oily, gooey, slick, smooth

slobbery
  slimy, slippery, slurpy, salivating, frothy, dribbling, drooling, runny

sloppy
  slushy, slurpy, runny, watery, messy, sludgy, oozy, muddy

slurpy
  slushy, sloppy, runny, watery

smooth
  creamy, velvety, silky, mellow, rich, buttery, soothing

soapy
  sudsy, bubbly, tallow, waxy, foamy, lathery, frothy

soft
  chewy, delicate, doughy, buttery, tender, squishy, fluffy, spongy, mushy

soggy
  mushy, pulpy, sloppy, squishy, runny

TASTE: MOUTHFEEL *and* TEXTURE

soupy
watery, thin, runny, slurpy, soppy

sparkling
effervescent, lively, bright, invigorating, refreshing, bubbly, fizzy

stale
hard, dry, musty, rancid, fusty, flat, moldy

starchy
glutinous, doughy, bready, heavy

steamy, steaming
moist, hot, juicy, baked, succulent, piping hot

sticky
gooey, gummy, syrupy, tacky, sugary, gluey

stinging
biting, burning, scorching, piercing, tingling, prickling

stringy
pulpy, rough, woody, fibrous, stalky

succulent
tender, delectable, delicious, luscious, mouth-watering, juicy, toothsome, enticing

sudsy
bubbly, soapy, foamy, lathering, frothy, hoppy

sumptuous
luscious, delectable, lavish, juicy, succulent, savory, tempting

supple
creamy, velvety, silky, mellow, rich, buttery, smooth, soft

tallow
waxy, soapy, sudsy, fatty, smeary

tender
succulent, ripe, juicy, moist, delicate, soft, supple

tepid
cool, lukewarm, flat, dull, lifeless

thick
full, rich, smooth, plump, meaty, hearty, bulky, chunky, heavy

tingling
prickling, stinging, bubbling, itchy, biting

toasted, toasty
crusty, crispy, dry, roasted

velvety
creamy, smooth, buttery, silky, luscious, whipped, rich

watery
runny, thin, soupy, weak, slurpy

waxy
soapy, tallow, sudsy, foamy, sticky

whipped
creamy, foamy, frothy, whisked, sudsy, smooth, bubbly

whisked
whipped, creamy, frothy, sudsy, bubbly, foamy

woody
tough, rough, stringy, pulpy, fibrous, stalky

zingy
zesty, flavorful, rich, tangy, spicy, peppery, lively

zippy
flavorful, tangy, spicy, bright, flavorful

EATING, CHEWING, *and* FOOD

appetite
hunger, craving, thirst, yearning, desire, famished, ravenous

belch
burp, vomit, spew, spit, sputter, gush, disgorge, hiccup, erupt

binge
gorge, guzzle, devour, gulp, gobble, scarf

bite
chew, gnaw, chomp, munch, morsel, nibble, maul, gobble, tear, crunch

blend
concoction, soup, brew, tonic, extract, infusion, potion, tincture, remedy, elixir

brew
concoction, soup, blend, tonic, extract, elixir, infusion, potion, tincture, remedy

burp
belch, vomit, spew, spit, sputter, hiccup, erupt

chew
bite, gnaw, grind, munch, crunch, chomp, nibble, gobble

chomp
bite, gnaw, grind, munch, crunch, chew, nibble, gulp

clench
grit, grind, gnash, grate

Taste: Eating, Chewing, *and* Food

concoction
  brew, soup, blend, tonic, extract, elixir, infusion, medley, potion, tincture, remedy

connoisseur
  epicure, gourmet, foodie, aficionado

crave
  desire, appetite, hunger, thirst, yearn, pine, lust, hanker

crumb
  soupçon, bite, nibble, morsel, dollop, tidbit, pinch, dab, sliver

crunch
  munch, chew, bite, chomp, grind, gobble, bite, gnaw

delicacy
  gourmet, treat, luxury, nectar, tidbit, feast

devour
  gobble, gulp, wolf, voracious, ravenous, gnaw, maul, gorge, relish, swallow

distaste
  aversion, disgust, repellent, repulsion, revulsion

dollop
  bite, nibble, spoonful, morsel, tidbit, glob, soupçon

drool
  salivate, slobber, dribble, spit, spittle, drivel

elixir
  extract, infusion, potion, concoction, tincture, remedy, tonic, brew, blend

epicure
  gourmet, foodie, connoisseur, aficionado

extract
  elixir, infusion, potion, concoction, tincture, tonic, brew, juice

famished
  ravenous, hunger, hungry, starving, voracious

feast
  delight, treat, banquet, spread, delicacy, indulgence, gorge, gobble, gulp, devour, binge, maul

gag
  burp, belch, vomit, purge, spew, spit, sputter, gasp, choke, retch

glutton, gluttonous
  ravenous, voracious, greedy, insatiable, starved, wolfish

gnash
  grind, grate, chew, gnaw, crush, chomp, mince

gnaw
  chew, bite, chomp, munch, nibble, devour, maul

gobble
  devour, gulp, gorge, nibble, munch, maul, scarf, bite, chew, gnaw

gorge
  gobble, gulp, devour, binge, maul, scarf, guzzle, wolf

gourmand
  epicure, gorging, glutton, gourmet, guzzler, binge

grate
  grind, gnash, mince, crumble, crush

grind
  gnash, chew, crumble, pulverize, grate, crush

grit
  grind, gnash, clench, grate, mince

gulp
  devour, gobble, slurp, wolf, guzzle, swallow, swig, slosh, chug

gusto
  zest, vigor, relish, appetite, delight, brio

gut
  visceral, instinctive, deep-seated, inherent, ingrained

guzzle
  gulp, swill, slurp, swig, gorge, bolt, slosh

hanker
  crave, desire, appetite, hunger, thirst, yearn, lust, pine

hunger, hungry
  ravenous, voracious, craving, lusting, yearning, longing, thirsty, desiring, greedy, famished

indulge, indulgence
  feast, treat, luxury, delicacy, extravagance, excess

infusion
  concoction, brew, blend, tonic, extract, elixir, potion, tincture, remedy, immersion, soup

insatiable
  unquenchable, ravenous, voracious, gluttonous, wolfish, yearning, greedy, unappeasable

juice
  tonic, sap, nectar, liquor, extract, milk, essence, spirit

Taste: Eating, Chewing, *and* Food

lick
suck, lap, tongue, slurp, sip

mince
grind, cut, chop, grate, crush, pulverize

morsel
bite, nibble, dollop, tidbit, soupçon, taste

mouthful
bite, nibble, spoonful, morsel, tidbit, chunk, gulp

nibble
chew, bite, gnaw, grind, munch, crunch, chomp, tidbit

nourish, nourishing
sustain, nurture, satiate, satisfy, rejuvenate

palate
appetite, flavor, taste, zest, gusto

potion
concoction, blend, tonic, extract, elixir, infusion, brew, tincture, remedy, soup

pucker, puckering
purse, tighten, smack, kiss, crinkle

purge
vomit, burp, belch, gag, spew, spit, sputter, cleanse, expel, heave

quench
satiate, indulge, assuage, appease, gratify, relieve, satisfy

ravenous
famished, hungry, starving, insatiable, voracious, wolfish

retch
vomit, purge, spew, spit, burp, belch, sputter, gag, gasp, choke

salivate
drool, slobber, dribble, relish, spit, spittle

satiate, satiating
fill, satisfy, quench, fulfill, indulge

satisfy
nourish, quench, satiate, appease, indulge, fulfill

savor
relish, delight, revel, sip, enjoy

scarf
gobble, devour, gulp, gorge, nibble, munch, guzzle

sip
slurp, suck, savor, swirl, swallow

slobber
salivate, slurp, dripping, dribble, slaver, drool

sloppy
slushy, slurpy, runny, watery, slimy, oozy

slurp
suck, sip, slosh, swirl, lick, guzzle, gargle, swig

smack
relish, lick, slurp, savor, suck

smorgasbord
buffet, variety, spread, medley

soupçon
bite, nibble, morsel, dollop, tidbit, crumb, pinch

spit
drool, slobber, dribble, spew, sputter, spittle, slaver

sputter
burp, belch, gag, spittle, spew, spit

starve, starving
ravenous, hungry, famished, voracious

suck
slurp, sip, drink, gulp, lick, lap, smack

sustenance
nourishment, refreshment, edibles

swig
gulp, gargle, guzzle, sip, swill

swill
gargle, swig, guzzle, gulp

thirst, thirsty, thirsting
unquenchable, parched, craving, burning, unfulfilled, yearning, dry

tidbit
bite, nibble, spoonful, morsel, dollop

tincture
concoction, soup, blend, tonic, extract, elixir, infusion, potion, brew, remedy

unquenchable
parched, insatiable, voracious, ravenous, yearning, unappeasable, thirsty

vomit
burp, belch, gag, purge, spew, spit, sputter

Taste: Eating, Chewing, *and* Food

voracious
> devouring, ravenous, insatiable, gorging, unquenchable, greedy

wolfish
> ravenous, voracious, gluttonous, greedy

yearning
> thirsting, craving, burning, lusting, unfulfilled, desiring, wanting

SMELL

*Even as I think of smells, my nose is full of scents that start awake sweet memories
of summers gone and ripening grain fields far away.*
—*Helen Keller, American author, lecturer, and activist*

AROMATIC *and* FRAGRANT - DISTINCT *or* INTENSE -
REPULSIVE *or* NOXIOUS

Smells are histories. An invisible cloud of aftershave, pipe tobacco, and
shoe polish signals a visitor was here. A scarf carries the scent of latte
and spice cake. An old book smells damp and salty.

Smells are trails. Not the source itself but a trail of the source—a secret
message billowing out along an unknown path. Follow the swirling trail back
to the source. A sugary, vanilla-drenched, confectionery trail. A whiff of
lilac with a long, seductive reach. The sudden sting of smoke from a fire
smoldering somewhere. A repulsive stench. All leading you somewhere by
the nose to itself.

Smells are memories. Of a childhood house, Grandma's kitchen, incense
at a funeral, a baby's delicate skin, a path in a pine forest. Precise, distinct
gateways beckoning you back to the past.

Smells are assessments. *I smell a rat. That stinks. She's smelling like a rose.*

Smells are warnings. One sniff and we reject the milk. Gas leak danger.
Skunk alert. *I'd turn back if I were you.*

Smells are reminders. To come alive, to experience, to rejoice (and perhaps to bathe). Uplifting, warm, sharp, revitalizing. Inviting us to engage, expand, and explore.

In this section, we examine the aromas and fragrances that delight us; the distinct, intense, and unmistakable odors that sharpen our senses; and the repulsive, noxious smells that revolt us and warn us of potential harm.

AROMATIC *and* FRAGRANT

airy
light, fresh, breezy, brisk

allspice
spicy, cinnamon, fragrant, aromatic

apple
fruity, sweet, berry, aromatic

aroma
whiff, scent, smell, odor, bouquet, perfume, fragrance, incense

aromatic
perfumed, scented, fragrant, odoriferous, spicy, redolent

banana
fruity, sweet, tropical, starchy

berry
fruity, sweet, plum, apple, tart

botanical
herbal, grassy, weedy, mossy, floral

bouquet
flowery, floral, perfumed, scented, incense

buttery
sweet, candied, honey, caramel, creamy

candied
sweet, honey, syrupy, sugary, confectionery

caramel
candied, buttery, creamy, honey, syrupy, sweet, toffee

cedar
piney, woody, mossy, woodsy

chocolaty
cocoa, sweet, rich, coffee, burnt, roasted, creamy

Smell: Aromatic *and* Fragrant

cinnamon
  spicy, apple, sweet, allspice

citrus
  lemony, fresh, clean, citron, sharp, orange

clean
  fresh, refreshing, crisp, bright, pure

cocoa
  chocolaty, sweet, rich, coffee, burnt, creamy

earthy
  rich, robust, woody, woodsy, herbal, muddy

evergreen
  piney, cedar, woody, weedy, mossy, grassy, rosemary

floral
  flowery, herbal, perfumed, bouquet, botanical, blossomy

flowery
  floral, herbal, perfumed, fragrant, blossomy

fragrant
  aromatic, perfumed, scented, floral, flowery, incense

fresh
  clean, minty, refreshing, pure, crisp, invigorating

fruity
  apple, berry, sweet, honey

grassy
  herbal, botanical, weedy, mossy, earthy

herbal, herbaceous
  botanical, grassy, weedy, floral, minty

honey, honeyed
  sweet, candied, syrupy, sugary

incense
  fragrant, smoky, spicy, exotic, perfumed

lemon, lemony
  citrus, clean, sharp, fresh, refreshing, invigorating

lilac
  floral, perfumy, bouquet, fragrant, flowery

lime
  citrusy, clean, lemony, sharp

menthol
  sharp, minty, wintergreen, crisp, invigorating, refreshing

minty
sharp, fresh, herbal, crisp, invigorating, refreshing, menthol

mossy
herbal, woody, moist, grassy, damp

nectar
sap, honey, sweet, wine, ambrosia

odoriferous
scented, fragrant, aromatic, perfumy, pungent, spicy

odorous
flowery, aromatic, fragrant, scented, spicy, smelly

orange
citrus, clean, sweet, tangy

perfumed, perfumy
aromatic, scented, fragrant, herbal

piney
cedar, woody, mossy, grassy, evergreen, rosemary, earthy

powder
sweet, fragrant, soft, perfumy

redolent
rich, fragrant, sweet-smelling, reminiscent

rose, rosy
aromatic, perfumed, lilac, floral, flowery, sweet, blossomy

scent
aroma, whiff, smell, bouquet, odor, spice

spicy
complex, piquant, exotic, rich, fragrant, tangy

sweet
candied, cloying, honey, vanilla, fruity, buttery, berry, confectionery

sugary
honey, vanilla, candied, confectionery, toffee

whiff
aroma, scent, smell, odor, fume, puff, blast, waft, sniff, snuff

woodsy
cedar, piney, mossy, grassy, earthy

woody
cedar, piney, mossy, botanical, weedy, grassy, earthy

vanilla
sweet, honey, sugary, candied

DISTINCT *or* INTENSE

acidic
sour, citrus, burning, caustic, vinegary, sharp, biting

acrid
pungent, rank, sour, vinegary, acidic, sharp

ammonia
sharp, fumy, pungent, vaporous, bracing, piercing, burning

beefy
meaty, gamy, fleshy, savory, pungent, salty

biting
stinging, sharp, acrid, pungent, piercing, intense, burning

burnt
fiery, smoky, charred, blackened, scorched, seared

camphor
aromatic, mothball, sharp, intense, bracing, bitter

charred
burnt, scorched, smoky, blackened, seared, singed

cheesy
creamy, sharp, rich, buttery, milky, salty

coffee
bitter, burnt, roasted, chocolate, toasted, sweet

complex
spicy, rich, exotic

dank
damp, humid, musty, muggy, slimy, moldy

doggy
dank, sweaty, skunky, moist, musky

dusty
musty, sooty, stale, chalky, dirty, sandy, grubby

eggy
creamy, velvety, rich, buttery

exhaust
fumy, fuel, gas, gassy, vaporous

fiery
smoky, burnt, charred, seared, spicy, pungent

fishy
meaty, piscine, gamy, seaweed, briny, salty

fleshy
meaty, gamy, beefy, oniony, pungent, sour

fumy
gassy, vapor, fuel, exhaust, gasoline

fusty
stuffy, musty, stale, dusty, moldy, damp, mildewy

gamy
meaty, rancid, fleshy, beefy

garlicky
oniony, savory, pungent, sharp, sour

gassy
fumy, vaporous, exhaust, fuel

gingery
peppery, candied, sugary, aromatic

horsey
sweaty, musty, barnyard, doggy

leather
earthy, soft, musky

loamy
earthy, woody, clayey, muddy

meadow
grassy, herbal, earthy, mossy, muddy, blossomy

medicinal
sharp. piercing, artificial, chemical, synthetic

metallic
mineral, tinny, coppery

mildew, mildewy
moldy, musty, damp, stale

moist
wet, humid, dank, dewy, muggy

moldy
musty, damp, stale, mildew, funky

muddy
woody, sandy, clayey, earthy, loamy, grassy

mushroom
rich, earthy, muddy, savory, mossy, damp, sandy, woody

musky
sweaty, scented, perfumed, aromatic, skunky

mustard
pungent, sharp, spicy, oniony, garlicky, sour, bitter

musty
damp, stale, dusty, moldy, fusty

nutty
almondy, toasted, hazelnut, buttery

oniony
garlicky, savory, pungent, sour

penetrating
stiff, sharp, biting, piercing, permeating, pungent, intense, stinging

peppery
spicy, savory, fiery, gingery, pungent

pickled
salty, spicy, fermented, cured, vinegary, briny, sour

plastic
synthetic, metallic, rubber, fumy, chemical

pungent
sharp, strong, ripe, caustic, acrid, spicy, tangy

rain
earthy, clean, fresh, mossy, sweet, dewy, moist, humid, muggy

ripe
strong, intense, pungent, sharp, rich, sour

rubber
plastic, burnt, charred, chemical

savory
pungent, piquant, succulent, zingy, tangy, mushroom, earthy

seared
burnt, charred, crispy, blackened, toasted, scorched

seaweed
fishy, piscine, briny, salty, grassy

sharp
pungent, penetrating, intense, biting, piercing

skunky
musky, swampy, doggy, dank, fragrant, musty, odorous

smell (n)
aroma, whiff, scent, stink, odor, perfume, essence

smell (v)
sniff, detect, whiff, discern, inhale, snuff

smoky
burnt, fiery, ash, woody, sooty, smoldering

sniff
snort, whiff, snuff, inhale, snuff

soapy
waxy, perfume, powdery, frothy, fragrant

sooty
dusty, musty, chalky, powdery, moldy

sour
acidic, lemony, vinegary, tart, sharp, citrus, stale, rank

spicy
fiery, exotic, rich, pungent, sharp, salty

stale
musty, rancid, fusty, flat, moldy, sour

stuffy
fusty, musty, stale, dusty, airless

sugary
sweet, syrupy, candied, honey, gooey, confectionery

swampy
skunky, mossy, grassy, algal, dank, marshy, wet, humid

sweaty
musky, skunky, ripe, horsey, rank, dank, humid, muggy

synthetic
plastic, metallic, rubber, fumy, chemical

tart
acidic, lemony, sour, biting, sharp, tangy

turpentine
lacquer, metallic, synthetic, chemical

weedy
grassy, herbal, botanical, woody

yeasty
doughy, fermented, creamy, toasty

zesty
pungent, sharp, fresh, tangy

REPULSIVE *or* NOXIOUS

biting
stinging, sharp, acrid, pungent, piercing, intense, burning

cloying
sickening, nauseating, oversweet, overpowering, gooey, sappy

fetid
putrid, rank, rotting, stinky, stinking, foul, repulsive

foul
odorous, smelly, stinking, acrid, putrid, rank

miasma, miasmal
reeking, rank, rotten, stink, stenchful, odorous

nauseating
putrid, rank, sickening, repulsive, fetid, foul

noxious
repulsive, odious, putrid, foul, fetid

odorous
smelly, stinking, foul, acrid, putrid, rank

putrid
nauseating, rank, fetid, rotting, repulsive, repugnant, gagging

putrefied
rotten, decayed, decomposed, stinking, festering, spoiled

rancid
stale, spoiled, rank, putrid, stinking, rotten, sharp

rank
foul, repulsive, odorous, smelly, stinking, acrid, putrid, repugnant

reek
stink, smell, stench

repugnant
foul, repulsive, revolting, vile, nauseating

revolting
repugnant, foul, repulsive, abhorrent, appalling, vile

rotting, rotten
putrid, fetid, rank, moldy, tainted, decaying

smelly
odorous, stinking, foul, acrid, pungent, rank, rancid, putrid

spoiled
rotten, overripe, putrid, sour

stench, stenchful
reek, rank, odor, stink, miasma, foul

stinging
biting, sharp, acrid, pungent, piercing, burning

stink, stinky, stinking
stench, reek, rank, odor, odorous, smelly, foul, acrid, pungent

sulfur
rotten egg, metallic, skunky, burnt rubber

Resources

The following resources were helpful reference materials during the construction of *Thesaurus of the Senses*. See also the Notes section for references related to the senses.

Random House Word Menu, by Stephen Glazier; Random House: New York, 1997.

The DICT Development Group; http://www.dict.org.

The Synonym Finder, by J. I. Rodale; Warner Books: New York, 1978.

Thesaurus.com; *Roget's 21st Century Thesaurus*, 3rd ed.; Philip Lief Group: Princeton, NJ, 2009.

New Oxford American Dictionary, 3rd ed.; Oxford University Press: Oxford, 2010.

Oxford American Writer's Thesaurus, 3rd ed., by D. Auburn et al.; Oxford University Press: Oxford, 2012.

Roget's II Pocket Thesaurus; Houghton Mifflin Company: Boston, 1987.

20,000 Words; compiled by Louis A. Leslie; McGraw-Hill: New York, 1965.

A Dictionary of Synonyms and Antonyms, by Joseph Devlin; Popular Library Inc.: New York, 1961.

The New International Webster's Pocket Thesaurus of the English Language; Trident Press International: Naples, FL, 2002.

Notes

Connecting with the Senses: Exercises

Exercise 12: For advice on using all of your senses in connecting with nature, including how to expand your sight using "splatter vision," see *Tom Brown's Field Guide to Nature Observation and Tracking*, by Tom Brown, Jr.; Berkley Trade: New York, 1986.

Exercise 19: For a look at what people with synesthesia experience, see "Rare but Real: People Who Feel, Taste and Hear Color," by Ker Than, livescience.com, February 22, 2005; http://www.livescience.com/169-rare-real-people-feel-taste-hear-color.html.

Exercise 23: In her delightful book *A Natural History of the Senses* (Vintage Books, 1990), Diane Ackerman notes that we often describe smell based on what something "smells like" rather than its actual scent. See also "Why So Few English Words for Odors?" by Jessica Love, *The American Scholar*, January 16, 2014; https://theamericanscholar.org/why-so-few-english-words-for-odors/

Hear

For a fascinating discussion about what the Big Bang and early universe may have sounded like, based on research by astronomy professor Mark Whittle, see "Listening to the Big Bang" by Brandon Keim, WIRED.com, 9/28/08, https://www.wired.com/2008/09/listening-to-th/

Touch

In his book *Touch: The Science of Hand, Heart, and Mind* (Viking Press, 2015), neuroscientist David Linden explores the many unique dimensions of touch, including its compelling connection to language and emotion.

Taste

"How does our sense of taste work?" *Pubmed Health*, January 6, 2012; see http://www.ncbi.nlm.nih.gov/pubmedhealth/PMH0033701/

Smell

In Helen Keller's book *The World I Live In* (1908), she discusses her exquisite sense of smell that allowed her accurately perceive distances, coming storms, distinct places and their various rhythmic activities, plants and animals, and the individual scents of people. She writes, "In my experience smell is most important, and I find that there is high authority for the nobility of the sense which we have neglected and disparaged."

Acknowledgments

Writing is an inner journey fueled by persistence and inspiration. I am grateful for the kind support and encouragement of family and friends who have helped me in this journey. Special thanks to Don Hart, writer and word lover *par excellence*, for guidance and brilliant creative insight; Tonya Foreman for her artistic eye and invaluable collaboration; Mary Ann Hart for huge moral support and helpful feedback; Kerry George for inspiration and advice; Connee Draper for always delightful writing discussions at Zen Cha teahouse; and Susie, Gemma, Coo Coo, and Maggie of Four Cats Publishing LLC for helping make everything run so smoothly. Lastly, thanks to the many readers who have provided thoughtful feedback on how they are using the thesaurus for their own writing. May your literary creations enrich the world.

Word Index

257

Word Index

Word Index

nutty, 224, 247
nuzzle, 164, 203

O

oaky, 224
oblique, obliquely, 40
obliterate, 204
obnoxious, 90
obscure, obscured, 106
obstructed, 107
ochre, 30
octave, 121
odd, 90
oddity, 90
odious, 90
odoriferous, 244
odorous, 244, 249
off-flavor, 224
off-key, 118
off-putting, 164
ogle, 107
oil, 164
oily, 164, 181, 224, 231
olive, 31
onerous, 90
oniony, 224, 247
onslaught, 136, 204
ooze, oozing, 182
oozy, 182
opalescent, 31
opaque, 25, 107
open-mouthed, 66
operatic, 90
oppressive, 164
opulent, 90
orange, 244
ornamented, 56
ornate, 56
oscillate, 75, 204
oscillating, 75
ossified, 182
ostentatious, 90
other-worldly, 90
outburst, 137
outcry, 137
outlandish, 90
outrageous, 91
outstretched, 204

overflow, 75, 204
overflowing, 36, 75, 204
overgrown, 99
overhear, 147
overpowering, 224
overripe, 224
oversized, 37
overt, 107
overtone, 121
overwrought, 66
oyster, 224

P

pacify, 164
pained, 164
painstaking, 164
palatable, 224
palate, 237
pale, 31
pallid, 31
pallor, 31
palpable, 164
palpitate, palpitation, 164
paltry, 37
pandemonium, 75
pang, 165, 204
panicked, 67
panicky, 67, 165
panoramic, 37
pant, 137
pantomime, 107, 204
papery, 47, 182
paralyze, 204
paralyzed, 75, 165
parched, 165, 182, 231
parrot, 137
passionate, 91, 161
pastel, 31
pastiche, 57
pastoral, 91
pasty, 31, 231
patchy, 56
patina, 57
patrol, 107
patter, 204
paunchy, 47
peaked, 31
peal, 115

pearly, 31
peculiar, 91
peek, 107
peep, 107, 125
peer, 107
peevish, 67
pell-mell, 204
pelt, 145
penetrate, 204
penetrating, 67, 165, 224, 247
pensive, 67
peppered, 57
peppermint, 224
peppery, 224, 247
perceive, 107
perceptive, 107
percolate, 145, 204
perforated, 47
perfumed, perfumy, 224, 244
perfunctory, 204
perilous, 91
peripheral, 40
periwinkle, 31
permeate, 204
perplexed, 67
perplexing, 91
perturbed, 165
pervade, 204
pervading, 91
petty, 37
pewter, 31
phantom, 107
pickled, 224, 247
picturesque, 91
pierce, 204
piercing, 67, 118, 148, 165, 246
piffling, 37
pinched, 165
piney, 224, 244
ping, 125
pining, 67
piquant, 224
pitch, 121, 137, 204
pitch-black, 31
pitched, 137
pithy, 148
pitted, 57
pivot, 204

Word Index

Word Index

Word Index

Y

Z

Subject Index

SUBJECT INDEX

Big Bang, 111, 253
listening, 17-18, 146-147
music, 120-122
noise and discord, 116-120
onomatopoeia, 122-127
percussions and vibrations, 113-116
volume, 147-150
Space, location, and position, 38-41
Speech and utterances, 127-143
Speed
and movement and touch, 188-216
Splatter vision, 253
Structures
and shapes, 21, 41-53
and textures, 53-59
Synesthesia, 14, 19, 253

T

Tactile, 14, 151-152, see also Touch
skin and visceral responses, 14, 20, **152-174**
textures and structures, 174-188
Taste, 217-239
acquired taste, 218
aesthetics, 217
chewing, 234-239
connection to smell, 217
decorum, 218
eating, 234-239
flavors, 217, 218--228
food, 14, 20, 217-218, **234-239**
mouthfeel, 228-234
and smell, 217
texture and mouthfeel, 228-234
Textures
and mouthfeel, 228-234
and seeing, 53-59
and touch, 174-188
The World I Live In, 254
Tom Brown's Field Guide to Nature Observation and Tracking, 253
Touch, 14, 18, 20, **151-216**, 253-254, see also Feeling(s)
feeling, 17, 18, 151-152
kinesthetic, 14, 151
movement, 188-216
pressure, 188-216
skin and body sensations, 14, 20, **152-174**
speed and movement, 188-216

tactile, 14, 151-152
textures and structures, 174-188
visceral responses, 14, 20, **152-174**
Touch: The Science of Hand, Heart, and Mind, 253-254
Turrell, James, 21

U

Utterances and speech, 127-143

V

Vibrations and percussions, 113-116
Visceral responses, 14, 20, **152-174**
Vision
eyes and sight, 14, 20-21, **102-109**, 253
using splatter vision in nature, 253
Volume, 147-150

W

Writing, 9, 13-15, 17
characters, 19-20
creativity, 13
description, 9, 13, 17
dialogue, 14, 112
language, 13, 20, 151
poetry, 9, 13, 15, 18
prompts, 9, 13
prose, 19
readers, 13-15
words, 9, 13-15, 17-20, 253

CPSIA information can be obtained
at www.ICGtesting.com
Printed in the USA
LVHW061947160723
752503LV00006B/394